The Real Jesus

David L. Edwards is the author of many books which have been well received. "Here once again", wrote a reviewer, "is that marvellous fluency and lucidity, that ability to present complex and conflicting facts and situations completely fairly, those magisterial judgements which combine penetrating insight and down-to-earth common sense, and with it all a sheer readability" (*Church Times*). "He seems to tackle each subject as it arises as though he had spent half his life studying it and the other half perfecting a way in which to write about it, which is always lucid, invariably balanced and never boring" (*Contemporary Review*). "I stand back in admiration of a man who, if the world could be saved by books alone, would already have saved the world six times over" (*Methodist Recorder*). His recent books include three volumes of a history of *Christian England*.

Now Provost of Southwark Cathedral in London, he was formerly a Fellow of All Souls College, Oxford, Dean of King's College, Cambridge, Sub-Dean of Westminster and Dean of Norwich. He has served the ecumenical movement as Editor of the SCM Press and Chairman of Christian Aid. While at Westminster Abbey he was the Speaker's Chaplain in the House of Commons. He has been honoured by a Lambeth Doctorate of Divinity.

Books by the same author
available as Fount Paperbacks

Christian England, Vols 1–3
Christians in a New Europe
A Key to the Old Testament

David L. Edwards

THE REAL JESUS

Fount
An Imprint of HarperCollinsPublishers

Fount Paperbacks is an Imprint of
HarperCollins*Religious*
Part of HarperCollins*Publishers*
77–85 Fulham Palace Road, London W6 8JB

First published in Great Britain
in 1992 by Fount Paperbacks

3 5 7 9 10 8 6 4 2

Biblical references in this book are
taken from the Revised English Bible,
and are used by kind permission of Cambridge
University Press and Oxford University Press

A catalogue record for this book is
available from the British Library

ISBN 0 00 627637 7

Printed and bound in Great Britain by
HarperCollinsManufacturing Glasgow

Contents

To Sybil and Southwark Cathedral,
who again made it possible

Preface

In this book I try to discuss the truth about Christianity. I offer it to those who have not read my other books, and to those who may have read one or two of them but who might be interested in a non-technical summary of the theology in them, with many fresh reflections and almost no references to individual theologians. In the 1960s, when I was a publisher, I was responsible for the publication of a controversial book which became famous, *Honest to God* by John Robinson. This is a very different book, but it began when it was suggested that I might try to write something not entirely unlike it in intention.

This seemed to be an opportunity to sum up the results of my dialogues with Third World, Evangelical and radical theologians published by Hodder and Stoughton in four volumes, *Religion and Change* (1969), *The Futures of Christianity* (1987), *Essentials* (with John Stott, 1988, the US title being *Evangelical Essentials*) and *Tradition and Truth* (1989). I have used, after much revision, some material first published by Collins in an introduction to the gospels, *Jesus for Modern Man* (1975), and in an introduction to current discussion about the challenge of science in *A Reason to Hope* (1978). I mention a few truths about politics which became clearer when I edited *Christianity and Conservatism* with Michael Alison (Hodder and Stoughton, 1990). In the background are other books written over thirty years, including *A Key to the Old Testament* (Collins, 1975 and 1989), although here I concentrate on Christianity, and *Christians in a New Europe* (Collins, 1990), although there I concentrate on the Christian response to humanity's crisis; and in these years I have reviewed with care, and learned from many hundreds of other people's books in the wide field of theology. In the background also is a good deal of instructive travel which has been my privilege in recent years amid equally instructive duties in a busy London church.

I believe that theologians ought to explain themselves to the public and be as constructive about Christian faith as they can be honestly. So I am very grateful to all my teachers whose insights have contributed to this little book which has those great purposes. Although I must not claim that they altogether agree with me, I am particularly indebted to Bishop Hugh Montefiore and Dr Anthony Harvey for commenting on a draft of the book as New Testament scholars with a wide range of other interests, and to Dr John Polkinghorne for his comments as a scientist-theologian.

I have not burdened this book with footnotes, but suggestions for further reading may be found in two recent books by Professors at King's College, London: G. N. Stanton, *The Gospels and Jesus* (OUP, 1989) and J. L. Houlden, *Jesus: A Question of Identity* (SPCK, 1992).

D. L. E.

Confusion in Christianity

AFTER MODERNITY, WHAT?

TO be modern is, it seems, not enough. As the twentieth century nears its end, the term "post-modern" has come into use. I am never quite sure what is meant by it, but often its meaning seems to lie in its ambiguity. "Post-modern" architecture uses modern materials and methods of construction but avoids the simplicity of squared glass and concrete. It also avoids making a statement which is a definite alternative to what is instantly recognizable as modern. It adds touches of what may be decoration or nostalgia or decadence or the architecture of a new age. "Post-modern" novels use many twentieth-century techniques but they avoid realism. The alternative is a kind of dream, which may be nonsense or a probe into a deeper reality.

Many people have a sense, however vague, that the modern period is beginning to end. Of course "modern" is another word which has been used to suggest all sorts of things since it came into use in English shortly before Shakespeare's day, but probably few would now exclude it from these developed meanings: everyone ought to be free, everyone ought to be truthful (meaning mainly by that, scientific), everyone ought to be reasonable (reasoning together in a free democracy), and because economic growth based on modern technology is one of the happy results of honest and reasonable people being free to use science in a democracy, everyone ought to be prosperous and healthy. All that progress seemed to be symbolized by confidently modern buildings or modern literature, and in areas which have been modernized there is a general desire to keep most modern achievements. Most people do not want to be enslaved, unrealistic, irrational, poor or ill. But . . .

The freedom won in modern times – say, since Tom Paine's manifesto *The Age of Reason* accompanied the French Revolution in the 1790s – has led to far more confusion and fear than was expected by the progressive pioneers, and the failure of nerve during and after the First World War has never been totally reversed. The modern period has not produced a complete agreement between people who are truthful about what is reasonable. Nor has it sustained much solid optimism about the world's prospects. Marxism, once claimed to be modern, scientific understanding of human progress, is now discredited almost everywhere. It is often said that modern capitalism using science-based technology has also failed to deliver the goods of justice and happiness, and that science itself is guilty. The new platitudes are these: human nature continues to indulge its old habits of war, greed and incompetence when priority ought to be given to food and jobs for a world population of staggering size; technical progress there must be, but it must be subordinated to human rights and humane values; economic growth there must be, but it must be disciplined by the need to conserve our fragile planet's resources. Whether poor or rich in material things, modern humanity faces a disaster which cannot be avoided without a new moral and spiritual vision, but no vision is accepted widely and deeply enough to generate the necessary moral and spiritual power.

Most people, however, cannot adopt the kind of attitude that is recommended by some "post-modern" intellectuals in response to that often-diagnosed disillusionment. The recommendation is that we should accept a general lack of meaning in life; that we should sceptically "deconstruct" the meanings on offer in the old religions and the old literature; that we should privatize religion, deregulate morality and work out a do-it-yourself meaning if we want one, but that all our hymns of hope can be no more than songs to allow us some illusions and diversions. But human nature as most people have it continues to find it difficult to live without a worldview possessing both coherence and depth, both consolation and power. What seems to most people to be their best instincts are the instincts that life is significant and good, with a meaning that sometimes hits them.

What is this meaning? Around the world there are many groups and whole societies which reject modernity far more thoroughly than the "post-moderns" do. There are traditional societies which are determined to remain traditional and are often envied. There are religious fundamentalisms which claim that error is absent from the spiritual systems which they have inherited. The most obviously successful is militantly conservative Islam, but Christian fundamentalism remains a feature even in the world's most modern country, the USA. In conservative Islamic countries, as in the USA, among Hindus as among Jews, even among Buddhists, this reaction is often allied with a fierce nationalism, for where an emotionally powerful response to the chaos and anxiety of modernity is needed, it can be supplied by blood-and-soil cults of national or ethnic identity. In Africa "nation building", often in a one-party state, has arisen on the ruins of colonialism; in the former Soviet Union, national independence is the popular cry as the slogans of Communism become the feeble mutterings of defeated men; within many nations, regions or tribes belligerantly assert their own heritages. In areas such as Western Europe, where nationalism has lost much of its appeal, other alternatives to modernity may be found. In disgust at what industrialism has created, many dream of an age which is "new", moving towards the earth rather than the stars, listening to the body rather than the brain, wealthy in love not possessions. Other alternatives, still further away from modern ideas, flourish within modern societies. Occult magic retains its fascination. Many people who would call themselves modern consult horoscopes to find what fate holds in store for them, while others, poor or rich, use chemical drugs or alcohol or gambling or sex as a necessary escape from the boredom of living in a world which is as meaningless as the stars.

These are some of the many alternatives on offer if we sense that the modern age is dying or dead because its heart no longer pumps blood. But in many societies there remain many people who continue to insist that there cannot be an adequate alternative to modernity if the strong modern achievements are rejected. They feel sure that something more than modernity is needed now – but what was won by humanity in modern times at great cost must be taken into the future. The vision they want would be seen by one eye which is modern and by another eye which is . . . what?

In this human crisis, Christians claim to have the answer – or at least to be able to make an important contribution. Certainly there is an opportunity. Yet Christianity itself seems to be confused in this age of confusion. To give one current example: as I write, the denomination to which I belong, the Church of England, is often depicted in the media as thoroughly confused. It seems to be tearing itself apart as it debates such questions as whether women or "practising" homosexuals can be priests. Another example may be found in the Roman Catholic Church. The Pope says one thing and most married Catholics do another, at least in Europe and the English-speaking world: they use contraceptives. The twentieth Christian century seems to be bequeathing a legacy which will be of little use to post-modern people because it is a legacy of disagreement and division. And one thing is certain: chaos cannot speak to chaos. The fundamentalists are right to say that.

It is often said that Christianity is now confused about what is true. This has not been the best of beginnings for the attempt, requested by the Pope and by the many other church leaders, to make the 1990s a "decade of evangelism" or "of evangelization" (it seems that Christians cannot even agree on the appropriate term in English). In history when a religion has persuaded many people to believe its message, it has been because the message was believed to be true. Many pressures, including politics and fashion, may have encouraged such a belief, and specially influential encouragement has come from parents and teachers, but the belief has been in the truth of what was proposed. A religion has not been accepted merely because it was advertised, attractively packaged or efficiently organized. Spreading a religion has not been like selling a brand of soap. Those who want Christianity to be spread in our time would therefore be wise to concentrate more on the question of its truth. I do not mean merely the truth which the intellect acknowledges. I mean truth which illuminates a universe and changes a life.

Some Christians can be confident that the answer which they know best is the right answer. People may be pretty sure that what matters is Christian morality as they understand it, or the way it helps them to think in private about the mystery of life, and such people may not think it necessary to ask whether other Christians see things the same

way. Regular churchgoers may be inclined to consider what
goes on in one church to be normal. But nowadays there
are not many places where Christians are totally sheltered
from the variety which has grown with modernity. In almost
every city the existence of numerous denominations adver-
tises Christian disunity. Into almost every village radio, if
not TV, brings echoes of a world where religion is questioned
or ignored. The school has often ended the pulpit's mono-
poly. Even where life seems little changed by modern confusions, people are often aware that at least two versions
of Christianity are on offer, Catholic (or Orthodox) and
Protestant. Different Protestant movements, historic or lib-
eral or Evangelical or Pentecostal, are active. But what is
really convincing in any of these traditions? What is truth?
Modern or post-modern people who are prepared to think
seriously about the claims of Christianity to be true must
often feel bewildered by the variety of the teachings about
what Christianity is, like shoppers who enter a strange
supermarket.

The twentieth century has not merely been uncertain
about the best way to organize church life or to express
Christian doctrines. Political and personal questions which
few people can escape have received different answers. Does
Christianity stress justice for the poor and therefore solidarity with the powerless – or the individual's freedom and
responsibility? Does it lead logically to capitalism or to
socialism? What is meant by "capitalism" or "socialism" as
a morally desirable society? Is a third way best as an application of Christianity to politics? Or is Christianity a message
about eternity, not economics? Does it supply any inspiration
or guidance for the grind of daily work? Can it guide our
personal decisions? Is sexual intercourse outside marriage
ever right for a Christian, heterosexual or homosexual? Is contraception? Is abortion? Is divorce? Is alcohol? Is gambling?

Is revolution? Is war? It can seem that on the questions which really interest people, the answer is a debate.

Increasingly Christians are in contact with adherents of other religions. Should they expect to learn something from those neighbours? Do the holy books of other religions contain important truths? Do all worship the same God? Or will all non-Christians end up in hell? Do the wicked among the Christians end up there? What is hell anyway? Is anyone thoroughly wicked or are all sinners only sick?

It can be said that despite their disagreements Christians are united in prayer. But are they? When they pray, many address God as they would in talking with a human friend; for others, the "holy" and "transcendent" God may be more majestic and remote. Some find no problem in prayer as a person-to-person contact; for others "God" is something much more mysterious than a "person", and thinking in impersonal categories (God as the Depth of the World or the Source of the Universe or the Ground of Being or, to be a bit Buddhist, Emptiness or No-thing) may seem less trivial. Many believe that God answers prayers by intervening to alter the normal processes of nature and history, while for others it is childish to expect miracles. Many find it easy to pray to God as "Almighty Father"; for others, both those words are difficult, for God is not a monarch and not a man. Many think of Jesus Christ as "God and Saviour" in a traditional way; but others do not. Many consciously rely on the Holy Spirit to make them pray or to pray in them; but to others such a traditional expression means little, and the unleashing of the emotions in dependence on the Spirit is very dangerous. Many, as they worship God, think that life before death is only a preparation for life after it; others are extremely uncertain about what may lie beyond death. Many find it helpful or delightful, or at any rate their clear duty, to spend hours in concentrated prayer; others find that real prayer is an arrow shot up from the midst of everyday life. Many go to church regularly; many do not feel so obliged or inclined. These are not differences which arise solely because one Christian is conventional or shallow, or the other heretical or lazy. Whether we agree with them or not, these seem to be different paths which the sincere and serious Christian can take in our time.

I became more sensitive to the diversity in modern Christianity when I was a young publisher of religious books as Editor of the SCM Press, particularly when in 1963 I published a bestseller, *Honest to God* by John Robinson, then Bishop of Woolwich. That paperback aroused storms of protest or enthusiasm spreading out from London, eventually in many languages. People who had seldom bothered with theology were among those who discussed its challenges, often without reading every word. For many, *Honest to God* was a symbol (welcome or unwelcome) of the end of a consensus about what Christianity is (whether believed or not). Part of the fascination of the book was that the author seemed to be debating with himself, being partly traditional and partly radical. Could he rightly be a bishop? Also fascinating was the question whether the religion that seemed to be emerging out of the radical side could rightly be called Christian. The newspaper article in which Robinson summarized his book on publication was given the headline "Our Image of God Must Go". Did that mean that any current image of God was a mere figment of the imagination? Was the book's sympathy with the "new morality" a surrender to the old immorality? Different answers were found by different readers in the one little book and in their own reactions to its explosion. In 1963 I edited *The Honest to God Debate*, printing a few of the thousands of reviews and letters which had poured in; and in 1989 I offered my own reflections in *Tradition and Truth*, discussing Robinson along with some later radicals who made him look cautious.

For about forty years I have read at least one new religious book almost every week, often in order to write a review for the *Church Times* or the *Tablet*. The debate has moved on, away from the excited thoughts of the 1960s that God might be in some sense "dead" and Man in some sense "come of age". (Did the 1973 rise in oil prices after a dozen years when the world's economic output had increased by 5 per cent a year do something to end that mood of power, affluence and secularity?) But the ferment in Christianity has certainly not ceased.

In worldwide Christianity it has been spiritually creative to see in new ways how lovely and how vulnerable is this planet – and to see the human body, including the genitals, as the crown of the creation. I have seen the spiritually healthy growth of an insistence on the provision of the basic bodily needs – food, housing, health care, education, work – for all God's children. I have seen churchgoing in decline in many places, but a search for spiritual truth often growing. In other parts of the world I have seen churches decisively influencing nations. I have seen Roman Catholicism in a creative turmoil which has broken a pattern set by four hundred years – and the Evangelical movement gaining ground but becoming a federation, with some Evangelicals accepting many of the things which liberals were denounced for teaching, and some exploring Pentecostal experiences once regarded as too emotional. I have seen the Eastern Orthodox Churches beginning a new life, at last free of persecution, and burying doctrinal disputes which had lasted for fifteen hundred years. I have seen some Christians being more revolutionary than the Communists, and churches outlasting Communist governments. I have seen Christianity covered with the red dust of Africa or with the sweat of Asia's heat and poverty. I have seen it black as the preached, marched and danced theology of races once despised as Negroes. I have seen women clergy and theologians embodying another renewal of Christianity, potentially the most far-reaching of all. And I have heard all this vigour celebrated and communicated in an outburst of new hymns and songs, new communities and experiments.

I suppose I have lived through some of the most richly creative years in the whole history of Christian life and thought. Perhaps it is possible to sum up much of it by saying that over the last sixty years Christianity has creatively exploded in two hemispheres – the right hemisphere of the brain, which, we are told, is the birthplace of intuition, imagination and creativity itself, and the southern hemisphere of our planet, where live people who are poor materially but rich spiritually, many millions of them being Christians. But during these years I have had many conversations with people of many kinds – from university teachers in Oxbridge to residents in a poor part of London – who have the impression not that Christianity is alive and well but that Christians disagree about everything. The creativity which thrills me leaves many people utterly confused or bored by the controversies. Particularly is this true in the northern hemisphere of the world, where the rational, logical and soberly truth-loving left hemisphere of the brain is honoured.

Who can sort out such disagreements? To use a Catholic term, what is the *magisterium*? It appears to be foolish to hope that the scholars will agree, for there seem to be as many opinions as there are scholars – and more, for many scholars have divided minds because they refuse to oversimplify. If we look for a preacher to guide us, everything will depend on which preacher we choose to believe. If we are Roman Catholics we shall certainly look towards Rome – but many Catholics who consider themselves faithful do not entirely like what they see there, and many surveys of Catholic lay opinion have shown a lack of confidence that the Pope is "infallible" in any ordinary sense. In the 1960s the Second Vatican Council opened windows but did not close debates. If we are Orthodox we shall place our trust in Councils of the Church – but no council acknowledged as "ecumenical" (truly representative of the whole Church) has met since 787. At present, as for many centuries past, not even the date of Easter can be agreed by the whole Church. If the Orthodox Churches are no longer persecuted by atheist Communists, and are no longer needed to keep nationalism alive, many questions may be asked aloud. Since 1948 the World Council of Churches has done something to express Christian agreement in theology as well as in practical concerns; I have attended two of its Assemblies. But the Roman Catholic Church is not a member of it, and few ordinary Christians treat it as a weighty authority.

The most commonly invoked authority for Christians is, of course, the Bible. But Christians disagree about the nature of the Bible. What are its contents? Is the Bible "infallible" or "inerrant"? If so, does that traditional word mean that it contains no mistake at all? If the word means something else, what is that? If a passage is poetry (perhaps written as prose), how literally should it be taken? If only "what Scripture affirms" is authoritative, what does that include? What is the Bible's central message or "Gospel"? What belongs to a vanished culture? What belongs to the everlasting Gospel? As they wrestle with such questions, even Christians who are inclined to be conservative because they love the Bible are not so sure-footed as their predecessors were.

Fundamentalism survives and in some situations flourishes. It can seem to be true to people who know no alternative. Or its simplicity can appeal as an alternative to confusion, and its security can be very attractive in a time of

many rapid changes. Persecuting it, or insulting it, can make
it more obstinate. It can be the banner for the struggle of a
threatened nation or class. But in most parts of the modern
world, fundamentalism meets education as the sand meets
the incoming tide. More likely than fundamentalism's victory is the prospect of most Christians working out their
own beliefs without frequent Bible study or churchgoing.

At the opposite end of the spectrum of religious opinions,
Christian liberalism or modernism also survives. Instead of
rejecting modernity, it welcomes and learns from the age in
which it lives. It is critical of the Bible and the Church, and
is prepared to adjust tradition to newly perceived truth. It
can attract people who want to think for themselves. But it
is less confident towards the end of the twentieth century
than it was towards the beginning, for it has often been felt
to be too weak, too soft-centred, to stand up to the evils
which have raged since 1914. It has seemed to be too aca-
demic and too ready to compromise and complicate. It has
seemed like a rowing boat at home on a lake in a park but
now tossed on the ocean by a storm. The triumph of liberalism or modernism as we have known it has become as
improbable as the triumph of fundamentalism.

To be honest, the Christian scene often appears to be
confusion raised to the level of chaos. There may seem to
be many Christianities, led by many Christs. But is that the
whole of the truth?

DIVERSITY AND AGREEMENTS

My argument in this book will be that what appears to be
confusion in Christianity is to a large extent a diversity of
temperament and circumstance. Within this diversity, much
more agreement is possible than is often expected. It is
possible to discover what nearly all Christians now believe

to be Christianity's essential message – "the Gospel". And it is possible to find the truth there.

The diversity is inevitable unless there is to be a censorship worthy of a police state. In practice, Christianity could not be permanently controlled by European men, even if such men were to agree. If recent trends continue, in the year 2000 about 6¼ billion (thousand million) people will be alive on this planet, and almost a third of them will call themselves Christians. About 10 per cent will live in Asia, about 20 per cent in Africa, and about 30 per cent in Latin America – and (as always) most of the more active among them will be women. But some agreement has proved possible in the past, so that Christianity has an inherited identity. Opinions have differed about the exact contents of this agreement, but that is not to say that there has been no agreement at all. Certain perversions of Christianity have been seen – seen by almost every Christian who is aware of them – to fall outside the agreement, although this understanding may have taken some time to become fully formed and agreed. The Inquisition, which was set up to defend Christianity in the Middle Ages, is now agreed to have been an attack on it because it was so cruel. The attempt of some "German Christians" to bestow Christian blessings on Nazism has been condemned by nearly all Christians, as has been the attempt to find biblical support for European colonialism or South African racism. A preacher who interprets the freedom brought by the Gospel to mean sexual liberty for himself finds that not many people believe what he says on American TV. Almost universal Christian agreement on such points ought to encourage the attempt to answer the question: What now is the identity of Christianity amid the inevitable diversity?

It is also encouraging to remember that Christian diversity is no new thing. It existed in centuries when memories of the founder were fresh and there was a great sense of common loyalty to him, a loyalty in life and death. It is true that in the first Christian century there were no denominations. But there were heated disagreements between and within the local churches, as is proved by Paul's or John's correspondence or by the letters to the seven churches in the Revelation of John; and the differences between the local churches were such that the differences between the gospels in the New Testament originated in them. It is possible to believe very simply in the authority of "what the Bible says" and to proclaim "the Gospel" with complete confidence – but it is impossible to deny the fact that there are at least four gospels. Some of the disagreements of that first Christian century are said to have involved serious departures from the basic Christian faith, as Paul or John or the author of the Revelation which closes the New Testament insisted, although it is now hard to recover the arguments of the so-called heretics. But other disagreements of the early days were within the common loyalty of fellow-Christians and fellow-martyrs, who knew that they followed a Lord who could not be divided.

In later centuries, forms of Christianity which were denounced as heretical encouraged Christ-like prayers and lives – a hint that their opponents often spoke too hastily. It is striking that forms of faith in Christ condemned by the councils of the Church which defined orthodoxy in the fourth and fifth centuries proved capable of effective missionary work in Europe (the Arians), up the Nile to Ethiopia (the Monophysites) and across Asia to China (the Nestorians). The Eastern Orthodox Churches, rejected in their turn by the Western medieval Church, proved capable of maintaining their life and wonderful worship under hostile political pressures. In the sixteenth and seventeenth centuries Protestantism, rejected by the Roman Catholic Church, began an international movement which showed great vigour and sanctity – and so did a renewed Roman Catholicism in the "Counter-Reformation". In the twentieth century historic Protestantism has felt itself superior to the Pentecostal Churches; yet the Pentecostals have grown faster. The Vatican has tried to maintain order in the Roman Catholic Church which, however, has consisted largely of Christians with their own ideas. I conclude that Christianity would have been better served had there been less arrogance about who is truly Christian, and had fewer Christians excommunicated each other.

Recently, although many disagreements remain between Christians and many divisions have gone unhealed, it has been seen that hostility is disgraceful. Instead there has been a quest for unity. It has proved possible for members of different denominations to collaborate in many practical tasks. More strangely, it has also proved possible to reach agreements in many theological questions previously in dispute by listening patiently to each other's convictions, by respecting each other's experiences and by going together to the Bible and to the whole Christian tradition in order to reason together about the conclusions to be drawn. This patient theological work has been inspired by the conviction that other Christians are spiritually and morally authentic Christians, within the Church as the "Body of Christ". In the twentieth century this movement towards Christian unity has been called ecumenical. Because that word still arouses some suspicions, I repeat: ecumenical agreements are based on the Bible. And this is no accident.

It has proved possible to find this biblical basis for agreements because the Bible is marked by unity as well as diversity. The intensive study of the material made in the nineteenth and twentieth centuries has taught both lessons, and the next century ought to profit from them. If there had been no unity in the Bible, there could be no strong reason for assembling these books and treating them as a collection which means something, as almost all Christians have done. The Christian claiming the Bible's support would really be supported only by those bits which he or she fancied. Fellow Christians would be quick to draw attention to this flimsy basis but they, too, would be in no position to say that others ought to agree with them. Christianity would be no more than a collection of opinions, often incompatible with each other, held by people who like to call themselves Christians. But if there was no diversity in the Bible, its many books would not hold so many different meanings for so many different people, giving rise to the debate about which meanings are most Christian. Indeed, I hope to show in this book that many of the movements which have caused diversity in twentieth-century Christianity – genuinely Christian Christianity – have parallels in the diversity of the New Testament.

Although many Christians have been so prejudiced against the Jewish religion that they have often denied any connection with it, it seems to me a fact that the forms of Christianity which have been most successful have been deeply influenced by Judaism. This is not surprising. Jesus was a Jew not only by birth but also by formation, including all that he had of schooling. Every part of his message was expressed in a style which was as Jewish as his body. He protested against parts of the teaching of his Jewish contemporaries but much of his own proclamation was based on the Hebrew Scriptures or agreed with them. It ought to cause no surprise that the new movement which he began had many Jewish characteristics, both in its early days and in its more developed forms. Nor should it amaze us that in our own time strong features of successful Christianity are recognizable as features also to be found in the Jewish tradition.

The Roman Catholic Church is by far the largest body of Christians in the modern world. The Orthodox Churches – of Russia, for example, or Greece – also have a large and devoted membership. Among Protestants, often the greatest success has been achieved by those with a conservative theology, whether Lutheran or Reformed, whether Evangelical or Pentecostal, and although these Protestants are often highly critical of the Roman Catholic and Orthodox Churches their interpretation of Christianity does have features in common with those Churches. To some extent conservative Christianity is all of one type – and all of a Jewish character.

For all these conservative Christian bodies convey a powerful sense of the presence of God. Their greatest attraction is that they seem to set up ladders reaching to heaven. They convince millions that they can offer salvation from the sins and sorrows of the world. Their worship communicates this sense that God is real and near – whether it is the Catholic Mass or the Orthodox Liturgy or the more informal worship of the Protestants. That sense of God is a feature which is prominent in the Hebrew Bible and constitutes its perennial fascination. If Catholics and Orthodox tend to think of the Church as a great temple full of priests and incense, the Hebrew psalms are in the Bible as reminders of what the temple in Jerusalem meant to some worshippers; and if Protestants have in the mind's eye a small fellowship gathered round the Scriptures, that is the Christian version of the synagogue.

These conservatives, Jewish or Christian, know where they stand. They have respected teachers – rabbis, priests or ministers – who in their turn respect the Scriptures. In the Roman Catholic and Orthodox Churches there exists a great sense of continuity with the Church which first acknowledged or "canonized" the Scriptures. Roman Catholics regard the Pope as the successor of Peter, the chief of the apostles, and therefore as the head of the college which consists of the world's bishops. They are confident that Christ has guaranteed that his Church, built on this rock, will never fatally deviate from the truth. In the twentieth century disagreements about the nature and scope of papal infallibility and jurisdiction have surfaced. But in one sense or another everyone who is more than a nominal Roman Catholic has a sense that the Church is founded on the promises of Christ – and not only on the promise to be present in the Mass. In a way that is psychologically similar whatever the theological differences, all faithful members of the Orthodox Churches feel that they glimpse heaven when they worship with the saints in the Liturgy. They also feel confident that they inherit true teachings when they are loyal to the teachings of the Fathers of the Church. In the twentieth century many thousands of them have proved their love and loyalty by martyrdom; and many millions by a refusal to accept atheist Marxism. And although the conservative Protestants of whom I am thinking regard many of the practices and teachings of Catholics and Ortho-dox as strange or repulsive, they have the same sense that God has given a revelation which can be known clearly and expounded authoritatively – a revelation which calls for prayer and obedience. The Bible and the preacher proclaim a salvation which is accepted with all the heart. Psychologi-cally similar is the tradition of orthodox Judaism, which delights in obeying a definite law in response to a definite revelation. And the results of this strong orthodoxy in human lives are not only visible in any conservative Catholic, Orthodox or Protestant congregation or orthodox syna-gogue. They are also to be seen in the life of a family or individual whose love is shaped by the glad acceptance of moral and religious laws.

It has often been said that for Jews orthodoxy is mainly "orthopraxis" (it stresses the practical keeping of the food laws or the Sabbath or moral standards in daily life), whereas Christians have been more interested in defining doctrines. But this contrast can be exaggerated. Jews do have definite beliefs and they produce rival movements which argue about beliefs. Conservative Christians do emphasize practical (and not only theoretical) conformity to the tradition, for example, attendance at church or obedience to the bishops or preachers in sexual and other behaviour. In both religions orthodoxy is a collection of attitudes, theoretical and practical. That is why in the early history of Christianity the strongest features of Judaism could be adapted to serve the Church's needs. Inevitably the process involved uncertainty and controversy about the question of which Jewish teachings and practices were then obsolete. But "Early Catholicism" emerged out of these difficulties with remarkable speed and success. Its system of belief and behaviour mixed the Jewish heritage with borrowings from the Greek or Roman society which it gradually conquered – and one reason why it did conquer was that it was a firm system.

However, in every generation this obedience to a religious law does not satisfy the spirits of some who hunger for a more direct contact with God. Through Christian, as through Jewish, history there runs a small but golden thread of mysticism, in which the painfully purified soul claims direct access to the ultimate mystery. In Christian, as in Jewish, experience there is also a possibility open to people who would never think of themselves as mystics. These people say that the gifts of the living God have been poured into their hearts and lives, producing miracles, healings and extraordinary powers. The ecstatic "speaking in tongues" which can be heard by onlookers as babbling is only one phenomenon in this intense experience of God as miraculous energy – as "Holy Spirit". More important is the new warmth of joy and love, breaking down many barriers. And although onlookers may say that all this is the result of emotional excitements, to those who "believe" it is nothing else than a response to the thrilling acts of God. For Jews, this means responding personally to the acts of God in the long history of that unique and tragic people, including the modern resurrection of Israel. For Christians, it means responding personally to the acts of God in Christ, supremely in Christ's death and resurrection. For many Christians, the response has taken the form of believing that sinless Christ died as a substitute for sinners, accepting the punishment due (because the Father is just) for the world's sins. For the individual, this belief can have the focus: "Christ died for me." So the heart rises in gratitude and adoration – it may be when the bread, which is to the faithful Christ's body, is given in the Mass; it may be when the deeds and promises of Christ are taken to heart in a conversion. The Christian response also takes the form of believing that Christ's resurrection from the dead is a foretaste of the glory which awaits all who in their hearts are united with Christ. For the individual, this belief has the focus: "I too shall rise from death and be with Christ." So the light which dawns on Good Friday and Easter floods into a mortal life. We shall find that in the early years of Christianity Paul taught this profoundly personal understanding of what it means to be a Christian.

The intensity of this personal experience of being "saved" by Christ, particularly by his death and resurrection, is often contained within a traditional framework of beliefs and customs. But it may lead to a rejection of the regulations and practices which more conventional Christians regard as orthodox and respectable. Therefore the majority of Christians tend to be suspicious of the "enthusiasm" which claims to enjoy extraordinary gifts of the Holy Spirit. Such Christians may prefer to say that they quietly follow the teachings of Christ, attracted by his life, believing in his uniqueness but not paying special attention to his death and resurrection or to Pentecost. For such Christians, Christ is the messenger who announces the good news that God is real and that God reigns. He summons disciples in every generation, and these disciples find that his way is the way of the good life, the way of peace, health and joy.

That is a happy version of Christianity and we shall, I think, find that it is also expressed within the New Testament, in the material which the scholars call Q. Much sterner is the understanding of Christ which sees him as one who stands among those condemned to poverty, contempt and death – and as one who challenges all who would follow him to "take up" their own crosses among those who are still the victims of power. But this summons to suffering is also a summons to share in a victory over evil, and – even more strangely – a victory over death. Of course few will hear this call. Always it will be a mysterious call. But those who do hear it will not play around with ifs and buts. They will hurry after their strange Lord, with his suffering and triumph, for he is the Son of God who commands. The twentieth century, which has produced many more Christian martyrs than any previous age, is able to understand that Gospel.

That is a dramatic Gospel. Mark's gospel, which preaches it in the New Testament, is intensely dramatic: it is about a crisis and it creates a crisis for the reader. But many Christians have a calmer understanding of Christianity as a message about God's love for the humble in every section of humanity. God loves those who are often despised by people who are powerful in the world. He loves the women he created; he loves the poor and those who help them; he welcomes sinners and he clothes them with beauty. One by one, God's children who have been rejected find acceptance, peace and a new way of life. Such a version of Christianity appeals particularly to those who are marginalized by their societies. But it can also touch the hearts of the educated and the influential by its vision of the love of God for all. These are features of Luke's gospel in the New Testament – features which are understood wherever Christianity is understood as liberation. And as the twentieth century approaches its end, "liberation" has become the key in much Christian life and thought.

Some Christians, however, find that this emphasis on God's all-embracing love is not strenuous enough. Their understanding of Christianity may take either of two forms. They may hear the call of Christ as essentially a moral challenge to them – a challenge to a heroic level of morality. The perfection which they see in Christ and his teaching rises high above any level which can be reached by a law, for a law must take account of the unheroic and the problematic. The conscience is touched, the moral imagination is awakened, by a sermon on a mountain and a man on a cross; and so with him they climb the mountain. Or Christians may hear the call of Christ as an invitation to know peace in his love for them, feeding on him as branches feed, finding in him the one light amid the world's darkness, seeing his glory. They hear a call not so much to morality as to spirituality, not so much to a life which is busily involved in this world's tasks as to a more contemplative life which begins eternity. In the New Testament, the gospels of Matthew and John reflect this difference between morality and spirituality as they show Christianity moving beyond Judaism.

Those are the most important strengths of the healthy

forms of twentieth-century Christianity. The New Testament shows that they were also the greatest strengths of the varied reactions to Jesus Christ when Christianity was young. We complain about the difficulties which Christians experience as they dispute about the correct response to questions which are essentially modern, but we ought not to forget that it was difficult to reach an adequate agreement in New Testament times as Christianity moved from Galilee and Jerusalem to Antioch, Corinth and Rome. Unity was difficult – but not impossible. That ought to encourage modern and post-modern Christians.

The universal ("Catholic") faith of Christians was defined by St Vincent of Lérins, a monk who died before 450, as being "what has been believed everywhere, always and by all". He taught that development in doctrine was legitimate but should always be based on the truth proclaimed by the Bible. Much Christian theology in the twentieth century has been more exploratory and questioning than a fifth-century monk would have thought proper, and "what has been believed everywhere, always and by all" has shrunk considerably since his day. Even then he was not aware of the limits of what "all" Christians had believed. But I am one of those who think that he was essentially right to see the continuing task of theology as being a development which is not chaotic. It is an adventure with its base in a tradition which begins in the Bible, and it never loses touch with that base; therefore the adventurers can keep in touch with one another. The age of science and of freedom has indeed posed new challenges to traditional Christianity, inconceivable in the fifth century. I shall refer to some of the problems in the last two chapters of this book. But in the debates about such challenges it seems possible to discern the truths which remain the essential truths in Christianity while leaving less vital points to remain optional. That process must involve new thinking and new disagreements, but there can be new "gospels" which are truly Christian, matching the New Testament's diversity-within-unity, because in new situations they restate truths "believed everywhere, always and by all".

So I believe. I shall now try to argue in more detail. I ask for the reader's patience because much is at stake.

Eight Gospels

INTERPRETING JESUS OF NAZARETH

JESUS of Nazareth has been the most influential figure in the
history of the world. That is suggested by the vigour of the
debate about the significance of his life two thousand years
after his birth. But the attraction of Jesus, and the facing of
his challenge, can be seen far outside the circle of actively
debating theologians and churchgoers, and far outside the
third (almost) of humanity which calls itself Christian.
Whether or not he will have a similar, or smaller or greater,
influence after AD 2000 depends partly on people's assess-
ment of what the New Testament says about him.

At present two opinions often compete for popular acceptance. They are both, I think, mistaken.

It is sometimes said that the New Testament supplies
an account of Jesus which deserves to be received without
questioning because it is accurate in all its facts and permanently authoritative in all its verdicts on these facts. Such
fundamentalism, however, does not stand up to any honest
examination. A single careful reading of the four gospels –
or (to take an example) of what they say about the resurrection of Jesus – will show that at many points, small or large,

they do not agree with each other. A reading of the letters collected in the New Testament will leave much the same impression on an open mind: about opinions as about facts, Christians disagreed. Those whose curiosity has been stirred by such an experience and who are willing to embark on further reading will find that a very large library is composed of books and articles by scholars writing since the disciplines of "biblical criticism" and "biblical hermeneutics" had their origins among Protestants in nineteenth-century Germany. ("Criticism" here means the study of the literary composition and historical background of the Bible, while "hermeneutics" was well defined by Rudolf Bultmann as "the technique of understanding expressions of life set in a written form".) No one can truthfully claim to have studied all that literature – or to agree with it all, for it is vigorously argumentative. Suggestions for which there is no solid evidence are often put forward in waves of fashion, and are then contradicted or viewed as outdated. But no one who has taken seriously the reasons which are stated carefully and defended reasonably for the main, solid, conclusions of all that intellectual labour can remain an uncomplicated fundamentalist. Many Christians around the world do not have the education which would enable them to cope with such problems, but those who do possess the necessary equipment, and who live in an educated society, have a moral duty to think. They do Christianity no service if they cling to fundamentalism, for they imply that Christian faith is incompatible with an honest exploration of the truth.

Another opinion has got around which is, I consider, equally false. Many people are sufficiently educated to have picked up an impression that after "biblical criticism" nothing important can be known about the historical Jesus, and nothing convincing can be said about his significance. The New Testament is thought to be more or less a book of fairy tales. Every few years some new "discovery" gets reported to the public by the media. When it is not a "discovery" which is welcomed by fundamentalists because it is held to prove the truth of the whole Bible, it may be a "discovery" which is held to suggest that the Bible contains no truth at all. Here the intellectual situation is more complicated than it is in connection with fundamentalism, for whereas fundamentalism finds no support among genuine scholars some members of that learned profession have taken a very negative line about the reliability of the New Testament. It can be argued by some scholars that only a few facts can be known about Jesus, and that these support only a narrow understanding of his message for later generations – an understanding which can turn out to be what this particular scholar would have thought anyway. But such attitudes are felt by most scholars to be too pessimistic, and good reasons are given for this opinion. The majority opinion among those who have gone into the problems is that quite a lot can be known about Jesus as a matter of fact – and quite a lot can be said responsibly about what all this means.

What is plainly true is that the New Testament, our only major source of information, gives us several accounts and interpretations of Jesus – several "gospels". We are about to study not only the four gospels which are printed as such in any Christian Bible, but also four more traditions which I call gospels in a way which I hope can be justified. These gospels differ from each other because they are all accounts and interpretations which come to us from communities of Christians whose faith is being expressed, and to some extent shaped anew, by the individual writer. The Revelation of John includes powerful examples of the practice by which prophets spoke within churches, and to them, in the name of Jesus. The Acts of the Apostles is another book which shows how it was believed that the voice of the exalted

Christ who was "in heaven" could be heard from time to time, with fresh messages. Two such messages changed the life of Paul. One, reported only in Acts (9:5), taught that to persecute his disciples was to persecute Jesus. Another, reported by Paul himself (2 Corinthians 12:9), declared that "my grace is all you need; power is most fully seen in weakness". John's gospel seems to have been written with a similar sense that Jesus was still alive and speaking in John's mind and community, but not one of the accounts in the New Testament is an unedited record of what the historical Jesus actually said. We can see this if we examine the ways in which Luke and Matthew changed the words in Mark's earlier gospel. To get at the real history of Jesus, we have to compare all the accounts and then try to get behind the editorial additions and interpretations. Sometimes that can be done. But sometimes comparing the accounts leaves us merely guessing which is nearer to the truth about history.

One of the problems is that in the ancient world few people – if any – were deeply interested in finding out the details of what had really taken place. Modern people want to know who a witness, reporter or writer is, for this helps us to decide about the authenticity of the account. In the ancient world, however, the practice of attributing one's own words to some greater figure was not regarded as fraudulent. Ancient books were written mainly in order to be read out to an audience, and "history" was regarded more as a branch of edifying or entertaining story-telling than as a piece of scientific research. Even Josephus, the unusually careful Jewish historian who wrote at about the same time as Luke and Matthew, frequently twisted or omitted facts in order to suit his purposes as a Jew writing for Romans, whose side he had joined. The element of propaganda which was present in all ancient "history" was such that a controller of TV programmes would have classified most of it as drama, not news. This element was increased when the "historians" were evangelists instructing religious communities with religious opinions which they were prepared to defend to the death. Another problem is that when offering interpretations of the life of Jesus the authors of the New Testament were not systematic thinkers trained to argue a case with cool logic. As they proclaimed the faith that dominated them, they were story-tellers who hoped that the way in which they told a story would make the desired impact, which was usually spiritual or moral rather than intellectual. It was an impact which might send their hearers gladly to their deaths. If they wanted to be more explicit, more than story-tellers (as in the letters collected in the New Testament), they used an image, or a title or quotation borrowed from earlier literature, without discussing in any detail how they would justify the application to the central figure in the story. It was a signal. They did not explain it, any more than modern lyric-writers, poets, dramatists or artists explain. In these methods of teaching they were like Jesus himself, one of the world's greatest story-tellers and image-makers. Any modern quest for a systematic "theology of the New Testament" composed of abstract ideas is therefore doomed to considerable disappointment.

That is the Christian Bible which really exists. The character of that determines the character of the diversity-in-unity which exists in Christianity. Most of the claims which have been made by Christian groups or individuals for basing their own teachings or organizations on the Holy Scriptures actually depend on selecting from the Bible those parts which seem to deserve the most emphasis, and those parts are then interpreted. The needs to select and to interpret amid the variety of biblical material become obvious as Christians consider the Hebrew Scriptures, for the "Old Testament" includes such different books, written at such different dates and in such different styles, that one is bound to pick and choose, and to interpret, if one is to say that such material is relevant and authoritative. Even the question "What books belong to the Hebrew Scriptures?" cannot be answered without choosing. Different groups of Jewish scholars drew up different lists in ancient times, and in the fifteenth and sixteenth centuries Catholic and Protestant authorities took different sides. The exact text was often uncertain, particularly before the vowels were added to the consonants in the period AD 600–900. A close study of the Old Testament quotations in the New shows that Jesus and the early Christians adapted the Hebrew Scriptures to their own purposes, partly because they quoted from memory in almost all cases, just as the authors of what Christians call the Old Testament did not regard each other as infallible. The New Testament (with contents not officially agreed before 367) is also far from being one unified, uniform, text book. It is in some ways like a magazine in its variety, and like a film in being open to personal reactions. Accordingly long experience has shown that interpretations by sincere, honest and careful Christians can differ widely.

All these facts remind us that the Bible is the words of men. But experience has also shown that the Christian Bible, with its two Testaments, has a strange power to challenge, instruct and inspire – a power so great that it can be called the "Word of God". And it has at its centre the amazing claim that Jesus was this "Word" in a life. Let us therefore examine, as objectively as possible, the evidence about how the writers of the New Testament understood the significance of the life of Jesus. Let us be honest both about its diversity and about its agreements. Christians who disagree with each other often appeal to the Bible as the decisive authority. To the Bible we too shall go.

THE JEWISH GOSPEL

The great rebellion against the Romans which began in AD 66 and erupted again in 132 resulted in a destruction of the Jewish nation which lasted until 1948. It also brought fatal damage to the earliest form of Christianity. Early in the fourth century the church historian Eusebius recorded a tradition that the Christians had escaped from Jerusalem when the troubles began, but it is certain that they became a small group which was regarded by fellow Christians, as well as by all orthodox Jews, as heretical. Their version of Christianity came to be called "Ebionite". Yet it was based on the account of Jesus given by his own family and by his earliest followers. All these were devout Jews, as he had been. If their gospel was ever written down, the document has been lost; it may well have been destroyed by a later generation as heretical. (The later "Gospel of the Hebrews" and the "Gospel of the Ebionites" have also been lost, while the "Preaching of Peter" which has survived dates from about 200.) But something can be reconstructed.

Christianity, it is clear, began as one of the movements within Judaism which gave aloof onlookers the irritating impression that Jews argued endlessly between themselves about their strange god. In about 110 the Roman historian Suetonius recorded that Claudius, emperor 41–54, had expelled all the Jews from Rome because of disturbances among them "at the instigation of Chrestos". (The expulsion is also mentioned in Acts 18:1–4.) Oddly enough, the Christian writer who enables us to detect a little of the history of this troublesome Jewish movement was probably not a Jew. At least he conveys to us something of the atmosphere of those early days. At the end of his gospel Luke represented Jesus, freshly risen from the dead, as wanting to persuade his followers that his suffering had been predicted in the

Hebrew Scriptures. At the beginning of his gospel Luke told
stories about the births of Jesus and of his cousin, John the
Baptist, and these stories contain many touches which seem
to come from an early and very Jewish form of Christianity,
whether he was using material which came from the old
days or was composing in an old-fashioned style. The stories
begin in the temple in Jerusalem, to be called by Jesus "my
Father's house" (2:49). They feature a holy priest, a layman
who is "upright and devout" and a widow who is perpetually
in the temple. Mary and Joseph, themselves the finest fruit
of "Old Testament" piety, are also careful to respect the
temple and the religious law (2:22–24). Mary is promised
that her son will be given "the throne of his ancestor David"
(1:32). Her song of triumph (1:46–54) echoes Hannah's song
(1 Samuel 2:1–10), and Zechariah's song (1:67–79) is also
thoroughly Jewish. It is striking that Luke, who might have
been tempted to denigrate the religion which in his time had
bitterly quarrelled with the Church, here presents Judaism
most attractively.

In the first five chapters of the Acts of the Apostles (Luke's
Volume Two) the atmosphere is still thoroughly Jewish,
whether or not the historical details are accurate. In Jerusalem a substitute is chosen to replace the traitor Judas: at
this stage there must be twelve apostles, for there are twelve
tribes in the Israel which is the mission field. The twelve,
among whom Peter is most prominent, are joined by James
and the other brothers of Jesus in the leadership of the new
community. (Paul records that the apostles and the brothers
of Jesus were married but did not have to earn their livings: 1
Corinthians 9:5, 6.) These leaders worship in the Jerusalem
temple daily, at the time of the afternoon sacrifice (Acts
2:46; 3:1). The Holy Spirit is experienced dramatically while
they celebrate the Jewish festival of Pentecost, and this gift
is understood as the power to see "the great and terrible

day of the Lord" coming, as predicted by an ancient prophet of Israel. Peter preaches about Jesus as a man "singled out by God" whose resurrection was predicted in a psalm, but there is no similar emphasis on the positive value of the crucifixion. Later he says that Jesus was a prophet like Moses, and had been "appointed" Messiah, a title he does not need to explain. Although in his gospel Luke presents the later conviction that Jesus had been Messiah from birth, in this reconstruction of the original Christianity he seems to record an earlier belief, for he writes of God making his "servant" Jesus Messiah, apparently as a reward for a lifetime of good service (2:36; 4:27). As Messiah, Jesus is to be sent back from heaven at "the time for the universal restoration of which God has spoken through his holy prophets from the beginning" (Acts 3:21). So intense is the excitement of these Christians that they pool their possessions. It seems that only a short period was expected before that final day when Jesus would return to show his power as Messiah.

Essentially this appears to be a reliable picture of the origins of Christianity, for this small group is presented as one of the many movements which attempted to redefine Judaism in response to its great crisis. In the end the most influential Jews were the Pharisees, who understood Jewish identity as strict obedience to a religious law written in the Scriptures and interpreted or elaborated in a spoken tradition which was reduced to writing only gradually. That is what Orthodox Judaism means to this day. But there were other groups who seemed to be in a stronger position in the first half of the first century AD – the priests who controlled the immensely prestigious and rich temple which was then under Roman protection, supported by their wealthy and conservative Sadducean allies; the Zealots who sternly prepared to achieve the military liberation of Israel from those same Romans; the enthusiasts who relied on a miraculous liberation in the near future; charismatics or monks (to use modern terms) who withdrew from the stresses and despair of the time into spiritual excitements or dreams. It is entirely probable that the Jesus movement was first seen as an alternative answer to these acute Jewish problems, with something in common with each of the other movements but with its own hero, claimed to be the Messiah.

Later chapters of the Acts of the Apostles show this movement spreading hesitantly outwards from Jerusalem and even from Judaism. Within the holy city, Greek-speaking Jews who had been discontented got their own seven leaders. These criticized what the priests had made of the temple, although they still believed that the religious law was given to Moses "by God's angels" (7:53). They could be accused of hoping that in the future Jesus "will destroy the temple and alter the customs handed down to us by Moses" (6:14). One of them, Stephen, was lynched, and others were expelled from Jerusalem, to become missionaries elsewhere.

In the large, mixed, city of Antioch they extended their mission to non-Jews (Gentiles) and there the followers of Jesus were first nicknamed *Christianoi* (11:20, 26). Since *Christos* is the Greek translation of the Hebrew *Messiah* ("Anointed"), it seems that this name originated among Gentiles who mocked Jewish talk about the Liberator who had come or who was to come. The letters of Paul, however, suggest that *Christos* became increasingly detached from its Jewish origins and was used more or less as a surname. In those letters we can watch Christianity becoming increasingly Gentile, although in the movement's headquarters in Jerusalem most of the Christians continued to observe Jewish customs, including the sacrifices in the temple and the food laws at meals. As Paul told the Galatians (2:14) without any sympathy, while visiting Antioch Peter found himself in a dilemma. He no longer lived like an orthodox

Jew, for he realized that Gentiles must be included in the Christian community; yet he wished to remain on good terms with his fellow Jews, so that (on some occasions?) he kept himself apart from Gentile converts who would eat in a way that disgusted the orthodox. Some Christians believed that Paul himself still lived as "a practising Jew" (Acts 21:24; 28:17), but the tone of his rebuke to Peter makes that highly unlikely. His letters are only some of the documents in the New Testament which enable us to glimpse the pain and anger which surrounded Christianity's exit from Judaism.

Other documents appear to preserve some of the moral teaching of the earlier phase. Two are letters attributed to James and Jude, brothers of Jesus. Whoever wrote them, all these documents suggest that these Christians understood Jesus as having reinforced the Jewish moral tradition as this was accepted by devout and good people who were not interested in the technicalities of temple worship or of the religious law. "A pure and faultless religion in the sight of God the Father is this: to look after orphans and widows in trouble and to keep oneself untarnished by the world" (James 1:27). Good people must expect troubles and not grumble; they should not want to be rich, for the rich are likely to be wicked; they must not be snobs or hypocrites; their words must be few and plain; they must not doubt that the bad will be punished and the good rewarded. Enthusiasm about the End being very near has now declined and there is little excitement that a new age has already dawned. Nor is the crucifixion of Jesus emphasized. When an example of patient firmness under suffering is sought in the Letter of James, it is found not in Jesus but in Job (5:11).

There is also little or no conviction that God already loves sinners or declares them "just" while they are sinners. Instead, for James the message is "come close to God, and he will draw close to you" (4:8). Christians are urged to remember that "faith divorced from action is dead", so that "it is by action and not by faith alone that a man is justified" (2:24, 26).

The Revelation of John was, it seems, written when the Jerusalem temple had been demolished for some twenty years, but it gives us some last glimpses of the Jewish origins of Christianity. The whole book is a mosaic made up of references to the Hebrew Bible, and its style (in clumsy Greek) is adapted from Jewish "apocalyptic" documents about the end of the world. The coming overthrow of enemies is imagined with relish. The climax is a vision of a new age in the near future, when claims such as those of the persecuting emperor Domitian to be acknowledged as "Our Lord and God" will be answered by the true God's complete triumph. There will be a new, pure, deathless Jerusalem, with twelve gates which are never shut. Twelve thousand from each of the twelve tribes of Israel have been preserved from destruction and are mentioned first. The snatches of song preserved in this book as "the prayers of God's people" are of a Jewish character although Christians now sing to the Lamb of God: "By your blood you bought for God people of every tribe and language, nation and race" (4:9). In one sense the Revelation of John is revolutionary. In another sense it remains Jewish.

PAUL'S GOSPEL

In this period many who had been born Jews could not be pure by the standards of the full religious law, and many Gentile "Godfearers" were attracted by the Jews' teachings about the one God and about morality, but were not interested in their legal and sacrificial systems. That combination of publics can be seen as a market waiting for a

Gospel. But the revolutionary and international character of Christianity was first fully appreciated by one individual, not by a group; by a late-comer into the circle of the apostles, who became a missionary commissioned by the church in Antioch not Jerusalem; by one who was naturally conservative (as he showed in his period of Jewish orthodoxy, in his insistence on order in his churches, or in his respect for the Roman empire); and by one who used rabbinic methods of argument in order to claim that a Christian need not also be a Jew. Paul is the only personality among the early Christians known to us through his outbursts in letters. He is also the only early Christian who can be recognized by theologians as a member of their profession. But his was a theology arising out of life, not study. It was charged with emotion and directed to the practical needs of churches. Even his most elaborate exposition of his theology, his letter to the Christians in Rome, was dictated to a secretary, Tertius (16:22), not written and revised. Here a heart beats.

He was, of course, not entirely original. From his ancestral religion Paul had inherited many glories which he praised when writing to the Christians in Rome (chapters 9–11). "Theirs is the glory of the divine presence, theirs the covenants, the law, the temple worship, the promises" (9:4). Supreme in his Jewish heritage was faith in the one "true and living God". The converted Thessalonians are reminded in Paul's earliest surviving letter that they "turned from idols" to serve God (1:9). The Christians in Corinth are reminded that the pagan gods are not God, although since belief in them has been so strong Christians should refuse to eat meat which has been sacrificed to them, if challenged to do so (1 Corinthians 10:28). The Christians in Rome are reminded that the worship of idols has had horrifying effects on behaviour; the first two chapters of this letter burn with a clean-living Jew's indignation. God, the one God, created

the world and created it well. "Ever since the world began
his invisible attributes, that is to say his everlasting power
and deity, have been visible to the eye of reason in the things
he has made" (Romans 1:20). And the human body, so far
from being the prison or the tomb of a soul which was
fortunately detachable as some pagan philosophers taught,
is good enough to be called a "temple of the Holy Spirit"
(1 Corinthians 6:19). Paul is himself unmarried, but he
admits in the same letter that he has "no instructions" to
teach that it is wrong to have sex within marriage, for he
inherits the Jewish assumption that almost everyone ought
to enjoy marriage (7:25–28). His general awareness of his
debt to Judaism, and to the first Christians who lived inside
that tradition, is shown by his anxiety to make a success of
a collection to be raised in the congregations he sponsored
(shown in chapters 8 and 9 of 2 Corinthians). It was for
the benefit of Christians in Jerusalem, now poverty-stricken
because the resources pooled in the earlier enthusiasm had
been exhausted.

Within this Jewish tradition Paul writes to the Galatians
that "God sent his Son, born of a woman, born under the
law, to buy freedom for those who were under the law"
(4:4). Paul's gospel, he tells the Christians in Rome, is about
Jesus the Messiah: "on the human level he was a descendant
of David, but on the level of the spirit – the Holy Spirit –
he was proclaimed Son of God by an act of power that
raised him from the dead" (1:3,4). The tradition which Paul
"received" (1 Corinthians 15:3–11) was that "Christ died
for our sins, in accordance with the Scriptures" – a formula
which does not enter into any theological theory about the
atonement. Christ was buried but was "raised to life on the
third day" – a formula which seems to imply a physical
resurrection, although one of a "spiritual body". Paul tells
the Romans that "the God who raised Christ Jesus from the

dead will also give new life to your mortal bodies through his indwelling spirit" (8:11), and he promises the Philippians that "the Lord Jesus Christ will transfigure our humble bodies, and give them a form like that of his own glorious body" (3:21).

The evidence for Christ's resurrection, as given to the Corinthians about twenty-five years after his death, is found in six appearances – including appearances to Peter, James, "over five hundred of our brothers" and Paul himself, none of which is mentioned in the gospels written later. In those gospels women who found the tomb empty are key witnesses. But they are not mentioned by Paul – which may reflect an attitude that women are not reliable witnesses. His own meeting with the risen Jesus is referred to in his letter to the Galatians: God "chose to reveal his Son to me and through me" (1:16). In the Acts of the Apostles there are three slightly different accounts of this experience on the road to Damascus. None of them says that he saw a body, and Paul does not mention that he did in his own surviving letters. He tells the Galatians that he waited for three years before consulting the other apostles (1:17, 18). Yet it is crucial to his self-identification that he can exclaim: "Am I not an apostle? Have I not seen Jesus our Lord?" (1 Corinthians 9:11). There is therefore uncertainty about exactly how Paul understood the "spiritual body" of the risen Jesus. But he was clear that "if Christ was not raised, your faith has nothing to it" (15:17).

It has been claimed that Paul tells us very little about Jesus except what has just been quoted; and it is true that we cannot be sure that all his references to "the Lord" refer to the historical Jesus, not to the spirit of the risen Christ. But when he taught that those who preached the Gospel should be paid for doing so, he said: "the Lord gave instructions" (1 Corinthians 9:14). His first letter to Corinth includes another reference to the "tradition which I handed on" – about the Eucharist. According to this tradition, at his last supper Jesus said that the bread "is my body, which is for you; do this in memory of me" and that the cup of wine "is the new covenant sealed by my blood. Whenever you drink it, do this in memory of me" (11:24,25). He implied that Jesus envisaged a community with its own full-time preachers continuing after his death and celebrating a new "covenant" or agreement with God. But it was expected that the end of the world would come quickly, and this tradition is also derived from Jesus, as in the first letter to the Thessalonians (4:15). Paul ends his first letter to Corinth with a prayer in Aramaic, the language which Jesus and the first Christians used: *Marana tha*, "Come Lord!" And he never abandons his hope that Jesus will return in triumph quickly. When writing to the Philippians from prison, happily expecting death (1:23), he still looks forward to "the day of Christ" and assures them that "the Lord is near; do not be anxious" (2:16; 4:5, 6). This expectation has helped to detach him from normal human concerns – as it had detached the earliest Christians in Jerusalem. "The time we live in will not last long. While it lasts, married men should be as if they had no wives; mourners should be as if they had nothing to grieve them, the joyful as if they did not rejoice; those who buy should be as if they possessed nothing; and those who use the world's wealth as if they did not have full use of it. For the world as we know it is passing away" (1 Corinthians 7:29–31). But Paul has also received a tradition that no one knows when the Lord will "come like a thief in the night" (1 Thessalonians 5:2). So Christians remember Christ's death and resurrection "until he comes" – whenever he will come (1 Corinthians 1:26). They can afford to wait because already this "is" the day of deliverance (2 Corinthians 6:2). Already Paul and other Christians are filled with love for "the Son of God, who loved me and gave himself up for me" (Galatians 2:20).

Although Paul does not seem to refer to any written collection of the words of Jesus, Christians already know what is essential in his character and his commands. They see "the glory of God" in the face of that man (2 Corinthians 4:6). When Paul wants to speak about Christian confidence in God's love, he quotes Jesus in the language which Jesus spoke, "*Abba*! Father!", to the Galatians (4:6) and to the Romans (8:15). When he writes about his love for the church in Philippi he says: "God knows how I long for you all, with the deep yearning of Christ Jesus himself" (1:8). When he teaches right behaviour he says: "Let Christ Jesus himself be the armour that you wear" (Romans 13:24). In particular he quotes as authoritative the teaching of Jesus against divorce, although he adds his own opinion that a Christian may divorce an unbelieving spouse who has deserted (1 Corinthians 7:10–16). These are some of the implications of the creed which is quoted to the Romans (10:9) and in the first letter to Corinth (12:3): "Jesus is *Kurios* (Lord)!" Paul wrote that "it is not ourselves we proclaim but Christ Jesus as *Kurios*" (2 Corinthians 4:5). He used a word which may well have originated when in Palestine Jesus had been called *mari* – a term like our "sir", although it was also used about God himself in the Greek version of the Hebrew Bible.

Yet Paul the Jewish disciple of Jesus the Jew was also a radical innovator, because among the disciples his spiritual experience had an unprecedented depth and his mind a unique power. He wrote fiercely to the Galatians (2:1–14) that in Antioch he had contradicted "messengers from James" and had opposed Peter "to the face" because his "conduct did not square with the truth of the Gospel". The importance of apostles "reported to be something" – "those super-apostles" (2 Corinthians 11:5) – mattered little to a man who claimed to be "an apostle commissioned not by any human authority or human act, but by Jesus Christ and God the Father" (Galatians 1:1). Although the Acts of the Apostles reports a decree by "the apostles and elders" in Jerusalem which solved the problems presented by Christians not keeping the Jewish religious law (chapter 15), in his surviving letters Paul nowhere mentions that solution.

The Gospel which he preached had first been experienced personally and painfully. He shared with the Christians in Rome a memory of his deepest feelings about the Jewish religious law. He had found that no one could obey that law perfectly. So the law produced despair in his ultra-sensitive conscience, a "state of death" (7:24). The emotional strain continued when he became a Christian. He could explode with the wish that the "agitators" opposing him would castrate themselves (Galatians 5:12). He was often too touchy about his personal position. He formed intensely personal and long-lived relationships with the congregations which he founded. In his correspondence with them he could sound like a bully or like a man using emotional blackmail in order to arouse their pity for him. But his letter to Philemon about the runaway slave Onesimus was a masterpiece of diplomatic tact. The last chapter of his letter to Rome, a city he had never seen, was full of the names of men and women who had remained his friends. He wrote the greatest description of Christian love ever written (1 Corinthians 13), and it was a portrait of his Lord, for "I have been crucified with Christ: the life I now live is not my life, but the life which Christ lives in me" (1:20). To the Philippians he exclaimed: "to me life is Christ" (1:21), for once "Christ took hold of me" (3:12). All his assets in which he took pride were "far outweighed by the gain of knowing Christ Jesus my Lord, for whose sake I did in fact forfeit everything" (3:8). When he had finished dictating his letter to the Galatians, he wrote in big letters: "God forbid that I should boast of anything but the cross of our Lord Jesus Christ, through which the world is crucified to me and I to the world" (6:14).

In his mission as an ambassador of Jesus Christ he used both Jewish and Greek ideas. He knew that "Jews demand signs, Greeks look for wisdom, but we proclaim Christ nailed to the cross" (1 Corinthians 1:22, 23). But "I have an obligation to Greek and non-Greek, to learned and simple". So he told the Christians in Rome, believing that the Gospel which he proclaimed was "the saving power of God for everyone who has faith – the Jew first, but the Greek also" (1:16). "I have become everything in turn, so that in one way or another I may save some" (9:22). On this frontier between two cultures, he had two names: Saul of Tarsus became in Greek Paulos.

From the Jewish tradition he took the idea of "faith" as trusting commitment and obedience: if that is real, God can reach the human heart and the human life. Chapter 4 of the letter to Rome is the classic exposition of this, going back to Abraham. He also took the idea of "justification" from the Jewish picture of God as the Judge who judges justly. But the "faith" in God's decision to "justify" sinners moved beyond any picture of a hostile Judge. "All are justified by God's free grace alone" (Romans 3:24). "God was in Christ reconciling the world to himself, no longer holding people's misdeeds against them" (2 Corinthians 5:19). This is the strange "righteousness of God", he writes to the Christians in Rome (3:21, 25). The best English translation is probably "God designated Christ to be the means of expiating sin", although Paul does not explain the Greek word he uses (*hilasterion*). This probably implies a reference to the "sin offering", a sacrifice made in the temple in Jerusalem on the Day of Atonement. Yet Paul draws back from saying that

God needed to be appeased or reconciled to the world – ideas which would have made Christ's sacrifice "propitiation" not "expiation". The Jewish law pronounced a curse on a hanged man – and Christ came "under the curse for our sake" (Galatians 3:13), becoming "one with human sinfulness" (2 Corinthians 5:21). Yet Paul also draws back from saying that God punished Christ in our place in order to satisfy his justice. "Christ died for us" – the Greek makes it clear: *for* not *instead of* us – "while we were yet sinners, and that is God's proof of his love towards us" (Romans 5:8). In other words, Christ's death was the sacrifice which God himself had provided in order that sinners might be reconciled to him and draw near to him. The Evangelical leader John Stott discussed the doctrine of the Atonement somewhat more fully with me in our dialogue published as *Essentials* (1988).

What chiefly interests Paul is not the mechanism by which God achieves our reconciliation to him, but the result of the reconciliation – a new "covenant" or agreement with us, a new age which we can enter. In the terms of the Hebrew Scriptures, it is an age when one man has secured "acquittal and life for all", reversing the death sentence pronounced on the wrongdoing of Adam (Man). As predicted in those Scriptures, it is the age when the Holy Spirit is poured out (2 Corinthians 3) and inspires "justice, peace and joy" in the kingdom of God (Romans 14:17). And as is sometimes said in those Scriptures, this gift is intended for all. Paul's hopes are therefore universal. "In Christ all will be brought to life" (1 Corinthians 15:22). "Once the Gentiles have been admitted in full strength, the whole of Israel will be saved . . . In shutting up all mankind in the prison of their disobedience, God's purpose was to show mercy to all mankind" (Romans 11:25, 26, 32).

Other ideas prominent in Paul's teaching have often been

called "Hellenistic" by scholars who see closer connections with the religions of the Greek-speaking Roman empire of that time than with the Hebrew Bible. This description "Hellenistic" points to the effectiveness of these ideas in reaching the minds and hearts of the Gentiles whom Paul was addressing. The ideas were in the air in that world of religious thought. But in his surviving letters he never mentioned that he was a Roman citizen. Instead he confessed to the Christians in Rome, who included many Gentiles: "As an apostle to the Gentiles I make much of that ministry, yet always in the hope of stirring those of my own race to envy, and so saving some of them" (11:13, 14). Most of the modern experts in Pauline studies agree that he was completely a Jew and completely a Christian, sometimes expressing his Gospel in Hellenistic ways but not changing it basically in order to be fashionably Greek or Roman.

For example, he uses the word *gnosis*, "knowledge", and he tells the Christians that they can know God's *musterion*, "secret plan". While he was at work a religious movement was beginning which modern scholars call Gnosticism. New cults which modern scholars call "mystery religions" were making many converts. Jews would not be attracted by the gods worshipped in the mystery religions, but if intellectually or mystically inclined they could think about their own religion as knowledge of *sophia*, "wisdom", another term which Paul uses. Jews who were strongly traditionalist could claim "knowledge" of the glorious future, when Israel would at last be liberated, and many "apocalyptic" prophecies about that future, in coded language largely derived from the Scriptures, were treasured.

These movements did not produce a single creed or clear theology which Paul or anyone else could take over. Gnosticism, for example, did not create in his lifetime any literature which he could study alongside the Hebrew Scriptures – or at least, none of which we have any knowledge. (More than fifty Gnostic documents found near the Egyptian village of Nag Hammadi in 1947, our earliest substantial evidence, come from the second century or later.) The mystery religions differed from each other and were secretive. To outsiders they seemed silly or disgusting. Jewish speculation about the future created various scenarios but nothing that would greatly attract an intellectual such as Paul. He was convinced that only the Christians "possess full knowledge" since "God has made the wisdom of the world look foolish" (1 Corinthians 1:5,19). However, it is also evident that he welcomed the contemporary interest in what was called *pneuma*, "spirit" – a way of knowing and living that rose above the flesh and the everyday world, experienced as prisons. The Roman empire had brought a degree of political and cultural unity to that world. It had not brought content-ment. Many groups and individuals looked for something which could not be provided by the official religions, based on the sacrifices of animals in temples which meant little to the people, and on mythologies which did not impress the educated. Philosophical movements – Cynics, Epicureans, Stoics – attempted to fill the gap by teaching that people must reduce their wants, or at least their emotional agi-tations, to the minimum. But many who were religiously ardent looked for a new *soter*, a "saviour", who would bring light into their darkness, life into their deaths, power into their impotence. They hoped that by understanding some new message which their neighbours could not understand, or by undergoing some new ceremony which would create an intense religious experience for the few, they would be initiated into the secret that they were not doomed. Here was a spiritual search which Paul could meet.

He proclaimed the conquest of the evil powers which brought death to the "flesh" and the "world". Often these "powers" were believed to be Fate or Chance, or the stars which decided human destinies, or water, fire and air, the elements dictating life on Earth. Many mystery religions were based on myths about gods who were killed in the course of epic struggles with such evil powers, but who then won the victory by rising from death. Paul regarded the death and resurrection of Christ as facts in recent history, and therefore as a real victory over evil in the stars or anywhere else. He offered Christians a share in this victory although they, too, had been "subject to the elemental spirits of the universe", as "slaves to gods who are not gods at all" (Galatians 4:3, 8). A largely undistinguished and often quarrelsome congregation, the scene of various scandals, could be told: "everything belongs to you – the world, and death, the present and the future, all are yours – and you belong to Christ, and Christ to God" (2 Corinthians 3:22, 23). In his letter to Rome, a city full of monuments advertising the glory of the empire, he rose to the peak of his eloquence about "the glory, as yet unrevealed, which is in store for us . . . , the glorious liberty of the children of God" (8:18, 21).

He proclaimed that Christ was the revealer and redeemer who although "the image of God" (2 Corinthians 4:4) had come among men "in the likeness of our sinful nature" (Romans 8:3). In his second letter to Corinth (8:6) he wrote that Christ "was rich, yet for your sake he became poor, so that through his poverty you might become rich" – and to the Philippians (2:5–11) he quoted a hymn in which "Christ Jesus" descended to Earth and ascended "to the heights". Such images would appeal to people familiar with stories about gods visiting Earth, although Paul always put at the centre the God revealed in the Hebrew Scriptures, to whom Christ was "obedient" before "God raised him". He quoted the hymn about Christ's descent and ascent not in order to develop a myth about a descending god but in order to encourage humility: "take to heart among yourselves what you find in Christ Jesus". He believed in what theologians call Christ's "pre-existence" – that is, he believed that the reality which he had encountered as "Christ" had not begun with the human birth of Christ. But so far as we know, he did not work out this belief in any detail. "For us there is one God, the Father, from whom are all things, and we exist for him; there is one Lord, Jesus Christ, through whom are all things, and we exist through him." That reference to Christ's role in creation occurs in Paul's first letter to Corinth (8:6) when he is discussing whether a Christian may eat meat which comes from the sacrifices in pagan temples. Probably scholars have been right to connect this belief with the Jewish belief that Wisdom was the "agent" (in Greek *technitis*) of God in creation; the Corinthians have already been reminded that Christ is the wisdom of God and "our wisdom" (1:24,30). But Paul does not stop to provide his own explanation. He hurries on to give practical advice.

He proclaimed that Christians could be united with Christ by the sacraments of Baptism and the Eucharist. It seems that "proselytes" or converts to Judaism were often baptized before being circumcised. Many mystery religions offered other initiation ceremonies followed by a meal which was understood as communion with the god. Paul used such ideas, but only in connection with the idea of union with Christ. He declared that baptism brought union with Christ in his death and resurrection (most fully in Romans 6), and that the Eucharist was a spiritual "eating" and "drinking" of the "body" and "blood" of Christ (1 Corinthians 11:23–29). He so emphasized this intimate union with Christ that he could tell the Christians living in a notoriously disreputable port, Corinth: "you are Christ's body and each of you a limb or organ of it" (2:27). More than 160 times in his surviving letters he called the Christian life life "in Christ" or "in the Lord". It was a life where "we are being transformed into his likeness with ever-increasing glory, through the power of the Lord who is the Spirit" (2 Corinthians 3:18). Because Christ is now active as a spiritual force ("Christ" and "Spirit" not being clearly distinguished), "the harvest of the Spirit is love, joy, peace, patience, kindness, goodness, fidelity, gentleness and self-control" (Galatians 5:22). In Christ and his continuing body (the Christians), Paul saw a new humanity, a new creation. He reminded the Galatians that a revolution had broken down the divisions between the races, the classes and the genders. "There is no such thing as Jew and Greek, slave and freeman, male and female, for you are all one person in Christ Jesus" (3:28). In the last analysis everything before Christ had been made redundant, for "the only thing that counts is faith expressing itself through love" (4:6). And the believer's love for Christ finds that "the only thing that counts is new creation" (6:15).

THE EARLY CATHOLIC GOSPEL

The passionate originality and depth in Paul's teaching are indeed remarkable. No less remarkable is the fact that his distinctive teaching was soon eclipsed, and his emotionalism calmed, by what is called by modern scholars "Early Catholicism".

At the centre of this development is a reconciliation between "the Gospel" and "the law". The Christian message is seen more clearly than before as involving a decisive break with the Jewish religion and its law – partly because the rabbis have made the break from their own side, but partly because of the Pauline revolution. However, the

Gospel is now seen to involve also teachings which in spirit
come close to the Jewish heritage. There is great confidence
in the lordship of Christ – confidence like the Jewish trust
in the God of Israel. For Christians as for Jews, there are
designated leaders and authorized Scriptures. There is great
pride in the Church – pride like the Jewish pride in membership of the People of God. There is a high and stable, but
rather dull, standard of morality – for Christians as for
Jews. In a phrase which is never quite uttered in the New
Testament, the Church is "the new Israel".

Some of the themes of Early Catholicism are announced
in the Acts of the Apostles. If the author travelled with Paul,
as the "we" passages suggest, he cannot have understood
much of his theology. He never calls him an apostle and
never says that he defied the Jewish religious law. He claims
that the apostles made Paul compromise over the Gentiles'
obligation to keep that law (15:22–31), which Paul
vehemently denies (Galatians 2:1–10). He has no clear doctrine of "atonement" or "justification". For him the Spirit
enables the apostles to speak foreign languages and to predict the future (2:3–21); the international character of the
Church, reversing the divisions of Babel (Genesis 11:1–9) is
a foretaste of the unity of all the human race under God.
But no description is given of the ecstatic excitements known
to Paul. The Christian life is not the Spirit-filled "new
creation", it is respectable both by Jewish and by Roman
standards, and the elders who "keep guard" over this
"flock" are firmly in charge (20:28). Paul tries preaching to
the Jews, and when he is rejected he turns to the Gentiles
without any thought that even now the mission to the Gentiles will stimulate the Jews to repent (13:44–48). Thus he
leads the Church's advance from Jerusalem to Rome. Everything else in his controversial thought is pushed into the
shadows. Wherever possible, Luke likes to think that "the

whole company of believers was united in heart and soul"
(4:32).

The New Testament letters to the Colossians and the
Ephesians have often been held by modern scholars not to
be genuinely Pauline, although of the two the former is the
more widely accepted as at least the work of one of Paul's
disciples, Timothy, with a postscript in Paul's own hand.
What matters for our present purpose is that both letters
come from a time when the Church can be said to be growing
"the whole world over" (Colossians 1:6), on a foundation
established by "the apostles and prophets" (Ephesians
2:20). The spirit of Christ is believed to fill the Church, and
the argument is that Christ also fills the rest of the universe
now; his triumph does not have to wait until "the day of
the Lord". This argument is necessary because there still
lingers a pagan belief that human destinies are controlled
by "powers" other than Christ. But the writer proclaims
that because Christians died with Christ and so passed
beyond reach of the elemental spirits of the universe, "Christ
in you" is the hope of glory (Colossians 1:27; 2:28). The
Christians may now "attain to mature manhood, measured
by nothing less than the full stature of Christ" (Ephesians
4:13). In two poetic passages (Colossians 1:13–20 and
Ephesians 1:3–10) it is said that Christ is "the image of the
invisible God" in whom "God in all his fullness chose to
dwell". "In him everything in heaven and earth was
created" and "all things are held together in him." Here
Christ is clearly substituted for personified Wisdom, which
in the Hebrew Bible is said to "hold all things together" as
"the native cause of all things". "Like a fine mist she arises
from the power of God . . . She is initiated into the knowledge that belongs to God, and she chooses what his works
are to be" (Wisdom of Solomon 1:7; 7:25; 8:4–5).

That confidence in Christ and his Church inspires the rest

of the surviving literature of Early Catholicism, but the mood is less exalted. The Letter to the Hebrews begins with the teaching that the universe was created through Jesus, who sustains it by his power as "the radiance of God's glory", but the emphasis is on what Christ did and became, not on his divine "pre-existence" before his human birth. He became the perfect high priest, who sacrificed himself and inaugurated a "new covenant" between God and Man. He has entered heaven, bringing a large family of "brothers" with him, and so "bringing many sons to glory". The Jewish religious law and temple sacrifices are now obsolete, and no Christian priests have replaced the priests of the temple. The writer fully shares the insistence of the Hebrew Scriptures on a courageous faith in God's promises and on high moral standards. It is "impossible" for Christians who have "fallen away" to be forgiven, even after repentance (6:6) – an extremism of austerity which is contradicted elsewhere in the New Testament. Christians who are undergoing suffering should rely on the help of Christ, who was made "perfect through sufferings" (2:10, 18). Christians who are tempted to despair should look forward not to the imminent end of the world but to heaven, to the "rest" that awaits the people of God (4:9–11).

Essentially the First Letter of Peter (often thought to be not authentically Peter's) has much the same message. Christians are a "chosen race, a royal priesthood" although in the New Testament no individual Christian is called a priest. Amid their sufferings Christians must hold fast to "the hope of an inheritance reserved in heaven for you" 1:4). Later, the Second Letter of Peter (definitely not his) is explicit in saying that enthusiasm about the imminent End has cooled. Scoffers ask Christians: "What has happened to his promised coming? Our fathers have been laid to rest, but still everything goes on exactly as it always has done since the world began" (3:3, 4). That author tries to warm up the old enthusiasm, but the First Letter of John offers the answer that persuaded most Christians in the long run: however long the world's end is delayed, we cannot for ever enjoy the world. "Everything in the world, all that panders to the appetites or entices the eyes, all the arrogance based on wealth, these spring not from the Father but from the world. That world with all its allurements is passing away, but those who do God's will remain for ever" (2:16, 17).

The letters said to have been written by Paul to Timothy and Titus may include some authentically Pauline passages (such as 2 Timothy 15–18 and 4:9–22) but are usually thought by modern scholars to date mostly from a time considerably later than his death. The supremacy of Christ is briefly asserted against all rival ideas. "Innumerable myths and genealogies which give rise to mere speculation are 'demon-inspired doctrines' " (1 Timothy 1:4; 4:1). People who are "contentious" despite being warned are to be thrown out of the Church and ignored (Titus 3:10). Leading heretics are to be "consigned to Satan" (1 Timothy 1:20). In such passages may be seen the rise of the authority of the ordained ministry which is to dominate later Catholicism. But the main theme is a development of the morality of quiet obedience and respectability which had been taught to the Colossians. The "law" over which Paul had agonized is now Roman law and it is "an admirable thing" (1 Timothy 1:8). Christians must be obedient to the empire in politics and to their own leaders ("bishops" and "deacons") in religion. Slaves must please their masters. The rich whom James had denounced are now more mildly told to be "rich in well-doing" (1 Timothy 6:18). The attitude to women has changed. A third of the names of leading Christians listed by Paul at the end of his letter to Rome had been the names of women, including Phoebe, a deacon who had work to do in Rome, and Junia, who was "eminent among the apostles". In Paul's view women decently covered could pray aloud or "prophesy" in the congregation (1 Corinthians 11:5). But now the role of women is much more restricted. It is "to learn, listening quietly and with due submission" (1 Timothy 2:11). Many modern scholars think that Junia's name was now changed to the masculine Junias, and the instruction that "women should keep silence at the meetings" (1 Corinthians 14:34) was added to Paul's authentic teaching.

These new attitudes to the ordering of society were dull in comparison with the earlier radicalism. But they paid off. In about 110 a Roman provincial governor, Pliny, wrote to the emperor Trajan in some puzzlement. The Christians were reputed to be troublemakers, a "depraved and extremist superstition", and they refused to offer prayers to the image of the emperor. Yet all he had been able to discover was that after a common meal and a hymn to Christ they took an oath not to commit any evil deed. At about the same time, the Roman historian Tacitus recorded that Nero (emperor 41–54) had been able to blame a great fire in Rome on the Christians, a group "loathed for their vices" and "hatred of the human race". It was vital to the reputation of Christianity that the impressions received by Pliny, rather than by Tacitus, should prevail.

There is now a firm tradition, doctrinal and moral, and the plea is: "Timothy, keep safe what has been entrusted to you" (1 Timothy 6:20). The local Christian leaders are now "elders in each town" appointed by Paul's agent (Titus 1:5). A means of keeping this deposit safe is the study of the Hebrew Bible, which was "inspired" (the Greek means "God-breathed") and "has its use for teaching the truth and refuting error, or for reformation of manners and discipline in right living" (2 Timothy 3:16). In the letter to Titus the ascendancy of Christ, the supreme leader, is such that there may be a reference to "our great God and Saviour Christ Jesus" (2:13), although the Greek more probably separates "the great God *and* our Saviour".

In the document called the Second Letter of Peter, "our God and Saviour Jesus Christ" is mentioned clearly (1:1), and the leadership by ordained men has now been joined by the authority of Scriptures. The Hebrew Scriptures are not "a matter for private interpretation" (1:20), and among the new Scriptures which have authority for Christians are the letters of Paul, although they contain "some obscure passages" (3:16).

When that letter was written, almost certainly in the second Christian century, the Christian Scriptures included the four gospels which appear in our New Testament, but the author made no clear reference to them: it is a reminder that they were slow to be acknowledged by all Christians as authoritative. For a time the authorized contents ("canon") of the New Testament varied from place to place: the contents, although more or less settled by the end of the second century, were not fixed finally until the middle of the fourth. The *episkopoi*, elders (in Greek *presbuteroi*, later contracted in English as "priests") and deacons addressed in the literature of Early Catholicism could already be expected to base their teaching on written authorities. But when these leaders consulted reports of the teaching of Jesus, there was no completely clear source of instruction. Different churches treasured different gospels, and even a church's favourite gospel could be quoted by both sides in a struggle for leadership – a situation which seems to be reflected in the Letters of John.

Luke wrote that "many writers have undertaken to draw up an account" of the life of Jesus (1:1). Some of the gospels which the orthodox Church was to discard as heretical have survived into modern times. The most interesting, a collection of 114 sayings called the Gospel of Thomas, was discovered in the 1940s. Other "apocryphal" gospels are known only through quotations by other ancient writers. Some gospels present Jesus either as a very Jewish, or as a decidedly Gnostic, teacher, although they may incorporate some authentic sayings; others take a childish delight in miracle stories, including tales of wonders done by Jesus as a child. Even the gospels which were in the end brought together and authorized as orthodox or "canonical" are far from unanimous in their presentation of the historical Jesus. And even Christians who wished to be orthodox sensed this. When in the second century Tatian tried to combine the four gospels, his synthesis did not find much favour.

THE GOSPEL IN Q

About 230 verses which with minor variations are common to the gospels of Luke and Matthew have been called Q (from the German *Quelle*, "source"). This material is itself a gospel in a sense, although since it is preserved only in fragments used by others we can know little about it.

Conceivably Bishop Papias in the second century was referring to the beginnings of Q when he wrote that the apostle Matthew "compiled the oracles in the Hebrew language", but the fact that the Greek gospels of Luke and "Matthew" so often agree in their quotations from Q shows that it too, was in Greek by the time it reached them. Quotations here will be from Luke's version, which sometimes (but not always) seems likely to be closer to the original. There is no likelihood that Mark or John used it, but a passage found only in one of the later gospels may have been already in Q. If it was a document, Q may have gone through more than one edition, which would help to explain the differences between the gospels of Luke and Matthew. Some scholars have argued that Q was a tradition handed on by the spoken word, although this seems unlikely because of the extent to which Luke and Matthew do agree when using it. They also disagree, but that applies to their use of Mark's gospel, which was unquestionably a document. Q is very different from the letters of Paul; for example, it contains no clear references to the trial, death or resurrection of Jesus. This may well explain why it was not preserved as (for example) Mark's gospel was, but it may have been intended as a companion to at least one lost document which did cover those events. Although mainly a collection of the sayings and parables of Jesus (in contrast with Paul's teaching), it contained at least one story of a miracle.

As presented by Q, Jesus had the feelings and thoughts of a Jew. He longed to convert Jerusalem, "as a hen gathers her brood under her wings" (13:34). But he was more than one rabbi among many. He was not primarily a scholar, teaching by quoting other scholars. Nature had taught him and he observed that "even Solomon in all his splendour was not attired" like a wild flower (12:27). And his Father had taught him, making what his Father was doing through him "greater than Solomon" (11:31). People called him "Lord, Lord" and were right to do so (6:46). He referred to himself not as "Messiah" but as the Son of Man, as in the saying: "Foxes have their holes and birds their roosts; but the Son of Man has nowhere to lay his head" (9:57). But when alone in the wilderness after his baptism he had conquered temptations to concentrate on material needs, to gain political power and to impress by miracles. He knew what mattered most in the Scriptures, so he knew God's will and depended on him in complete submission and trust (4:1–13). Later it is claimed that "everything is entrusted" to him by the Father, and that he alone knows "who the Father is"

(10:22) – although the capital letters in that saying come only in modern printed Bibles, and the original saying probably meant that Jesus understands God as a son understands his father. Many wise men had desired to know such things, but they had been hidden (10:21). Many prophets had desired to see the deeds of Jesus, but had not seen anything like them (10:24). In particular John the Baptist, although admired by Jesus as "greater than all who have been born", was merely his "herald" or announcer (7:27, 28). The disciples who carry the message of Jesus are heralds but also more. "Whoever listens to you listens to me; whoever rejects you rejects me. And whoever rejects me rejects the One who sent me" (10:16).

In Q there was, it seems, no explanation of titles such as Lord, Son of Man and Son of God. One can only assume that the explanation was left to preachers. But much was implied by warnings about the dangers of rejecting Jesus. Little Galilean towns which have rejected him (and which are named, although presumably unknown to most users of Q) will be judged more severely than notoriously wicked cities (10:12, 13). Jerusalem which rejects him will be forsaken by God (13:34–35). His arrival brings not peace but a sharp division (12:49–53). It begins a "fateful hour" (12:54–59), and his parables teach that it is no excuse to say that the crisis was never expected (12:39–48) or that the risk of a wholehearted response was too great (19:12–27). The crisis will end in God's judgement which will separate "two people in one bed, two women together grinding corn" (17:34, 35). With so much at stake, the disciples are warned that they must put Jesus above family. They must "leave the dead to bury their dead" instead of arranging a father's funeral (9:60). They must "hate father and mother, wife and children, brothers and sisters" (14:26). But those who rely on their own respectability to avoid the crisis are warned in even more terrible words. Experts in the Jewish religious law may wash hands and cups punctiliously, may include garden herbs in the tithes which they pay to God, and may build monuments to honour dead prophets – but they have not penetrated into true "knowledge". Indeed, they have rejected the prophets' teachings and have taken away the key of knowledge from humbler folk who were trying to know God (11:37–54). They are taunted: "Can one blind man guide another?" (6:39).

Those who do understand what the crisis which has begun means must "make every effort to enter through the narrow door" of obedient trust (13:24). On the other side of that door they will find a kingdom where God rules. They will find that they have only to ask for God's good gifts in that kingdom and they will receive. They can trust the Father, for even a human father will not give a stone when asked for a loaf, or a snake when asked for a fish, or a scorpion when asked for an egg (11:9–13). They will be welcomed by God, as it were to a banquet; Q includes the parable of the Great Feast (14:15–24). They will be welcomed even if they have been society's outcasts (14:15–24). Indeed, God will rejoice over their safety precisely because they have been like dirty and bleating lost sheep (15:3–7). Amazingly "blessed" or happy are the poor, the hungry, the mourners, the unpopular (16:20–26). Even more amazingly befriended by Jesus are the "tax-collectors and sinners", the racketeers who collaborate with the occupying regime to extort harsh taxes out of their own people (keeping a large slice for themselves), and the prostitutes (often deserted wives) who are despised even by their customers (17:22).

In Q there was, it seems, no explanation in abstract terms of what the "kingdom of God" meant. But the announcement was about a dramatic change to be experienced soon in this life. The messengers of Jesus were to warn that it was imminent (10:2–20). The deeds of Jesus were signs of its dawning: "the blind regain their sight, the lame walk, lepers are made clean, the deaf hear, the dead are raised to life, the poor are brought good news" (7:22). "If it is by the finger of God that I drive out the demons, then be sure the kingdom of God has already come upon you" (11:20). But the arrival of the kingdom must change the whole person; otherwise his plight will be "worse than before" (11:24–26). Of all the miraculous healings which were hinted at in such passages, only one is known to have been in Q. It was recounted both by Luke (7:1–10) and by Matthew (8:5–13) – and, in a different form, by John (4:46–53). An army officer who was a Gentile is said to have shown a greater faith than Jesus had found among his fellow Jews. Being a soldier who both received orders and gave orders, he understood that Jesus obeyed the Father and therefore was able to command the devils who caused diseases. Jesus had only to say the word, and the centurion's servant, who was ill at home, would be cured.

The stern warnings given by Q should be set in this context of health and joy, pictured as a feast to which the Gentiles will come "from east and west, from north and south" (13:29). The emphasis in the message of Jesus is different from the condemnation pronounced by the Baptist: "Vipers' brood! Who warned you to escape from the wrath to come? Prove your repentance by the fruit you bear . . . !" (3:7, 8). The message of the Baptist suggests a children's game of funerals; the message of Jesus suggests weddings (7:31–5). Because the coming of Jesus had not meant the coming of wrath, Q indicated some disappointment in the imprisoned Baptist, who sent disciples with the question: "Are you the one who is to come, or are we to expect someone else?" (7:19). And other holy men were disappointed. Their contempt was quoted: "Look at him! A glut-

ton and a drinker, a friend of tax-collectors and sinners!"
(7:34).

Q gave the teaching of Jesus about two features of life
under God's rule, when "whoever loses his life will gain it"
(17:33). All anxieties about material needs must be put
away, for each day God gives enough bread (11:3; 9–13;
12:22–34). He, not *mammon* (the Aramaic for "money" is
kept), must be served: "no slave can serve two masters"
(16:13). And all hatred must also be put away. In his great
love God forgives our sins and those who wholeheartedly
receive this pardon will of course love and forgive their own
enemies, if necessary "seven times a day" (6:27–30; 11:4;
17:4). Non-resistance is taught in terms which totally challenge poor people who are often insulted: "If anyone hits
you on the cheek, offer the other also; if anyone takes your
coat, offer him your shirt as well" (6:29). Forgiveness is
taught in terms which leave no room for any condescension:
"Be compassionate as your Father is compassionate. Do not
judge, and you will not be judged . . . Why do you look at
the speck in your brother's eye, with never a thought for the
plank in your own?" (6:36; 7:41).

These fragments of Q which have survived by being
quoted are therefore precious. They show the early Christians recalling that Jesus had a unique relationship with God
the Father; that he was connected with, but superior to,
John the Baptist; that he proclaimed a "kingdom of God"
which began in his own cures of diseases; that, although
thoroughly Jewish, he did not exclude Gentiles from his
work; that people's eternal destiny depended on their
response to him; that in this crisis many, including some
who were highly respectable by the standards of the Jewish
religious law, rejected him; that many who were Israel's
outcasts accepted his emphasis on trust in God's love and
forgiveness; that he looked forward to Gentiles joining them

in the kingdom; and that he demanded that people should love and forgive each other as they lived in this new joy. It is possible to see how this teaching could inspire all the gospels which we considered previously – but it was not identical with any one of them, which provides some evidence that it was a genuine attempt to reconstruct what had been said and done by Jesus. It may have been compiled in the form which has survived within thirty years of his death. Was it a successful attempt to present the historical Jesus? Some evidence that it was is provided by the universal use by Christians of the Lord's Prayer. The version in Q seems to be reproduced by Luke (11:2–4); Matthew's version seems to be a slight expansion. In this strikingly brief prayer Jesus calls God *Abba* or "Daddy"; he prays for the coming of this God's kingdom; he teaches trust in this God for daily bread and forgiveness; he makes his followers say that they forgive others; he prays that they may not be exposed to a "test" which would be too much for them.

Many other themes appear in the New Testament. The most likely reason why these are mentioned in the Lord's Prayer is that they were the themes which mattered most to Jesus.

MARK'S GOSPEL

Mark's gospel is very different from every other surviving document in early Christian literature, although it has been linked by modern scholars with the gospels of Luke and Matthew as the "Synoptic" gospels, using a Greek-based word which means that they can be seen together. For Mark has told the story of Jesus in a style that reads like history, while carefully arranging his material in order to put across his own perception of the significance of Jesus. He links originally disconnected sayings because they include the same striking words (as in 9:38–50), but his editorial work goes far beyond that. Much more than Q, his gospel is a careful work of art.

Probably written shortly before 70, it is anonymous like the next three gospels which we shall consider. It was believed in the next century by two bishops (Papias and Irenaeus) that its author was John Mark, a Jew brought up in Jerusalem who became Peter's assistant in Rome. The report about a young man who followed Jesus to Gethsemane in his nightshirt and ran away naked (14:51, 52) is, like much of the rest of the gospel, both mysterious and stark – but it may be a kind of signature. However, Mark was a very common name in the Roman empire, and instead of staying within the Jewish heritage or within Early Catholicism, this gospel seems closer to Paul. It depicts a Jesus who is opposed to the religious and political authorities. As early as 3:6 he manages to unite a very strange coalition of enemies: the Pharisees whose very name means that they are "separated" from all that is unclean combine with the agents of the far-from-clean local ruler, Herod Antipas, in a plot to bring about the death of this man who disturbs the peace. The coalition is seen again at 12:13, when they try to trap Jesus with the question about taxes. "Scribes" trained in the religious law attack Jesus as a man who is devil-possessed (3:22). Such experts would not have been shocked if an untrained layman such as he was simplified the religious law (12:28–34) and did not keep himself always ritually pure as the Pharisees did. But Jesus claims that he shares God's power to forgive sins (2:10) and has the right to set aside laws and customs regarded as sacred. Thus he has the freedom to heal and (although in a very small way) to harvest on the Sabbath when there is no real emergency entitling a Jew to work on that day of rest (2:23–3:6). He declares all foods "clean" in defiance of traditions about purity (7:1–23).

In a society which is anxious never to eat meat with blood still in it, he tells his followers to drink wine which "is my blood" (14:24). He cancels the law permitting divorce (10:1–10). (In reporting this, Mark seems to have extended the condemnation of divorce to cover a woman divorcing a man, something permitted in Roman, not Jewish, law.) He performs miracles in areas which an orthodox Jew would avoid, for example in the neighbourhood of the Gentile city of Gerasa where a demented man lived "among the tombs" near a "large herd of pigs" – a situation horrifyingly unclean (5:1–20). He is violently indignant about conditions in the temple, and can be accused of advocating its immediate destruction (10:15–19; 14:56–9).

So far from teaching respect for the apostles, Mark seems to have ended his gospel before saying how Jesus appeared to them after his death. He depicts them as fools and cowards. They are called to be the "companions" of Jesus, to be "fishers of men", to have power over evil (1:17; 3:14). Yet they very seldom seem to understand his teaching, and in the end, following Judas the traitor, they all desert him (14:46). They are ridiculously ambitious and try to stop others sharing their work (9:33–40). Peter, James and John are their leaders (9:2) but Peter is rebuked with the words "Out of my sight, Satan!" (8:33), and is left in tears when he has denied even knowing Jesus (14:72). James and John are rebuked for asking for thrones (10:35–40). In this gospel people to be imitated are not the apostles but the trustful children (10:13–16). The adult to be admired is a widow who gives God all that she has (12:41–44).

Still more surprising is Mark's emphasis on the humanity of Jesus. There is no interest in any existence of Jesus before his birth or in any miracle at his birth. Certainly Mark's Jesus is a miracle-worker like Moses, Elijah and Elisha in the Hebrew Scriptures, and he can be compared with the

miracle-workers praised in the pagan literature of the
Roman empire. But he is also unlike anyone else. "Even the
wind and the sea obey him" (4:41) and he can bring the
dead back to life (5:40–43) because he is the "Son of God",
acclaimed as such by God at his baptism (1:11) and in
the mystical experience known as the transfiguration (9:7),
acclaimed also by demons (3:11; 5:7). This seems to go
beyond the status of Jesus in Q. Yet Jesus could be moved
to anger (1:41; 3:5) and so tired that he slept through a
storm, with his disciples thinking that he did not care that
they were sinking (4:38). He protested: "Why do you call
me good? No one is good except God alone" (10:18, which
Matthew 19:17 tones down). Mark also stresses that Jesus
was unpopular – not only with the Pharisees, the religious
leadership and the Romans who condemned him to death,
but also in his home town. Nazareth's reaction "astonished"
him and made it impossible for him "to do any miracle
there" (6:1–6). He was estranged even from his own family,
who thought "he is out of his mind" (3:21, 31–35). In
Gethsemane "horror and anguish overwhelmed him", and
he longed for his friends' company (14:32–40). While dying,
the only words he spoke were a cry, quoted from Psalm 22:1,
that he had been forsaken by God (15:34).

Mark of course believes that he was the Messiah. He tells
us that Jesus said "I am" when solemnly challenged about
it by the High Priest (14:62); he makes Peter's acknowledgement of it another turning point (8:29); he says that the
demons with their supernatural knowledge cried aloud this
truth, as did a blind beggar (10:46); he even puts into the
mouth of Jesus a description of the disciples as "followers
of the Messiah" (9:41). But he stresses that Jesus did his
utmost to keep secret miracles which might lead to talk of
him as the Messiah – even when a girl surrounded by people
mourning her death had been brought back to life (5:43).

He often says that Jesus was secretive: he explains the lack
of response to the parables by saying that the parables were
designed to conceal the Gospel (3:10, 12). But in a book of
1901 William Wrede began to shatter the belief that Mark
had written unadorned history and he explained this insistence on the "messianic secret" as an imaginative attempt
to cover up the fact that no one, not even the man himself,
thought that Jesus was Messiah until the Church proclaimed
him as such after his resurrection. Just possibly that explanation may be true. The later gospels represent Jesus as
making this claim to be the Messiah only on two occasions
– and both passages clearly arise out of the faith of the post-
resurrection Church (Matthew 23:10, John 4:26). Both Luke
(22:67) and Matthew (26:64) report that Jesus refused to
confirm or deny the High Priest's accusation that he made
the claim. But many reports of what Jesus did or said suggest
that it was inevitable that he should be called "Messiah".
If so, the likely explanation of his own reticence would be
that the title was wide open to misunderstanding. At that
time the Messiah could be regarded as no more than the
heir of the great King David, the national hero, and there
were many would-be nationalist leaders who claimed the
title (12:35–37). Because of this, the Romans were bound to
regard the claim as high treason. If Jesus accepted the title,
he virtually signed his own death warrant.

Martin Kahler was obviously right to call this gospel "a
passion narrative with an extended introduction". That is
its unity. The contrast between what we know to have been
in Q and the emphasis which Mark places on the "passion"
(sufferings) of Jesus is great. It seems that he was not always
successful in unifying the material at his disposal: in
6:30–8:21 we are given two accounts of Jesus feeding thousands and then crossing the lake. (It may be significant that

the second feeding takes place in Gentile territory, but if so Mark does not explain this.) However, descriptions of this gospel as a mere scrapbook, or as a feeble stringing together of pearls, are wrong. Its frequent use of "immediately" leaves the impression that Jesus hurried to his cross, calling on his friends to follow. Predictions of the sufferings unify the narrative once Peter has declared that Jesus is the Messiah (8:30–32; 9:12, 31; 10:33–34, 39, 45; 12:8). The theme of a summons to self-sacrifice in the footsteps of the rejected Messiah is clear and strong. Mark writes for Christians who know the sons of Simon of Cyrene, the man who carried the cross to Calvary (15:21). "Anyone who wants to be a follower of mine must renounce self; he must take up his cross and follow me" (8:34). Childlike humility and a readiness to be "the slave of all" are needed (10:15). Faith is needed, for "everything is possible to one who believes" (9:23). The renunciation of wealth is needed, for "it is easier for a camel to pass through the eye of a needle than for a rich man to enter the Kingdom of God" (10:25). Purity is needed. "If your hand causes your downfall, cut it off; it is better to enter into life maimed than to keep both hands and go to hell" (9:43). Constant vigilance is needed. Jesus addresses "all" as well as "you" with his warning: "Watch!" (13:37). No wonder that when Jesus was leading the way the disciples were filled with awe, while "those who followed behind were afraid" (10:32)!

Some of the most thought-provoking of all the touches in Mark's story-telling come at the very end, if (as most scholars think) his gospel originally ended at 16:8: "They said nothing to anyone, for they were afraid." The women who had found the tomb of Jesus empty did not report this to the apostles, presumably because with such a strange message they might be both mocked by the apostles and punished by the authorities. This seems to be the end of the gospel

as Mark wrote it, although presumably he believed that the
risen Jesus had nevertheless appeared to his followers as he
had promised (16:7), for he believed in the resurrection in
Jerusalem (14:28). If he ended his gospel on a grim note, it
was because it was a grim gospel, well called "a gospel for
martyrs".

Yet, using one of Paul's favourite words, he wrote about
"the *gospel* of Jesus Christ the Son of God" (1:1). The good
news which Jesus had brought remains ultimately good as
Mark interprets it. The title of "Son of God" is never
explained, but it means something more than being a prophet and thus a servant of God (12:6). And the Son of
God, for all his reticence about himself, proclaims that "the
kingdom of God is upon you" (1:15). This kingdom, whether
understood or not, whether accepted or not, grows as a small
seed grows into a big plant (4:30–32). It invades history as
a burglar breaks into a house (3:37). It is new and joyful,
so that fasting is now as inappropriate as storing new wine
in old wineskins would be (2:18–22). It brings no political
liberation for it involves no rebellion against Rome
(12:13–17), but it brings health (as 156 verses of miracle
stories testify). It brings courage to cowards and eloquence
to simple folk: "it is not you who will be speaking, but the
Holy Spirit" (13:11). And it will end in miraculous glory
(8:38; 13–26; 14:62). The glory will, it is hoped, soon be full
on earth, so that "there are some of those standing here who
will not taste death before they have seen the kingdom of
God come with power" (9:1) and "the present generation
will live to see it all" (13:30). And the glory will be complete
in eternity where the dead whom God loves will live "like
angels" (12:18–27). To this material Mark adds more
sombre passages. Jesus warns his hearers that the full arrival
of the kingdom on earth is subject to delay and to rejection
(in a number of parables); that the preparation for it will

include many tribulations (13:3–23); and that he himself does not know when the preparation will be completed (13:32). Yet for Mark the certainty of the triumph of Jesus amid suffering – a triumph whether quick or slow – is what constitutes the good news. After celebrating in the Passover festival the liberation of Israel from slavery (14:12), the Son of God gave his life as a ransom for many, liberating humanity from evil (10:45). Jesus the chief of martyrs shed his blood "for many", as he made possible a new covenant between God and humanity (14:24).

LUKE'S GOSPEL

Luke's gospel, probably written about fifteen years after Mark's, has a sunnier climate. Here the worst troubles of the world become signs that the kingdom of God is near, like buds on a tree which show that summer is near (21:30, 31).

Probably Luke was not a Jew. Mark writes rough Greek and can quote the original Aramaic in his stories (5:41; 7:11, 34), but Luke uses Greek more elegantly and almost exclusively. Mark gives details about Jewish controversies, but Luke seems to hold himself somewhat aloof. While he provides attractive pictures of the origins both of Jesus Christ and of the Church within Judaism, he seems to regard that as a more-or-less closed chapter once Paul has turned to the Gentiles in the Acts of the Apostles. In his gospel he simply places side by side contradictory sayings which have come down to him through the heated debates of others. "The law and the prophets were until John: since then the good news of the kingdom of God is proclaimed" – but "it is easier for heaven and earth to come to an end than for one letter of the law to lose its force" (16:16, 17). He begins this gospel by confessing that he was not present at these

events, and he is vague about the geography of Palestine;
he can write that "in the course of his journey to Jerusalem
he was travelling through the borderlands of Samaria and
Galilee" (17:11).

A new community has arisen, with new leaders. Mark
emphasizes the foolishness of the apostles but Luke takes
from Q the promise that "you have stood by me in my times
of trial; . . . in my kingdom you shall eat and drink at my
table and sit on thrones as judges of the twelve tribes of
Israel" (22:28, 29). His gospel is accompanied by a sequel,
a celebration of the acts of the apostles – or, rather, of those
of the apostles' acts which fit in with his theme. When
he mentions seventy-two missionaries who supplement the
apostles (10:1–12, 17–20), he seems to have in mind a category similar to the assistant ministers who appear in Acts
in order to help the Christian expansion into the Mediter-
ranean world. He omits Mark's report that the family of
Jesus thought him mad. On the contrary, "his mother treasured up all these things in her heart" (2:51), and the
"things" included her son's conception by "the power of the
Most High" while she was still a virgin. Jesus' Messiahship
is for Luke no secret: angels proclaim it to shepherds (2:11).
His life was no example of human frailty; he "saw Satan
fall, like lightning, from heaven" (10:18). He was a king,
greater than all the kings of the world, although his glory
was his love.

Luke seems to write after the fall of Jerusalem to the
Romans in AD 70. We cannot be certain because he may
have been drawing on descriptions of sieges in the Hebrew
Bible, but the catastrophe of 70 may be reflected in his
account of predictions by Jesus. "Your enemies will set up
siege-walls against you; they will encircle you and hem you
in at every point; they will bring you to the ground, you
and your children within your walls, and not leave you one

stone standing on another" (19:43,44). "They will fall by
the sword; they will be carried captive into all countries;
and Jerusalem will be trampled underfoot by Gentiles until
the day of the Gentiles has run its course" (21:24). Jesus
predicts it on his way to a Roman execution: "The days are
surely coming, when people will say, 'Happy are the barren,
the wombs that never bore a child, the breasts that never
fed one'. Then they will begin to say to the mountains, 'Fall
on us', and to the hills, 'Cover us' " (23:29, 30).

Luke also seems to write when the split between the
Christian congregations and the Jewish synagogues has
become final. At some date in the last quarter of the first
century AD all orthodox Jews were instructed to pray when
they used the traditional "Benedictions": "May there be no
hope for the traitors, and may the arrogant kingdom be
rooted out soon in our days! May the Nazarenes and the
heretics perish quickly and may their names be erased from
the Book of Life!" But Luke was, it seems, not as bitter
about this separation between Church and Synagogue as
Matthew and John were to be. As we have noted, we owe
to him our clearest picture of the oldest form of Christianity,
which was thoroughly Jewish. One reason why he is more
relaxed and generous about the Church's Jewish origins is
that for him the sequel to the fall of Jerusalem is not the End
predicted in Mark's gospel (although with some caution). It
is "the day of the Gentiles" (21:24). In the song which Luke
puts into the mouth of a Jewish saint in the Jerusalem
temple, the order is significant: Jesus is to be "a light that
will bring revelation to the Gentiles *and* glory to Israel"
(2:32). The tragedies of rejection and martyrdom have been
lit up by the sunshine of the revealed glory, covering the
world. The response of the world is not guaranteed: "when
the Son of Man comes, will he find faith on earth?" (18:8).
But for Luke as for Matthew, the reign of Jesus the Son of

Man is not postponed to some future date. It is, Jesus
says before he dies, "from now on" (22:69, changing Mark
14:62).

Luke's whole gospel from 9:51 to 19:45 takes place on the
road to Jerusalem, for the bitter reason that "it is unthinkable for a prophet to meet his death anywhere but in Jerusalem" (13:33). But at the end, after that death, the risen
Jesus walks with two disciples on a road away from Jerusalem and says that "the forgiveness of sins is to be proclaimed to all nations beginning from Jerusalem" (24:13,
47). The Church embarks on a global mission which in
Luke's circumstances does not seem greatly hindered by any
persecution. The Church is not yet large, but "have no
fear little flock, for your Father has chosen to give you the
kingdom" (12:32).

About a third of his gospel is Luke's alone. About two-
fifths come from a version of Mark which apparently did
not include 6:45–8:26. The rest comes from Q. Probably Q,
like Mark, was changed by him in details, as when a passage
promising a gift from the Father refers to "good things" in
Matthew (7:11) but "the Holy Spirit" in Luke (11:13). In
his special material his themes are no less distinctive than
Mark's. They are reflected in many small changes to Mark's
wording but are summed up at the beginning of his account
of the public life of Jesus (4:14–30). The reference to "Jesus,
armed with the power of the Spirit" is one of the four
references to the Holy Spirit in this part of the gospel, and
is a foretaste of the time when the disciples will be "armed
with power from above" (24:49). In the synagogue at Nazareth Jesus preaches on Isaiah 61:1, 2, proclaiming that "the
spirit of the Lord is upon me . . . " He brings good news to
the poor, release for prisoners, sight for the blind, liberty for
"all broken victims". He does not mention the prophet's
"day of the vengeance of our God". But in Nazareth admir-

ation for words of such grace spoken by a local lad is quickly
replaced by fury when Jesus rebukes his home town's jeal-
ousy of Capernaum (where Mark's account of Jesus' work
begins). Jesus then points out that Elijah and Elisha performed miracles for Gentiles. And the status of these Gentiles
is significant: one is a woman, the other a general.

Luke's special material emphasizes Jesus' revolutionary
relationships with women. Women watched his crucifixion
when the men had all run away, and understood his resurrection when the men were all still in despair (23:49; 24:22).
His "heart went out" to a widow whose only son had died
(7:13); he allowed a prostitute to wet his feet with her tears,
dry them with her hair and anoint them with a luxurious
oil (7:38); he was accompanied on his journeys by a number
of "women who had been set free from evil spirits and
infirmities", and he was financed by them (8:2,3); he
accepted the careful hospitality of Martha but preferred
Mary's willingness to listen to his teaching just like the
young men who were students of the religious law
(10:38–42); he noticed in a crowded synagogue a woman
who had been crippled for eighteen years (13:11); he understood the distress of a woman who had lost one coin
(15:8–10). At that time respectable Jews, specially teachers
of religion, were far more reserved in their dealings with
women. Jesus asked a Pharisee: "You see this woman?"
(7:44). In his own case the answer to such a challenge would
be clear according to Luke, who wrote a gospel for women.
In this gospel Mary the mother of Jesus is the "most favoured one" (1:28) – yet when he hears "Happy the womb
that carried you and the breasts that suckled you!" Jesus
replies: "No, happy are those who hear the word of God
and keep it" (11:27, 28). For he offers to be born as God's
word in the heart of any woman.

Luke also delights to show how revolutionary was the

attitude of Jesus to foreigners. Jews hated Samaritans as
half-breeds, and Samaritans hated Jews. But when Samaritan villagers "would not receive him because he was on his
way to Jerusalem", Jesus rebuked James and John for wanting the village's destruction (9:51–56). In a parable the good
Samaritan put the Jewish priest and Levite to shame and
was a true neighbour to the mugged Jew, to be imitated
by a Jewish lawyer (10:25–38). Jesus was moved when a
Samaritan returned to give thanks for a healing and nine
Jews did not (17:11–19). As is indicated by tracing the
descent of Jesus from Adam (3:38), Luke's is a gospel for
all peoples. In his most famous parable (15:11–32) the
younger son represents the outcasts who receive from the
Father a son's robe, ring and sandals, and are welcomed
by the angels with "music and dancing", while dutifully
respectable but inwardly arrogant Jews sulk like the elder
son.

Although Luke presents Jesus as the champion of the
poor, he avoids saying that he was always totally
hostile to the rich. Few (if any) of the wealthy in Galilee or
Judea would have become rich in ways which devout and
moral Jews would respect, and Luke (18:25) repeated from
Mark the saying that camels would squeeze through needles
before rich men entered the kingdom of God. Yet according
to this gospel, Jesus admired astute businessmen and said
that his disciples could learn from them (16:1–12). He
thought that a tax-collector would be "acquitted of his sins"
if he humbly prayed for God's mercy (18:9–14), and he
stayed in the home of a "very rich" tax-collector before he
knew that Zacchaeus was more than curious about him
(19:1–10). He praised the persistence of a widow who had
a financial grievance (18:1–8) while himself refusing to get
involved in financial disputes (12:13, 14). It may be significant that Luke, when repeating Mark's story about the rich

"ruler" who was challenged to "sell everything you have and give to the poor", says that the man's heart sank but omits Mark's final touch that he "went away" (18:18–27). It is possible to imagine that the urban congregation which Luke knew best had members who were not poor and had prospects less grim than those envisaged in Mark's gospel for martyrs.

According to Luke, however, any sympathy which Jesus had for the rich was dwarfed by his love for the poor. By this Jesus meant the materially destitute: "the poor" were not, as in Matthew's version of Q, "the poor in spirit". The rich had had their "time of happiness" and now it was the turn of the poor (5:24, 25). The rich had been "sent empty away", the poor had been filled (1:53). The rich who relied on wealth for security were simply fools (12:15–21). Jesus urged the rich to invite beggars to their banquets (14:12–14). With relish Jesus retold an old story about a beggar who went to heaven and a rich man (who still thought that Lazarus could be ordered about) to the fires of Hades (16:19–31). Luke told his own story about a dying criminal daring to call the Lord "Jesus" (which is unique in the gospels) and being promised "Paradise today" (23:39–43). Luke's Jesus, born among the poor, dies among them.

Luke would not flatter the politically powerful. He gives a resounding roll-call of rulers and high priests as a mere prelude to saying that "the word of God came to John son of Zechariah in the wilderness" (3:2). Herod Antipas the ruler of Galilee is dismissed as "that fox" (13:32). But the politically powerful have their roles to play in this drama. Luke presents Pilate as the first of the Roman officials who, although too cowardly to take their side, are said in Acts to think Christians innocent of the charges brought against them. The centurion declares after the crucifixion: "Beyond all doubt, this man was innocent" (23:47). The gospel and

Acts are both dedicated to Theophilus, and "His Excellency" seems to be an educated and substantial citizen of the empire who is to be assured that the centurion was right. Luke believes that a census ordered by the emperor Augustus for the whole Roman world was the reason why Mary and Joseph were in Bethlehem (2:1). That announces a theme which becomes dominant in Acts: without any such intention, the empire which had established peace and good communications was helping the Church's mission. Luke thinks that Jesus came "to set fire to the earth" (12:49), and he incorporates in his gospel older materials which talk about the end of the world coming soon: but at the beginning of this gospel Mary expects many generations to count her blessed (1:48). Luke is prepared for a long mission which the world's human rulers can assist.

This is because he stresses the patience of God. God is entitled to punish everyone but does not, and it is wrong to think that those who are killed in an accident were singled out for punishment (13:1–5). God is entitled to uproot a barren fig tree but does not (13:6–9, in contrast with Mark 11:12–24). Preparing for the teaching that "it is not for you to know about dates or times which the Father has set within his own control" (Acts 1:7), this gospel insists that speculation about current events being signs that the End is near – a favourite activity of the early Christians – is pointless (17:20, 21). Instead of that waste of time, Christians ought to concentrate calmly on the ethical teaching which Luke gathers in the Sermon on the Plain (6:20–49). In simple trust they ought to commit their spirits into the hands of the Father for life or death, as Jesus did in a final cry far removed from the despair in Mark's account (23:46). What moves Luke deeply is not excitement about the coming end of the world or about the more sensational gifts of the Spirit, but the experience of knowing the risen Jesus. Jesus is known to Luke as in the story he is known to the disciples on the road to Emmaus – in the Bible-based preaching of the Gospel about the suffering Messiah, and in the quiet breaking of bread during the Eucharist. Luke is one of the Christians who have felt "our hearts on fire as he talked with us on the road" (24:13–32) – the road from Jerusalem into the world.

And his gospel has warmed the hearts of Christians in many times and places. This is the gospel that has given the Church its most popular teaching and its psychologically important calendar, for Luke's parables about the Good Samaritan and the Prodigal Son dominate most memories of the teaching of Jesus and his stories dominate the festivals of Christmas, Easter, the Ascension and Pentecost. At Christmas most Christians imagine chiefly the humble shepherds going to Bethlehem; at Easter, the risen Lord bringing joy as a gentle friend. The Ascension is imagined as Jesus going up to reign in heaven forty days after his resurrection, and the gift of the Holy Spirit is a separate and dramatic gift to the Church after another interval. None of these pictures is found in the New Testament except in Luke's gospel and the Acts of the Apostles. Nor is the love of God for all – the graceful love which inspires human love and the liberating love which inspires human justice – ever pictured more clearly than in Luke's Christian humanism.

MATTHEW'S GOSPEL

More than Luke, the author of the gospel we know as Matthew's was deeply interested in the relationship between Christianity and Judaism. Almost certainly he was a Jew. Despite the early traditions that he was Matthew the apostle, and that his gospel was the first written account of Jesus, he does not seem to have been an eyewitness, for almost all

modern scholars agree that he reproduces ninety per cent of
Mark's gospel, and that half of the rest of his own gospel
comes from Q. But the quarter of the gospel which is his
alone has the Christian–Jewish relationship as its main subject, and the editorial changes and abbreviations which he
makes to Mark and Q are substantial, often in order to fit
this special material with its dominant theme.

Some passages in Matthew's own material seem to contradict each other. Bishop Papias, writing between 120 and
140, may have been uneasily aware that not everything was
simple: "Matthew composed the sayings in Hebrew and
each one translated them as he could." The most likely
explanation is that, like Luke, he preserves some sayings
from a tradition which took its shape when the Christian–
Jewish relationship was at an earlier, more friendly, stage,
but his gospel suggests that his own situation was much
more tense than Luke's. We read: "Do not suppose that I
have come to abolish the law and the prophets; I did not
come to abolish but to complete . . . Anyone therefore who
sets aside even the least of the law's demands, and teaches
others to do the same, will have the lowest place in the
kingdom of Heaven, whereas anyone who keeps the law and
teaches others to do so, will rank high in the kingdom of
Heaven" (5:17, 19). Here is a strong blessing on the rabbis.
This Aramaic term meant literally "my great one" and came
into use to describe teachers of the religious law. Rabbis
based on Jerusalem would be trained experts in the Scriptures and the spoken tradition. In respect of villages in
Galilee, the term "scribes", which has been used in most
English Bibles, is probably appropriate because it suggests
a more modest category of men good at reading and writing,
more familiar with the Scriptures than their neighbours
were, but not trained experts. However, in some passages
Matthew sweeps away all these finer points and pronounces

curses, not blessings. The very use of "Rabbi" as a title is attacked, and "scribes and Pharisees" are called "hypocrites" six times. They are "blind guides" and "blind fools" as they travel towards hell (23:1–34).

Efforts have been made to argue that such sayings are compatible with each other, suggesting that what Jesus wanted was life in accordance with the spirit, not the letter, of the Jewish religious law. But that is not what is actually said here, and it is not easy to iron out the contradictions within this gospel. It bears all the signs of having been written amid the confusions of crisis and controversy, so that these passages which contradict each other are the fall-out from an explosion. For Matthew, like Luke, almost certainly writes after the fall of Jerusalem and the excommunication of the Christians by the synagogues. He adds to an old parable this touch: "the king was furious; he sent his troops to put those murderers to death and set their town on fire" (22:7). He adds to old material about Jesus' instructions to the apostles – material which looks back to days when Jesus and his disciples would go to synagogue every Sabbath – the expectation that "they will flog you in their synagogues" (19:17; 23:34).

The suggestion that Matthew failed to reconcile sayings attributed to Jesus at different stages in the tradition may seem incredible. But his gospel does not only include contradictions about the merits of the Jewish religious law and its teachers. It also contains incompatible passages about the coming kingdom of God. The passage just quoted about floggings in the synagogue also warns that "you will be brought before governors and kings on my account, to testify before them and the Gentiles" (10:18), promising that "whoever endures to the end will be saved" (10:22). This seems to predict a long mission in the Gentile world before the perfect kingdom comes. Yet the apostles are also told: "do

not take the road to Gentile lands, and do not enter any
Samaritan town", for "before you have gone through all the
towns of Israel the Son of Man will have come" (10:5, 23).
This particular instruction was central to the theory of
Albert Schweitzer that Jesus taught without qualification
that the full kingdom of God was imminent. According to
this theory, he believed that it would come within a few
weeks of the apostles' first mission to their fellow Jews, and
after disappointment he changed to the belief that first he
had to suffer crucifixion. But Schweitzer seems to have been
wrong to think that Matthew's was the earliest gospel, reproducing the exact words of the historical Jesus. His theory
did not come to terms with the existence of contradictory
sayings – a fact most easily explained if these sayings reflect
different stages in the tradition about Jesus, as the Gentile
mission celebrated in different ways by Paul and Luke
replaced the Jerusalem church's expectation of a rapid End
within Judaism.

Quite often Matthew indicates loyalty to the old religion.
He reports that Jesus and his disciples paid the tax collected
each year to support the temple (17:24–27). He blames the
teachers of the old religion not for being wrong but for being
insincere. "The scribes and Pharisees occupy Moses' seat,
so be careful to do whatever they tell you", he says. "But
do not follow their practice; for they say one thing and do
another" (23:1–3). He retains some of the important customs
of Judaism, for example usually speaking about the "kingdom of Heaven" as being a more reverent expression than
"kingdom of God". In his version of the Lord's Prayer (6:9)
"our Father in heaven", to which no Jew could object,
replaces Luke's crude *Abba*. He also retains some Jewish
prejudices and puts them into the mouth of Jesus. The
heathen "go babbling on" when praying (6:7). Food, drink
and clothing are "the things that occupy the minds of the

heathen" (6:32). Christians are encouraged to expel an obstinate sinner from their congregation and their company: "treat him as you would a pagan or a tax-collector" (18:17) – although the commandment of unlimited forgiveness is quoted from Q (18:21, 22). Contempt for outcasts and the Gentiles seems to lie behind the advice: "Do not give dogs what is holy" (7:6). Without translation he expects his readers to understand Hebrew or Aramaic words such as *raka* and *Gehenna* (5:22, 29). His radicalism is not Paul's or Mark's.

But his gospel is also different from the original gospel of the Jerusalem Christians. He writes for people who use Greek – for example, the Greek translation of the Hebrew Bible which has a word which may mean "virgin" although the Hebrew original does not (1:23). And he writes with a belief that miracles, not reforms within Judaism, are needed. Thus Joseph is a "man of principle" with a proud ancestry traced through King David to Abraham – yet he is not worthy to be responsible for the conception of Jesus the Messiah (1:18). Matthew, like Luke, has no hesitation about miracles which disclose the unique power of Jesus. Both gospels begin with the virginal conception and end with miracles surrounding the supreme miracle of the physical resurrection. Luke, who is interested chiefly in the effect on Christians, gives the three miracles that Jesus was not recognized on the road to Emmaus, that he "vanished from their sight" and that later he ate fish before their eyes (24:13–44). Matthew tells of two public miracles, both accompanied by earthquakes and both anticipating a wider resurrection on the last day. Many saints, coming out of their graves, "entered the Holy City, where many saw them", and an angel was seen by the guards as well as the women, rolling away the stone from the tomb of Jesus (27:52, 53; 28:2–4). Holding such beliefs, Matthew is deeply sad that so many of his fellow Jews have rejected Jesus and the Messianic age which has thus begun. They – not Pilate – were responsible for the crucifixion. This account of the trial before Pilate includes words which have been used fatefully in the history of Christian antisemitism, when "with one voice the people cried: 'His blood be on us and our children' " (27:25). And Matthew laments that "the Jews" have refused to acknowledge the resurrection. The report that the disciples stole the body "is current in Jewish circles to this day" (28:15). When they object to outcasts and Gentiles receiving what they need from God, respectable Jews are like labourers who protest when a good employer pays the minimum wage to the unemployed who have been hired at a late stage of the work (20:1–16).

The main theme of this gospel is that Jesus both teaches a new morality and founds a new community, transcending the Jews' traditions. It differs sharply from the Letter of James. Before its account of the death and resurrection the gospel is arranged in five sections, each including a long speech. They are distinguished from each other by the words "when Jesus had finished . . . " This editorial arrangement may well be intended as a parallel with the five books attributed to Moses in the Hebrew Scriptures. The sections may be called *The Law of the Kingdom of Heaven* (5:1–7:29), *Messengers of the Kingdom* (8:1–11:1), *Parables of the Kingdom* (11:2–13:52), *Servants of the Kingdom* (13:53–18:35) and *The Coming of the Kingdom* (19:1–25:46).

When Jesus like Moses goes up a mountain in order to deliver commandments (5:1), Matthew's special material in the Sermon on the Mount presents a morality which is distinctive. "What I tell you is this" is repeated six times in chapter 5. Here Jesus addresses and blesses those who are poor "in spirit" and who "hunger and thirst to see right prevail" – not, as in Luke, those who are materially destitute. He blesses the gentle, the merciful, the pure in heart, the peacemakers. The purity commanded is, like the poverty, "in spirit". Not only have some disciples renounced marriage "for the sake of the kingdom of Heaven" (19:12), but "if a man looks at a woman with a lustful eye, he has already committed adultery with her in his heart" (5:28). The gentleness commanded is also in the heart: "anyone who nurses anger against his brother must be brought to justice" (5:22). The parable of the Unforgiving Servant (18:23–35) drives home the teaching that because the Father has forgiven there must be human forgiveness. The spirit of heartfelt reverence which is commanded means that oaths invoking God are now totally forbidden (5:33–37). Almsgiving and prayer must be "done in secret" and very simply, out of love for "your Father who is in secret" (6:1–8).

This religion of the heart, so profoundly challenging to so many human instincts and customs, is, however, now practised within a firm Christian community. Wrongdoers are to be reported to the new *ekklesia*, the word used in the Greek translation of the Hebrew Bible for the assembly of Israel (18:17). The *ekklesia* is the "church" which is to be built on Peter's leadership, "and the powers of death shall never conquer it" (15:18). The power to decide what is right or wrong and who is to enter heaven is thought to be given to Peter (15:19) and shared with the other Christians (18:18). This church feels itself to be filled by a spirit more than human, and so it baptizes new members "in the name of the Father and the Son and the Holy Spirit" (28:19). It experiences the continuing presence of Jesus: "where two or three meet together in my name, I am there among them" (18:20) – "to the end of time" (28:20). Part of the discipline is the practice of fasting (6:16–18) although Matthew knows that the disciples of Jesus did not fast in his lifetime (9:14). There will be a heavenly reward for anyone who gives a Christian a "cup of cold water" (10:42). The last of the parables in this gospel promises that those in "all the nations" who have fed the hungry and thirsty, welcomed strangers, clothed the naked and visited the sick and the prisoners are to be rewarded because the people in those categories were Christians (25:31–46). It is possible that this parable teaches that Jesus is present in *all* the poor, as has often been believed as an inspiration for justice and charity, but that is not an interpretation which is obvious in the gospel itself.

These Christians were told that "unless you show yourselves far better than the scribes and Pharisees, you can never enter the kingdom of Heaven" (5:10), and that "narrow is the gate and restricted the road that leads to life, and those who find them are few" (7:14). When we remember that many of these Christians were persecuted or at least harassed, and were so poor that it was not ridiculous to say they needed to be given cups of water, we will marvel that anyone became a Christian, to be told that what was really needed was that they should be poor "in spirit". But Matthew adds some gentle and merciful words as he records the new commandments. For example, he adds to the prohibition of divorce an exception when a wife has committed adultery (5:32; 19:9). He differs from Luke in his use of a parable taken from Q. Whereas Luke (15:2–7) stresses the joy when a lost sheep has been found, Matthew (18:10–14) has no such climax but emphasizes that the good shepherd is ready to suffer in order to reclaim one who strays from the group. The teachers of the religious law summoned Jews to accept "the yoke of the law", and for many of the laity this would mean obeying regulations too burdensome to be borne in complete detail: hence the gap between the Pharisees and the ordinary people. But this is the invitation in Matthew's gospel: "Come to me, all who are weary and whose load is heavy; I will give you rest. Take my yoke upon you, and learn from me, for I am gentle and humble-hearted; and you will find rest for your souls. For my yoke is easy, my load is light" (11:28–30).

So Matthew gave his church a gospel which like Mark's was ultimately good news. The church may well have been in Antioch, whose bishop (Ignatius) quoted this gospel in about 107; Peter's work in Antioch may explain his prominence here. Matthew seems to have been writing mainly for Christians of Jewish birth now frightened by the disaster which had overcome their own nation, and by their excommunication from the synagogues. He reminded them that they had discovered treasure although it was at present buried in a field, a very special pearl although it cost the earth; and their church was like a net full of fish destined for the final banquet although some of the fish were worthless (13:44–53). He produced old and new teachings out of the larder of his well-stocked mind, and it is at least possible that he had himself been a teacher of the Jewish religious law who had become a "learner in the kingdom of Heaven" (13:51–2). He knew that the old religion had been shattered. But "Jesus Christ, son of David, son of Abraham" was also "the Son of the Living God" (16:16), able to attract Gentiles, that was the meaning of the story of the "astrologers from the east" who did homage at his birth (2:1–12). Since Jesus had now been given by the Father full authority in heaven and on earth, people in "all nations" would join his disciples (28:18,19). Already the Christians could know his presence among them whether or not they were also Jews, even if only two or three "gathered" (18:20). And Matthew's gospel has had a history among the peoples of the world which he cannot have expected at all. It became the Church's favourite gospel for readings during the Eucharist, and many millions interested neither in the religion of the Jews nor in regular churchgoing have found in the ethics of the Sermon on the Mount the peak to which Christians must aspire.

JOHN'S GOSPEL

It is possible that John wrote without any knowledge of the gospels of Mark, Luke and Matthew. This may not seem probable because there are some similarities, but nothing in his gospel proves that John used any of the other three. If he knew them, he did not think it worthwhile to quote them.

We move into a world where there is no trace of Jesus making a secret of his Messiahship, as he does in Mark's gospel. Instead, the Jesus of John declares: "You will die in your sins if you do not believe that I am what I am" (8:24). He openly challenges the religious authorities by cleansing the temple at the beginning of his work (2:13–21). Mark, like Matthew and Luke, puts right at the centre the proclamation of the kingdom of God, with the promise that the End is coming. "Kingdom of Heaven" occurs thirty-four times in Matthew's gospel. But in John's, the kingdom is mentioned only in conversations with Nicodemus and Pilate (3:3,5; 18:36), and belief that the dead "will rise again at the resurrection on the last day" is clearly subordinated to the belief that Jesus already is "the resurrection and life" (11:24,25). There are many fewer human details and many fewer parables than in Luke's gospel; instead, we read long speeches arising out of spectacular miracles. In these speeches we find none of the sympathy with the poor shown in Luke's gospel, and little ethical teaching of the kind assembled by Matthew in the Sermon of the Mount. There is no reserve in the self-description of Jesus, as in Mark's gospel. Instead, the Jesus of John teaches at length about himself, his union with God and the disciples' union with him. Words such as "apostle" or "church" are absent. The foundation of the Eucharist is not described, and Christian

Baptism is referred to obliquely. We have seen that each of the other gospel-writers has a tendency shown by his choice of material, but that the other three do not put forward their own teaching in their own words. In John's gospel we are often at a loss to know whether we are reading the words of Jesus or of John – as may be seen by any reader of the conversation with Nicodemus in chapter 3. In the great prayer of Jesus in this gospel the sentence occurs: "This is eternal life: to know you the only true God, and Jesus Christ whom you have sent" (17:3).

No other gospel has aroused such uncertainty about who wrote it and what was his or their audience. There was a good deal of hesitation before this gospel was included in the New Testament, but these early doubts were as nothing in comparison with the heat of the modern debate about the authorship and purpose. This uncertainty is ironic, because the gospel says at 21:24 that the disciple whom Jesus loved "wrote it" and "his testimony is true". And we read at 20:31 that the gospel has been written in order that "you may believe that Jesus is the Christ, the Son of God, and that through this faith you may have life by his name".

The statement about the authorship comes in a chapter which seems to have been added as an epilogue when the gospel has already been completed by the climax just quoted. It declares that "we", the group publishing chapter 21, can vouch for the truth of what has been said. That may apply to this epilogue only. But since the language of this last chapter shows no remarkable difference from the rest of the gospel, the implication may well be that the group has in some way edited the whole, which was all written by one "disciple". At 19:35 there is a similar certificate: an incident is "vouched for by an eyewitness, whose evidence is to be trusted".

But who was the disciple? He appears at 13:23, close to

Jesus at the Last Supper; at 19:26, close to Jesus on his cross; at 20:2, with Simon Peter on the first Easter morning; and finally at 21:20, with Simon Peter when they meet the risen Jesus by the lake in Galilee. He may also be meant when "another disciple" is mentioned as being well known to the High Priest and as introducing Simon Peter into the courtyard of the High Priest's house (18:15,16). The belief that he was John the son of Zebedee depends not on this gospel (which does not mention the name) but on the fact that the other gospels often group Peter, James and John as the three intimates of Jesus who share some of his most private experiences. (James, who is also not mentioned, is ruled out as the beloved disciple because he was martyred long before the fourth gospel was written: Acts 12:2.) There is also support from the Church's tradition. Irenaeus (about 180) wrote: "John, the disciple of the Lord, who had leaned upon his breast, published his gospel while he was living at Ephesus in Asia." But events ignored in this gospel include those in which, according to the other gospels, John the son of Zebedee was most memorably involved: his call while fishing, his inclusion in the twelve apostles, the transfiguration of Jesus, the request of his mother for a place next to the throne of Jesus in the glorious kingdom, his presence close to the anguished prayer in Gethsemane. This gospel says very little about Galilee; everything after 7:10 takes place in Jerusalem. It is not at all what we should expect as the memoirs of the apostle John.

The authorship remains an enigma. If the author was John the son of Zebedee, he had no intention of recalling his experience of the historical Jesus in any detail. If he was another disciple, his identity is unknown. Perhaps he was "John the elder", whom Papias mentioned in addition to John the apostle. Another possibility is that the "we" mentioned at 21:24 created most of the gospel, using only a few memories from an eyewitness. What we call "John" may have been a group, and this group may have written at different times in response to different pressures. Some scholars have attempted to find in the gospel reflections of the history of a congregation on the frontiers of the Jewish and Greek thought-worlds. There are some similarities between this gospel and the Letter to the Ephesians. Alexandria, about which the New Testament tells us almost nothing, is another possible place of origin. A further puzzle is that some of the chapters seem to be in the wrong order, as if the gospel lacks a final revision. At the end of chapter 14 Jesus says, "Come, let us go!" before continuing his speech, and the geography would be improved if chapters 5 and 6 were reversed. Other features suggest that this is a gospel pondered deeply but not polished into a unified perfection. Here Jesus seems sometimes human and sometimes divine. There has been speculation that the "low Christology" survives from a period when the Johannine community had still worshipped in the Jewish synagogue. But the emphasis on the humanity of Jesus may also have come towards the end of the gospel's development, when the "high Christology" had gone too far away from the "flesh" of history. Or there may never have been much interest in any kind of clear Christology at any stage of the experience behind a gospel which is dramatic rather than philosophical.

We are left not with knowledge of the author or authors but with the gospel itself and with its claim to provide "knowledge" of the "truth" about Jesus. This knowledge is conveyed by telling stories about the life of Jesus, in contrast with Paul's teaching method – and sometimes the stories seem to contain "truth" in a straightforwardly historical sense. Often this gospel includes details – such as what time of day it was (1:39), how plentiful the grass was (6:10) or how many fish were caught in the net (21:11) – which may be symbols of spiritual truths or the products of a vivid imagination. But they may be accurate memories. The knowledge of Palestinian geography shown here is better than Luke's. More importantly, John does not say that Jesus was formally tried by any Jewish religious council – and does say that he was crucified by the Romans on the day before the Passover feast (13:1; 19:31). This may be compared with the report of the other gospels that he died on the actual day of the feast, a very extraordinary day for an arrest, trial and execution. What little we know of the hostile Jewish tradition agrees with John that Jesus had been executed "on the eve of Passover". John also states that during the public work of Jesus two other Passovers occurred (2:13; 6:4) – which may be compared with the impression left by the other gospels that the public work took only one year, leading up to the single Passover. (The only other indications of time in Mark's gospel are the ripening wheat harvest at 2:23 and the green grass at 6:39. These are signs of spring in Palestine.) John tells of three visits by Jesus to Judea and Jerusalem, the final one lasting for about half a year – which may be compared with the failure of the other gospels to explain why the city was so intensely interested in a Galilean. And John informs us that the first disciples of Jesus were recruited from among the disciples of John the Baptist (1:33–42) – which may be compared with the failure of the other gospels to explain why fishermen should respond to a preacher who suddenly appeared and told them to leave everything. He says that Jesus baptized people as John did (3:24), although the statement is soon withdrawn (4:2).

But imparting historical knowledge is clearly not the author's chief aim. He begins his gospel by stories which are historically improbable in comparison with the Synoptics – that Jesus performed the spectacular miracle of turning water into wine within a week of his baptism, that "not

long" afterwards he cleansed the temple in Jerusalem, and
that a leading Pharisee, Nicodemus, then said: "no one
could perform these signs of yours unless God were with
him" (3:2). Early in the second century Clement the scholar
of Alexandria was already describing John's as a "spiritual
gospel", and there can be no doubt that it was intended
chiefly to convey spiritual knowledge, as when Nicodemus
is told he must be "born over again" (3:3). John concen-
trates on the kind of knowledge which Mary of Magdala has
when she turns to the risen Jesus and exclaims *Rabboni* or
"Teacher!" She is told not to cling to him physically, and
later Thomas is told: "Happy are those who find faith without seeing me" (18:16,17,29). The speeches in this gospel are
very unlike the teaching in the other gospels, in substance as
well as in style. They seem to point to what came to be
called the "Incarnation" of God the Son, yet John's gospel
includes no narrative about the birth of Jesus and no clear
discussion of the relationships between the Father, the Son
and the Spirit. The gospel does not fulfil the promise made
to Nathanael (a disciple otherwise not known in the gospels):
"you will see heaven wide open and God's angels ascending
and descending upon the Son of Man" (1:53). Instead Jesus
reveals himself by "signs" with a practical purpose. John's
comment on the first applies to them all: "he revealed his
glory and led his disciples to believe in him."

These "signs" are: the turning of water into wine at Cana
– Jesus brings joy (2:1–12); the healing of the centurion's
son – Jesus gives life by his words (4:43–54); the healing at
the pool – Jesus frees from the paralysis of sin (5:21–31);
the feeding of the thousands – Jesus is the bread that God
gives so that the world may truly live (6:1–59); the healing
of the man born blind – Jesus has come so that the blind
should see and that those who "see" should be shown up
as blind (9:1–41); the raising of Lazarus – whoever believes

in Jesus will never really die (11:1–44); the "lifting up" and
the glory of the cross and resurrection of Jesus himself,
drawing all men (12:20–50). During his arrest, trial and
crucifixion Jesus remains in control until he has tri-
umphantly completed his work. Although he is "troubled"
he knows that the crucifixion is necessary in order that both
the Father and he should be "glorified" (chapter 17). He
knows beforehand everything that is to happen to him
(18:4). When he says "I am he", the men sent to arrest him
fall to the ground (18:6). Pilate "tried hard to release him"
and said to the Jews: "Here is your king" (19:12,14).

The spiritual knowledge which the disciples can gain from
these signs – and which they can pass on to people who have
not seen them (4:48;20:29) – is explained in the speeches of
Jesus as given by John. In these speeches, Jesus declares
that he is the Son of Man, "who came down from heaven"
(3:13); the Messiah (4:26); the Son of God (5:19); the bread
of life (6:35); the light of the world (8:12); the eternal "I
am" before Abraham was born (8:58); the door into safety
(10:9); the good shepherd, willing to die for the sheep
(10:11); one with the Father (10:30); "the resurrection and
life" (11:25); the making visible of the Father (12:45;14:9);
the conqueror of the world (16:33). Finally Jesus prays at
length for the unity and glory of the disciples and of those
who will believe in him because of their message (17:1–26).

It has often been asked: are the wonderful words in this
gospel the words of Jesus? It seems that we cannot honestly
say that both the other gospels give a broadly reliable
account of the life of Jesus, and that he so openly performed
astounding miracles and so explicitly made such super-
human claims about himself. We must choose between the
others and John. The conclusion of almost all who have
studied and pondered the matter with a modern honesty is
that we cannot always rely on the "signs" or the speeches in

John as historical evidence. Instead, most modern scholars
would say that the signs of Jesus in the fourth gospel are to
be regarded chiefly as dramas to show the glory of Jesus,
and the speeches are to be read mainly as sermons communicating a very deep understanding of who Jesus is in eternal
reality. But that is not to say that this gospel gives us no
information about who Jesus was in Palestine under Pilate.

It has often been asked: was John a Greek or a Jew, and
did he write for the Church or for the soul? But John's
gospel refuses to be put into any of these categories. It was
thoroughly Jewish but included Gentiles in its audience. It
was thoroughly churchy but it saw the Church as a community of spiritually minded friends.

The fact that its prologue began with "the Word" (in
Greek *logos*) shows that the gospel, at least in its final edition,
was aimed at fairly well educated people familiar with the
phrase and acquainted with the philosophy in its background. Indeed, most of this prologue may well have existed
as a kind of hymn before it was adapted for the gospel's
purpose. The idea of the Word of God giving shape to all
creation – the source of life, the light shining on all – was
popoular with many reflective and religiously minded people
in the first Christian century. To Gentiles such as the Stoic
philosophers and their pupils, *logos* was the Reason, Vitality
and Order in all things. It made a universe which rational
men could contemplate. And the audience for John's gospel
included Gentiles who needed the elementary information
that *Rabbi* meant 'Teacher" and *Messiah* meant "Christ"
(1:38,41), and that the Passover was a Jewish feast (2:13).
But many Jews would also understand John's terminology.
To Greek-speaking Jews such as Philo of Alexandria, *logos*
was the equivalent of the Wisdom of God in the Hebrew
Bible. Luke had already used the ideas that Jesus and John
the Baptist were both "children" of God's wisdom (7:35),

and that the same "wisdom" had sent the prophets before them (11:49). This understanding of John's terminology would include Jews living in Palestine, where Greek was used extensively (as has been shown by modern archaeology). For example, the contrast between the Sons of Light and the Sons of Darkness occurs prominently in the "Dead Sea Scrolls" left by the Essene monks of Qumran. The gospel's thought is from first to last steeped in the Hebrew Scriptures. In it, Pilate and his soldiers are the only Gentiles in contact with Jesus. The main reason why it can seem to be a gospel for the Gentiles is that John is preoccupied, like Paul and Matthew, with the tragedy of the rejection of Jesus by "his own people" (1:11). This gospel was written at a time when "the Jewish authorities" had already agreed that anyone who acknowledged Jesus as the Messiah should be "banned from the synagogue" – as was not the case in the lifetime of Jesus (9:22). Indeed, it is said that "Anyone who kills you will suppose that he is serving God" (16:2) – a reference to Jewish, not Roman, hostility. Jesus the Jew can even be made to distance himself from "your law" (8:17). So to "the Jews" this gospel declares: "Your father is the devil and you choose to carry out your father's desires" (8:44).

What this gospel explores at depth is the love of Christians for each other and for their Lord – a love which responds to Jesus' love.

Jesus, John proclaims, "had always loved those who were his own in the world, and he loved them to the end" (13:1). So chapters 13–17 move from one exultant affirmation to another about what Jesus does for Christians who are "born again from water and spirit" (3:5) and who "understand" now that he has been "glorified" (12:16). He makes them clean; he sets them an example of humility towards each other; he gives them his new commandment to love one another; he prepares a heavenly place for them; he promises that on earth they will do mightier works than his own; he does whatever they ask for in his name; he sends the Spirit of truth to stay with them for ever; he teaches them everything that really matters; he gives them his own peace; he remains united with them as a vine is united with its branches; he calls them his friends; he has chosen them so that they no longer belong to the world; he fills them with the kind of gladness no one can take away from them; he gives them a unity as close as his own union with his Father; he protects them so that not one of them is lost; he puts his joy in their hearts in all its fullness; he gives them the glory which his Father gave him; he lives in them with the love which his Father has for him.

The Christians about whom such things can be said now include Greeks such as those who "came to Philip . . . and said, 'Sir, we should like to see Jesus' " (12:21). Some of the most solemn words in this gospel are spoken in response. "Unless a grain of wheat falls into the ground and dies it remains that and nothing more; but if it dies, it bears a rich harvest" (12:23,24). The glorified because crucified Son of Man will "draw everyone" (12:32). This Word which existed in "glory before the world began" (17:5), which was what God was (1:1), is "the light of mankind" and "the Saviour of the world" (1:4;4:42), "my Lord and my God" although the Roman emperor claimed that title (20:28). But this Jesus attracts because in his life the Word "became flesh" (1:14). This gospel is about eternal glory, but also about a man who is a friend. In its epilogue Peter is reduced to words which are universal in their simplicity: "Lord, you know everything; you know I love you" (21:17). Jesus leads Peter into life and death with words equally simple: "Follow me" (21:19,22). This gospel about glory transcends any report about what has happened in history, but its intention is not to ignore the history in which a man lives and dies. This gospel also transcends morality, but it does not ignore the morality in which "there is no greater love than this, that someone should lay down his life for his friends" (15:13). Here "Jesus son of Joseph, from Nazareth" (1:45), the crucified Word, commands: "As I have loved you, you are to love one another" (13:34).

Tragically, this command to love seems to be restricted to loving friendly fellow Christians. "The Jews" are insulted grossly, to the extent that it becomes difficult to remember that the historical Jesus was a Jew. It has been left to modern Christians, who have witnessed the Holocaust as the climax of antisemitism wearing a Christian disguise, to realize just how dangerous are many of the words put into the mouth of Jesus by this gospel. And in the First Letter of John, a document which seems to come from someone involved in writing the gospel, the command to love seems to be confined to loving those members of the congregation of whom the author approves. Within that circle, love is strenuous and profoundly revealing. "No one who dwells in Christ sins any more'" and "we know we have crossed over from death to life, because we love our fellow Christians" (3:6,14). This love must be practical, "not a matter of theory or talk", because "whoever claims to be dwelling in him must live as Christ lived" (3:18;2:6). But the gap remains great between this faithful, loving community and those outside. The outsiders do not "possess" God or truth or life, we are told, and prayer for them would be useless (5:16). Another example of the bitterness seems to come in the Third Letter of John, where the writer gives his testimony to the merits of Demetrius ("and you know that my testimony is true") and attacks Diotrephes (who "enjoys taking the lead"). John, it seems, reacts so vehemently because the position of his deputy Demetrius has been undermined. That is understandable, but it is not the Christianity of the Good Samaritan or the Sermon on the Mount.

However, in this First Letter of John two other defects in the gospel are corrected. One defect has been described as a tendency to present Jesus as "God striding over the earth". This seems to have encouraged some former members of the Johannine community to become Gnostics, in that they have denied the humanity of Jesus. Such heretics are now denounced as "many antichrists" who have "left our ranks, but never really belonged to us" (2:19). More positively, the letter expands what the prologue meant by "the Word became flesh." It meant being down-to-earth. "We have seen it with our own eyes; we have looked upon it and felt it with our own hands" (1:1). "The way to recognize the Spirit of God is this: every spirit which acknowledges that Jesus Christ has come in the flesh is from God" (4:2).

Another defect often noted in the gospel is a tendency to push God the Father into the background. This criticism can be exaggerated, for the Jesus of John refers to God as "Father" or "the Father" 173 times, while there are only four such references in Mark's gospel. But a critical reader can understand why it has been said that the Jesus of John's gospel "reveals only that he is the Revealer" – so intense is the concentration on the mission of the Son. In contrast, the First Letter of John does not obscure the concentration on the Father to be found in all the other gospels. "Here is the message we have heard from him and pass on to you: God is light and in him is no darkness at all . . . It is by keeping God's commands that we can be sure that we know him . . . Consider how great is the love which the Father has bestowed on us by calling us his children! . . . My dear friends, let us love one another, because the source of love is God . . . This is what love really is: not that we loved God, but that he loved us and sent his Son as a sacrifice to atone for our sins. If God thus loved us, dear friends, we also must love one another" (1:5;2:3;3:1;4:7,10,11).

THE QUEST FOR JESUS CHRIST

John's astonishingly independent gospel is not the only one that many Christians have thought defective. All the other gospels have their limitations: if they did not, one gospel would have sufficed as the complete New Testament. Paul's letters record criticism of the original message of the Jerusalem church – fierce criticism which he thought devastating. But the literature of Early Catholicism shows that it was thought necessary either to develop or to forget Paul's own insights. Apparently some of Paul's own disciples, who wrote letters using his name, thought this when he was dead. The compilation of Q is, however, evidence that it was not thought enough to leave the teachers of the churches entirely free to convey the message of Jesus as they understood it: there must be a record of his own words. But Mark added his own interpretation as he told the story of Jesus from his baptism to the finding of his empty tomb (as Q, so far as we know, had not done). His gospel did not satisfy either Luke or Matthew. But if the author of Luke's gospel and Acts was indeed the Luke who accompanied Paul, what he wrote showed little trace of Paul's influence – and Matthew's understanding of the impact of Jesus on Judaism was very different from the Jerusalem church's or Paul's or Mark's or Luke's. It is clear that the writers of the New Testament thought it necessary to criticize each other, at least implicitly.

Yet the quest for the real Jesus Christ, historical yet alive, is not hopeless. There is diversity in the evidence provided by the New Testament – but not a total confusion about him. All these documents seemed to agree sufficiently to be brought together as the New Testament. Luke's gospel and Acts made Paul a hero yet presented Jewish Christianity attractively and belonged in a number of ways to Early Catholicism, using both Mark and Q as material. There is a substantial overlap between other documents. If in the twentieth century we want a Christianity which has developed authentically out of the life and teaching of Jesus, it is possible to find a basis which is solid although not as large as we might hope. We can address to ancient and modern historians the request: "Sir, we should like to see Jesus" (John 12:21).

CHAPTER
THREE

The Historical Jesus

WE have looked at Jesus through the eyes of Christians in the second half of the first century AD. It may seem that in our quest for truth we cannot honestly go any further; for it may seem that we have come to the end of the facts because the only facts accessible to us are the facts about the things – often different things – which those Christians believed.

These gospels are indeed like portraits painted by artists who interpret the character of their subject with their own concerns, insights and styles. But it does not follow that we can never know anything about how the man himself really looked. On the contrary, we can know a great deal and the artistry of the painter can help us. The modern study of Jesus, using historical methods only, can be taken further. It is like comparing a series of portraits with each other and with anything else available about the subject and his background. Sometimes one has to strip the varnish away to reveal the original colour and lines; at other times one has to resist the temptation to believe that just because a feature appears in a portrait it cannot be true to life. Sometimes one uses a magnifying glass on a detail; at other times one stands back and looks at all the material as a whole. At all times one must ask who painted each portrait, and when and why, and whether the artist used reliable evidence, and what kind of imagination was also used. What results is not an accurate photograph. But it does give the outline of the face of a man.

In this chapter I shall sum up what seem to be the solid results of the quest of the historical Jesus. I shall list what most scholars nowadays accept as knowable facts by making twelve very short statements in italics. Then I shall add some statements which few serious scholars today would reject although they are not quite so non-controversial. Sometimes in these additional statements I shall refer to probabilities, not knowable facts – but that is true about almost all study of the history of ancient times.

1. Jesus was crucified as a suspected rebel under Pontius Pilate, who was governor of Judea from 26 to 36
It is impossible that all the varied writing about Jesus which we have been considering in this book should refer to a man who never existed. It is equally impossible that the Christians should have invented the fact that he was executed as a criminal by crucifixion – for "Christ nailed to a cross" was an almost unsuperable obstacle in their evangelism. Tacitus, a historian who knew almost nothing about Christianity, did know that "Christus" had been executed by order of Pontius Pilate in the reign of Tiberius, emperor 14–37; and that was enough to brand the Christian movement as criminal.

Crucifixion was a Roman punishment administered only for the most serious crimes by slaves and people of low class. Suggestions have been made that Jesus was a political leader, in which case Pilate was right to have him executed as a rebel or potential rebel, alongside two bandits. But the only evidence which we possess suggests that Jesus and his movement avoided identification with the many rebellious plots of the time. There was, indeed, a tendency in Christian circles to play down Pilate's role in the execution, no doubt in order to minimize any suggestion that the founder of Christianity had been justly condemned for a political offence. But for Pilate the mere fact that Jesus had aroused talk that he was "king" would be enough of a crime. Pilate was exceptionally brutal even by the standards of the Roman empire, and was eventually sacked for excessive harshness.

Those who wish to present Jesus as a rebel naturally claim that there was a Christian attempt to gloss over the revolutionary origins of the movement. They cite the inclusion of Simon the Zealot among the twelve apostles. It is also possible that Judas Iscariot was also one of those who were (or supported) guerrillas or "freedom fighters", since his second name may come from the Latin *sicarius* or "dagger man". Certainly Jesus was surrounded by such men. Galilee was full of them, and it is not surprising to read that some "rebels who had committed murder in the rising" were in prison in Jerusalem (Mark 15:7). It is reasonable to suppose that he attracted some of them as a potential figurehead. John says that on at least one occasion, when the thousands had eaten together in an atmosphere of great excitement, "they meant to come and seize him to proclaim him king" (6:15). And certainly the enthusiasm of one entry into Jerusalem was enough to alarm the police. Mark (11:10) says that it was a demonstration chanting: "Blessed is the kingdom of our father David which is coming!" But against this must be balanced the strong evidence that Jesus made a special point of befriending tax-collectors and advocated the payment of taxes to the Roman emperor (Mark 12:13–17). We are told that a tax-collector was included among the apostles, although his name is uncertain (Mark 2:14; Matthew 9:9). Jesus is also reported as urging collaboration with the enemy on a people which seethed with rebellion. If one of the occupation troops forces a Jew to carry his pack one mile, he is to carry it another mile (Matthew 5:41).

There is a curious incident in Luke's gospel (22:35–38). At their last supper with him, the disciples are advised by Jesus that "whoever does not have a sword must sell his coat and buy one" – and two then say that they already wear swords (as most men did when travelling or in a strange city). Jesus replies: "Enough!" But Luke also reports that when arrested Jesus stopped the use of these swords when one had cut off the ear of the High Priest's servant: "Stop! No more of that!" (22:47–51) And it seems clear that the first piece of evidence is meant to be ironic, in keeping with the Scriptural reference that Jesus is now quoted as making: "He was reckoned among transgressors." Luke almost certainly interpreted the words in this way when he included them in a gospel intended to portray Jesus as the founder of a movement not aimed against the Roman state. And none of the evidence suggests that any of the disciples of Jesus were arrested at the time. They were not a Zealot gang.

We do not know for certain when Jesus "suffered under Pontius Pilate".

Another Roman official, Gallio, is mentioned in the Acts of the Apostles (18:12–17), and an inscription carved at the time shows that the date was 51–52 – the only date in the New Testament about which scholars cannot argue. The evidence which we have in the New Testament indicates that almost twenty years before that Saul of Tarsus became convinced that Jesus of Nazareth was alive although he had been crucified. Luke (3:1) records the tradition that John the Baptist began preaching "in the fifteenth year of the emperor Tiberius". This year of the reign began officially on 19th August 28, although some evidence suggests that

the year was reckoned from the previous autumn in the
eastern parts of the empire. As we have noted, hostile Jewish
references support the report in John's gospel (19:31) that
Jesus was executed on the eve of the Passover. Mark, Luke
and Matthew say that he died on a Friday, the eve of a
Sabbath which was not a Passover, but if John is right to
say that he was crucified in a year when the Passover feast
took place on a Sabbath, the year was 30 or 33. John seems
to date the cleansing of the temple by Jesus at the beginning
of his public work in the year 27–28 (2:20). If that is accurate
the third Passover in the public ministry of Jesus, the Passover of death, was on 7th April 30. The year 36, when
Passover also fell on a Sabbath, seems too late. Pilate was
sacked in that year. The Christians would not have failed
to record that spectacular downfall, had it occurred a few
months after Pilate's supreme sin, the crucifixion.

In the sixth century the monk Dionysius suggested that
all years should be dated either "Before Christ" or *Anno
Domini*. But if Matthew is right to say that Herod the Great
was alive when Jesus was born (2:1–21), that means that
Jesus was born before 4 BC. Luke also says that Herod was
king (1:5), but adds that the birth took place in the year of
the "first registration" when Quirinius was governor of Syria
(2:2). The only such census known to us took place in AD
6, when Judaea was brought under direct Roman rule. It
sparked off a revolt which was put down with many cruci-
fixions in Galilee; this is referred to in Acts (5:37). P. Sulpic-
ius Quirinius is known to have been in the Roman colonial
administration then but it is not at all likely that he organized an enrolment in the kingdom of Herod the Great,
believed by Luke to have been still reigning. Certainly there
is no evidence to support Luke in believing that "a decree
was issued by the emperor Augustus for a census to be taken
throughout the Roman world" (2:1).

It seems, therefore, that we have no reliable information about when Jesus was born. We have to be content to be told that during his public work he was "about thirty years old" (Luke 3:23) – or at least "not yet fifty" (John 8:57).

2. Although he identified himself with the holiness movement around John the Baptist, Jesus claimed that a greater and more joyful event was taking place around him

The work of John the Baptist, summoning Jews to repentance and to a greater holiness of life, is mentioned by the historian Josephus. In the Acts of the Apostles there is a report that in Alexandria and Ephesus about the year 50 there were still Jews who "knew only the baptism of John" (18:25,19:3), and other evidence indicates that this was not the end of the Baptist's movement. But the main evidence for the impact made by the Baptist comes from the agreement of the Christians that the Son of God, the Saviour, was himself baptized by John. To admit that Jesus submitted to an act which so obviously symbolized the washing away of sin was embarrassing. It was a fact which had to be reported but could be minimized. In John's gospel the embarrassment is put into the mouth of the Baptist, who has to be reassured by the voice of God (1:19–34). In Matthew's gospel the Baptist says: "It is I who need to be baptized by you" (3:14). In Luke's, the Baptist does homage to Jesus in the womb (1:39–45). These seem to be traces of attempts to iron out the awkward fact that Jesus was spiritually indebted to the Baptist and did not begin independent work until after the Baptist's arrest (Mark 2:14).

There are hints of tensions because the contrast between Jesus and the Baptist seems to show also the difference between Jesus and the Essenes. The probable site of Bathabara, the Baptist's headquarters, lies only eight miles from the monastery at Qumran, where the Dead Sea Scrolls were

discovered, and the Baptist may well have been influenced
profoundly by the Essenes' demand for purity in expectation
of the rapid intervention of God to end the world's corruption, including the corruption of the Jerusalem temple. They
took ritual baths every day. The message of Jesus also had
many points in common with this holiness movement, which
had its own "Teacher of Righteousness" (about whom little
is recorded). But Jesus did not withdraw into the desert. He
lived among the tax-collectors and prostitutes. He taught
the ignorant people where they were, in a language they
could understand. And the image of the banquet was at the
heart of his preaching. In contrast, the Essene monks
insisted that anyone who violated the Jewish religious law,
which they obeyed meticulously, had no hope of salvation.

*3. Although he had worked as a carpenter, Jesus of Nazareth was
widely welcomed as a teacher and a prophet*
In the Palestine where Jesus lived leadership in religion was
strictly regulated. Pharisees and Sadducees agreed that there
were no prophets any more. The priests and Levites in the
temple were hereditary. At least some of the "scribes" or
rabbis were carefully trained and solemnly ordained. No one
ever said that Jesus was either a priest or scribe. He was a
layman. When the author of the Letter to the Hebrews
wished to claim that Jesus was the perfect priest, he first
had to face the fact that it was well known that he was born
a member of the tribe of Judah, and no member of that tribe
ever served as a priest at the altar (7:13,14). When John
portrayed Jesus as teaching in the Court of the Gentiles in
the temple (as any Jew was free to attempt), he first had to
present the Jewish authorities as asking: "How is it that this
untrained man has such learning?" (7:15).

Jesus is described by Mark (6:3) as a carpenter who
belonged to a large family: he had four brothers (whose

names were remembered, presumably because they became Christians) and sisters as well. He is called more respectfully by Matthew (13:55) "the carpenter's son" but most jobs were then inherited. This need not mean that he was always poor. Carpenters were skilled craftsmen who made houses as well as agricultural implements (such as well-fitting yokes) and furniture. Since there is no mention of his father Joseph in the tradition after Luke 2:51 and Matthew 2:23, it is probable that Joseph died, and that Jesus had to support the family. They lived in Nazareth, a little hillside town fifteen miles from the Lake of Galilee. The town had no fame or prestige. When Matthew wanted to produce a dignified biblical reference to Nazareth, he quoted: "He will be called *Nazoraios*" (2:23) – a quotation which no one has been able to trace. In later controversy the Jewish rabbis called the Christians Nazarenes, implying the taunt of Nathanael in John's gospel: "Can anything good come from Nazareth?" (1:46). When Christians called Jesus of Nazareth "Messiah" they had to face the question: "Does not Scripture say that the Messiah is to be of the family of David, from David's village of Bethlehem?" (John 7:42). It was probably in response to that question that Luke and Matthew claimed that Nazareth did not even have the honour of being the birthplace of Jesus.

If we are taking historical considerations only into account, we have to say that Luke and Matthew were wrong to bring Bethlehem into the story of Jesus – and wrong to say that he was conceived without a father. The story of a virginal conception (the "Virgin Birth") of course contradicts our knowledge of how human lives begin genetically, and the evidence supporting it is not strong. The only material in the New Testament plainly relevant is provided by Luke and Matthew, and comes in the midst of material which is obviously legendary (and very beautiful also). Luke

(1:26–3:8) tells of the miracle from Mary's point of view, Matthew (1:18–2:15) from Joseph's; and their stories differ. To reconcile the stories it would be necessary to suppose that Mary did not tell Joseph, to whom she was betrothed, about the angel's visit which explained her pregnancy. But the two stories cannot be reconciled. Luke says that after the birth the family "returned to Galilee to their own town of Nazareth" while Matthew says that it was after a period as a refugee in Egypt that Joseph was guided to move to Galilee and to settle in Nazareth. The two gospels back up a tradition which Paul passed to the Romans (1:3), that Jesus was descended from King David. But they do so by providing different genealogies, both tracing the descent through Joseph not Mary although Joseph was not the father of Jesus. They give different names for Joseph's own father. We are taken into a world where (in defiance of the known practices in Roman census-taking for taxation purposes) Joseph has to take a terminally pregnant woman to a village where he has no property and no friends (they have to use the inn); where angels speak and sing; where a star stops to indicate a house which then cannot be discovered by a tyrant's agents; where the tyrant orders a massacre which no historian includes among his crimes; where strange Orientals bring costly gifts into a family which then treats Jesus without honour (Matthew 13:57); where no one outside that family – no shepherd, no Oriental – seems to become a disciple of the Son of God whose birth was manifestly supernatural. It is not a world known to history. What seems to be the reality behind the legendary embellishment is that because of their experience of the saving power of "God in Christ", Christians came to believe that the life of Jesus had been from its start the expression of God's love. To their faith it was more than the fruit of a man's love for a woman. Jesus was the "Son of God". They expressed this faith not by philosophical theology but by telling stories such as those told by Luke and Matthew.

The Galilee into which Jesus was born was (and is) a beautiful country. The historian Josephus, who once commanded the Jewish rebel army in Galilee, boasted of the land's fertility and the men's courage. There is some evidence that Galilee was also fertile in a courageous and enthusiastic kind of Judaism. We should call it a charismatic or spiritual religion, with no emphasis on rules and formalities. It could also be called provincial or naïve: it lacked sophistication and professionalism. This religion was mixed with social discontent. The government was foreign; taxation was heavy; tax-collectors (who were allowed to keep what they collected in excess of the official taxes) were hated; the population was too large for the land; too much of the land was divided into large estates with absentee landlords. In the background of the work and teaching of Jesus were many of the results of poverty – unemployment, begging, burglaries, unhealed illness whether physical or psychological, frantic worries over small losses such as one sheep or one coin.

It is all the more remarkable that Jesus was so widely acknowledged as a teacher and prophet – and not only in charismatic circles in Galilee. This tradition is preserved in the gospels although they might have been expected to divide the reactions between the hostility of the many and the acclamation of the few. Mark sums up the popularity of Jesus when he says that, in the last days in the Jerusalem temple, "there was a large crowd" (12:37). In the gospels Jesus is frequently called "Teacher". In Mark's gospel people say: "He is a prophet, like one of the prophets of old" (6:15;8:28). In Luke's gospel the reaction produced by the report that Jesus has brought a dead man back to life is: "A great prophet has arisen among us!" (7:16). And at the end, the disciples walking to Emmaus call him simply "Jesus of Nazareth, who by deeds and words of power proved himself a prophet . . . " (24:19).

One reason why it makes sense to think that Jesus was admired by many was that much of his teaching agreed with much that was taught in the Hebrew Scriptures and contemporary Jewish religion. The gospels, although concerned to emphasize the novelty of Jesus, often show how orthodox he was in his loyalty to the Scriptures which he loved. For example, Mark (12:28–34) gives the story that he quoted from the two books, Deuteronomy and Leviticus, in answer to the question, "Which is the first of all the commandments?" – and received the congratulations of a rabbi: "Well said, Teacher!" Jesus was a teacher who explained and simplified; in this, he must have seemed the successor of Hillel, the famous rabbi who flourished when Jesus was a boy and who was more sensitive to the difficulties of the common people than his sterner colleague, Shammai. But he was more than a scholar. He was a prophet who made the ancient message vividly immediate. It is not surprising to meet in the Christian tradition estimates of John the Baptist as a prophet like Elijah (as predicted in Malachi 4:5), and of Jesus himself as a prophet like Moses (as predicted in Deuteronomy 18:18,19).

The recorded teaching of Jesus includes a number of sayings which are similar to the recorded sayings of the rabbis. But almost all modern Jewish scholars who comment say that he had a genius for teaching. They agree, too, that he had a consistent style – pictorial rather than abstract, narrative rather than philosophical, direct rather than allusive, sharp rather than full, exaggerated rather than qualified, sometimes terrifying but often witty, sometimes quoting the Scriptures but more often based on his own observation of nature and human life and his own direct knowledge of God.

He did not waste words. What in an English translation looks like a certain amount of repetition was recognizable to all his first hearers as the "parallelism" which was the strongest feature of Hebrew poetry (as the psalms show): something is said, and then either something in contrast or else something almost exactly the same. This style of Jesus was not exclusively his own. Some of the rabbis sometimes spoke like this and so did some of the early Christians (unless all the sayings which "sound like sayings of Jesus" actually were his). But the two greatest thinkers of the first-century Church, Paul and John, had different styles, and almost all the Christian literature surviving from the second century and later is very different.

A prophet would be expected to speak with vividness and authority, as did the great prophets of Israel. Jesus did so. But he would also be expected to illustrate his teaching by symbolic actions. Jesus did this, too.

4. Jesus performed healings regarded as miraculous

The gospels are full of the deeds of Jesus – healings welcomed as miracles and understood as expulsions of the demons causing distress. Hostile Jewish references which have survived and which may be contemporary with the gospels (although they cannot be dated accurately) describe him as a magician. This should not surprise us. There were some doctors in that society, but not many – and they were not very effective. Mark (5:25–26) gives us a glimpse of a woman who had "become worse rather than better" although she had "spent all she had" on "long treatment by many doctors". A prophet would be expected to heal. Why, the followers of the Pharisees did it! The gospels make this point when reporting the Pharisees' objection that "it is by Beelzebul prince of demons that he drives the demons out". Jesus asks: "By whom do your own people drive them out?" (Luke 11:14–19). Outside the New Testament there is evidence that charismatic teachers in Galilee were also healers.

The accounts of these healings often mention the forgiveness of sins. The explanation seems to be that when God is believed to be real a sense that he is near and friendly can often be very important in the recovery of spiritual, mental and physical health, but first the barriers set up on the human side must be removed. Poison in relationships with other people can bring poison into the body, so that it is also often very important for a person who seems paralysed by bitterness to acknowledge that all are sinners and that God is himself ready to forgive all.

These accounts also often mention the presence of faith. Early in Mark's gospel (1:40–3:5) a skin disease is healed when Jesus is believed to be able to make a man clean; a paralysed man can walk when surrounded by excited believers; an arm which seems to be withered becomes healthy when held out in faith. "Everything is possible", Jesus says later, "to one who believes" (9:23). The explanation seems to be that many of these diseases were cured by strengthening the sufferer's will-power and sense of psychological liberation and calm. This method is often called "faith-healing". So many healings by the same method have been attested in so many periods, including our own, that it is not reasonable to be completely sceptical. We may add that many of the diseases may have been partly mental in origin, or psychosomatic. In particular the word "leprosy" was used of all kinds of skin diseases. In the absence of a medical diagnosis some people believed to have died may in fact have been in a coma or "sleep".

This is not to say that as a matter of fact all these healings took place as Christian preachers and gospel writers were saying many miles away and thirty or more years later. That is highly improbable. Nor need we accept as historical facts all the non-healing or "nature" miracles recounted in the gospels. Some of these stories may be linked with reports that Christian saints and non-Christian holy men have performed feats such as walking on water (Mark 6:45–52). It may be wise to keep an open mind there. Others of the stories may have grown in the telling. For example, we may ask: how many thousands were fed in the "lonely place" – five thousand (Mark 6:30–44), or four thousand (Mark 8:1–10), or fewer? And we may ask: was new bread created (as no doubt Mark thought) or were they fed by sharing their food when Jesus had taught and prayed? The strangest miracle in the gospels is often thought to be the cursing of the fig tree when Jesus found only leaves, "for it was not the season for figs" (Mark 11:12–14). The explanation may be that the tradition behind this story has misunderstood a parable which used the ripeness of the fig tree to teach about the ripeness of the time (Mark 13:28,29 is an example).

Another miracle which seems to be out of keeping with the character of Jesus is indicated by the report that Jesus told Peter he would find a coin in the mouth of the first fish he caught (Matthew 17:24–27). Fish do swallow shiny objects, but it seems more likely that Jesus told Peter to pay a tax out of the profits of everyday fishing. John's story that Jesus turned water into wine (2:1–11) sounds too like magic to be real history. It appears to dramatize the teaching that Jesus turns the ordinary into the glorious. The profoundly moving story that Jesus raised from the dead a friend whose body had lain in the tomb for four days is hard to reconcile with the evidence about the despair surrounding the death of Jesus himself, but it seems to dramatize the proclamation: "I am the resurrection and I am life" (11:25).

5. Jesus broke religious laws and severely criticized religious leaders
Probing modern investigation of the evidence shows that
it is highly probable that the gospels exaggerate Jewish
participation in the trial of Jesus, which no Christian
attended. The claims made by Jesus in the Synoptic gospels
do not amount to blasphemy as defined in the Jewish
religious law (despite Mark 14:36). It was not blasphemy
to claim to be "Messiah" or "Son of Man". It seems probable that the Jewish religious court, the Sanhedrin, was not
allowed to inflict the death penalty in that period, and that
the stoning of Stephen (Acts 7:54–60) was the act of a mob.
Mark's account of a trial in the High Priest's house during
the Passover night, speedily resulting in the death sentence
(14:53–64), can be said more definitely to be in conflict with
Jewish law and custom. It is probable that Jesus was
arrested by the temple police as a trouble maker and, after
interrogation, handed over to the Romans with the information that he was a rebel or potential rebel. There was
only one formal trial – before Pilate.

But it is certain that Jesus clashed with the official religion
of his day. The evidence surviving from the first century,
both from the Christian and from the Jewish sides, has been
shaped by the conflict of charge and counter-charge, in
growing controversies, but it speaks eloquently enough of the
fact that Jesus was officially rejected despite his popularity as
a prophet and healer. We have to explain this. In modern
times many Jews have taken pride in the sublime ethics, the
poetic genius, the courage and the faith of Jesus the Jew –
but clearly that was not the attitude of most of the religious
leadership of his own people in the first century AD. Had he
been executed by the Romans entirely on their own initiat-
ive, his followers would have taken pride in the support of
the Jewish leaders. Had the Jewish leaders' opposition begun
only when Gentile Christians failed to keep the Jewish

religious law, innovators such as Paul would have had to answer the charge that they alone had disturbed the peace. But every piece of evidence which we have tells us that Jesus and the movement he began aroused the Jewish leaders' hostility. As the controversy mounted it was Jesus, not Paul, who was attacked. Paul's own letters show that the attack was regarded by him as a religious duty before he became a Christian. That is very remarkable in view of the fact that great diversity was accepted (although not necessarily welcomed) in Palestinian Judaism at that time. How should we account for it?

All the gospels which describe his last days report that Jesus was accused of planning or predicting the destruction of the temple in Jerusalem. We cannot be sure what Jesus actually said. John thought that "the temple he was speaking of was his body" (2:21). But we know that the hope that there would be a new temple, staffed by pure Jews but attracting many Gentiles, burned brightly in the Essene monastery at Qumran. It seems likely that Jesus shared this hope and dramatized it in a demonstration. It is also likely that, being the heir of the great prophets of Israel and also a Galilean layman, he put righteousness before ritual, mercy before sacrifice. This was perfectly compatible with joining pilgrimages to the temple and paying the annual tax to support it. It would also have been compatible with some participation in the temple's sacrifices, although that is not reported of Jesus. Jesus is said to have told his disciples: "If you are presenting your gift to God at the altar and remember that your brother has something against you, leave your gift where it is before the altar. First go and make your peace with your brother" (Matthew 5:23–24). Christians such as Matthew recalled that vivid saying at a time when no Jew or Christian ever offered any sacrifice in any temple. It seems to be authentic.

But as four gospels recount, Jesus threw down a public challenge to the priests. They had allowed the open-air Court of the Gentiles in the Jerusalem temple to become a sordid market for the sale of sacrificial victims – and for the exchange of coinage bearing the Roman Emperor's head for approved coins. So in this temple sacred to all Jews, the preacher of non-resistance exploded in violent anger. Mark (11:15–19) gives the Scriptural quotation which Jesus used: "My house will be called a house of prayer for all peoples" – implying that the Gentiles had the right to a place for solemn worship. In addition to this misuse of the Court of the Gentiles, the very handsome profits made by the hereditary aristocratic priests out of sacrifices in the temple had no doubt aroused the indignation of Jesus, who "upset the tables of the moneychangers and the seats of the dealers in pigeons". Jesus is reported as crying: "You have made it a robbers' cave" (Mark 11:17).

In the New Testament the emphasis is also on conflict with the Pharisees, who although laymen took on themselves the obligation to live with a purity like that of the temple's priests. The Law or *Torah* (a word which means much more than "law") in the Hebrew Scriptures was reckoned to contain 248 positive commandments and 365 prohibitions, and on top of this there was a vast quantity of religious law or custom handed on in the rabbis' teaching based on the Scriptures. The ideal was to keep all these laws and customs with a total fidelity out of love for the gracious God of Israel. That ideal is stated very eloquently in Psalm 119 (for example). It is probable that the Pharisees were singled out for fierce criticism in the gospels because, as the group that led the reconstruction of Judaism after the destruction of the temple, they were largely responsible for the excommunication of the Christians. But it is also probable that Jesus bewildered, irritated or infuriated many of the Phariseees and rabbis who encountered him by his own attitude to the law.

A number of disputes with Jewish conservatives are reported in the gospels and are reflected in Matthew's repeated insistence in the Sermon on the Mount that Jesus put "what I tell you" above what "our forefathers were told". The gospels may or may not record the actual words of Jesus during these disputes. What seems clear is that the Christian defence of Jesus against his Jewish critics could not include claims that he had fasted piously and had strictly observed the customs which safeguarded purity while eating. On the contrary, it was admitted that he did not "conform to the ancient tradition" (Mark 7:5). Many regulations which orthodox Jews obeyed were not laid down in the Hebrew Scriptures and it can be argued that Jesus disregarded only laws which could be regarded as man-made. But it is striking that Matthew, who was no radical hothead, believed that Jesus had forbidden all oaths invoking God (5:33–37) despite the biblical provision for them (Leviticus 19:12). In the Letter of James (4:12) "do not use oaths" was placed "above all things". In our discussion of Jesus' attitude to divorce we have seen that he was remembered as having taught that all divorces were against the will of God despite the biblical permission for a man to divorce a wife, "who does not find favour because he finds something offensive in her" (Deuteronomy 24:1). And despite the Scriptures Matthew thought that "no one is defiled by what goes into his mouth" (15:11).

One of the most sacred institutions of the Jewish religious system was the Sabbath. From Friday to Saturday evening, every Jew was commanded to rest from all work and to concentrate on the worship of God in the temple, synagogue or home. More than anything else this rule made the Jews distinctive in the Roman empire, and Julius Caesar won much credit from the Jews for allowing it to be observed. Jesus, it seems, did not observe it strictly. Early in Mark's gospel comes the emphasis that Jesus made a point of performing on the Sabbath day cures which could easily have waited for the next day (1:21–28;3:1–6). The same emphasis is found in the other gospels. Mark includes an incident when a minor breach of the Sabbath law had no great humanitarian purpose but could be made the occasion for a radical declaration: "The Sabbath was made for man and not man for the Sabbath" (2:23–27).

The gospels of Luke, Matthew and John, almost certainly written after 70, are generally thought by scholars to add to the tragedies of that time by the bitterness with which they denounce the "scribes and Pharisees" and even the "Jews". Their evidence about the historical Jesus deserves to be read with a special caution at this point. But even this evidence includes reports that the rabbis were often in dialogue with Jesus, that he accepted invitations to dine with Pharisees, and that Pharisees warned him that Herod was planning to kill him (Luke 7:36;11:37;13:31). When "the scribes and Pharisees" are called "hypocrites" (a word which means "actors"), this was no doubt accurate about some of them some of the time, but we should also notice that Matthew tells us that these men were "greeted respectfully in the street" (23:7), and that Paul tells the Philippians that as a Pharisee he put the whole Torah into practice (3:5). It seems possible to glimpse the genuine attitude of Jesus in one of his parables (Luke 18:9–14). Here it is not alleged that the Pharisee who prays in the temple is himself "greedy, dishonest, adulterous". What is lamented is that he has separated himself from his fellow sinner by his contempt for "this tax-collector" and has separated himself from God by being so caught up in his own self-righteousness. He is not humble enough to receive God's free gift of forgiveness.

6. Jesus became the friend of those despised by others, teaching that God loves all

This is the special theme of Luke, as we saw, but it is by no means confined to Luke's gospel. Luke takes the prayer of Jesus from Q: "I thank you, Father, Lord of heaven and earth, for hiding these things from the learned and wise, and revealing them to the simple" (10:21). Three tender incidents occur in the middle of Mark's stern gospel, which may justly be called a gospel for male adults. Jesus heals a woman who for twelve years had been humiliated by bleedings. She had been isolated from her community because thought to be unclean, and therefore does not dare to speak to him (5:25–34). After a refusal Jesus, moved by her plight and delighted by her wit, responds to a foreign woman whose small daughter is ill (7:24–30). When the disciples have told them to get lost, Jesus welcomes children, saying: "Whoever does not accept the kingdom of God like a child will never enter it." "And he put his arms round them, laid his hands on them and blessed them" (10:12–16). The attitudes of Jesus to women and to children which are reflected in such traditions about him were revolutionary. They made Paul, who was no feminist, teach that there was no difference between male and female "in Christ". He told the Corinthians that he was glad that he had "finished with childish things", but he ended up with a priority for love which a child could understand.

It can be thought that the blessing of Jesus was confined to innocent women and children and to the deserving poor. But the evidence provided by Mark (2:16,17) and others is striking. "Some scribes who were Pharisees, observing the company in which he was eating, said to his disciples, 'Why does he eat with tax-collectors and sinners?' Hearing this, Jesus said to them, 'It is not the healthy who need a doctor, but the sick. I did not come to call the virtuous, but sinners.' " The fact is clear that Jesus took many meals with disreputable people such as prostitutes and the tax-collectors who collaborated with the Romans, risking his entire reputation and arousing gossip about sins worse than gluttony and an addiction to wine. This is not a fact which the early Christians would have invented about their holy Lord. Indeed, the gospels were written at the very time when Early Catholicism was doing its best to make Christianity respectable.

The explanation is given when we are told what Jesus taught about God. He taught that God forgave sins gladly – and to prove it, he himself would say without hesitation: "My son, your sins are forgiven" (as in Mark 2:5). The rabbis and Pharisees no doubt considered that this made the forgiveness of God cheap. According to the orthodox Jewish piety, God's mercy had to be entreated with many prayers and tears; it had to be sought by sacrifices in the temple, if at all possible; it had to be deserved by a life of obedient goodness. But according to Jesus God was like a father who actually ran to greet a rebellious son "still a long way off" and who instantly gave back all a son's privileges (Luke 15:20–23). Human love for God, including the forgiveness of fellow sinners, comes fully after, not before, God's pardon. About one ex-prostitute Jesus is reported as saying: "Her great love proves that her many sins have been forgiven; where little has been forgiven, little love is shown" (Luke 7:47).

In reaction against antisemitism, some Christian as well as Jewish scholars have recently stressed the elements in the religion around him which harmonized with the teaching of Jesus. But there was also conflict – and the way to avoid unfairness to Judaism is to confess that Christians, too, have often tried to narrow the wideness of God's mercy.

7. Jesus announced that the kingdom of God was near by telling parables

The actions of Jesus spoke louder than words. When he healed someone, that action shouted aloud that God was King. When he sat next to someone, that said very effectively that God was Friend. But he also used words as weapons. And they were not words which would have been chosen by the teachers of Early Catholicism in the period when their gospels were written by Mark, Luke and Matthew.

He was a master of the short story with a religious point. Some parables are to be found elsewhere in the New Testament and in other ancient Christian literature, but in comparison with those in the Synoptic gospels they are clumsy – for example, Paul's parable of the olive tree in his letter to the Romans (11:16–18). Parables are also to be found in the teaching of the rabbis and in the Hebrew Scriptures, but no teacher of Israel known to us used parables half as much, or half as well, as Jesus. The Synoptic gospels show that this was his favourite method of teaching the public. Even Mark shows this, although he has to claim that the parables were told in order that people should *not* see and understand (4:10–12).

The parables given to us in the gospels no doubt owe a good deal of their wording to the gospel-writers, although it is hard to believe that all or most of them had no connection with the historical Jesus. In those days when memories were not so burdened as they are today stories, like sharp sayings, might be remembered quite well. Many are reported with explanations (for example, Mark 4:13–20) or with shorter moralizing comments (for example, Matthew 20:16). Luke 16:9–12 is a miniature sermon. Almost certainly most of these explanations or comments were not added by Jesus but represent the work of preachers in the early Church, who have added other touches to show that they were con-

cerned with a problem which did not face the parables'
original audiences – the delay in the arrival of the End. It
is also almost certain that originally each of the parables
was told with one main point in mind; any elaborate explanations of what each detail meant came later. The parable
was told so that this one point would sink into the memories
of the first hearers, although many of them did not immediately understand or respond. They would sometimes be
stimulated by the unusual, even bizarre, character of the
tale – and sometimes attracted by the very familiarity of a
picture of village life. They would go away relishing the
story and thinking quietly about its significance. And it is
almost certain that originally the parables were told in order
to encourage or warn about the coming of the kingdom of
God. The message of Jesus through them was that God's
activity was about to reach a climax, proving his reality
and establishing his rule. And what Jesus meant by this
"kingdom" is most neatly stated in Matthew's version of
the Lord's Prayer (6:10):

> your kingdom come,
> your will be done,
> on earth as in heaven.

The idea of the kingdom of God has sometimes been misunderstood as advocating only a psychological change in the
converted individual. It is obvious that Jesus did seek con-
versions and did promise peace of mind. But it is highly
probable that the Greek of Luke 17:21 means "the kingdom
of God is among you" as in the Revised English Bible, or
"in the midst of you" as in the Revised Standard Version,
and not "within you" as in some other translations. It refers
to a public takeover of power by God, demanding a public
response. It is in keeping with Luke's references to a flash

of lightning, to a great flood and to the gathering of vultures which shows where a dead body is. It is also in keeping with the references to the "kingdom of God" in the surviving Jewish literature of the time, where what is longed for is the public, all-decisive intervention by God in history's tragedies. But Luke 17:21 claims (as do many other sayings and parables) that this intervention has begun, that the kingdom is dawning among the spectators, in the midst of history, illuminating the darkness, sweeping away the past, eating up the debris of all the centuries.

We cannot be certain about the original meaning of the parables retold in the gospels; they have not reached us in the exact words of Jesus but instead have been preached in order to meet the spiritual needs of the early Christians. In three gospels we can observe three different styles as these stories are retold: in Mark the stories are simple warnings or encouragements with imagery that is close to the earth, in Luke the stories are told with psychological insight and with faith in the Father's love, in Matthew the scenes are grander but hell is nearer. However, a broad understanding of the message about the kingdom of God can be gained from the collection as a whole.

Here I give what seems to be the most probable original meaning and I usually use the title in the Good News Bible. The Hidden Treasure, the Pearl and the New Wine show that the kingdom is entered with delight. The invitation to enter it implies a challenge to sacrifice much: that is taught by the Narrow Door, the Tower-builder, the King Going to War and the Return of the Evil Spirit. But the Great Feast, the Rich Fool, the Shrewd Manager, the Two House Builders, the Obedient and Disobedient Sons and the Wicked Tenants show that the invitation must be accepted without hesitation and without pretence. Pride must not stand in the way: see the Pharisee and the Tax-Collector. In this kingdom each receives what he needs, like the Workers in the Vineyard. In particular each receives God's forgiveness: that good news is given by the Lost Sheep, the Lost Coin and the Lost Son. In this kingdom we need one another and must forgive one another: that is commanded by the Good Samaritan, the Rich Man and the Beggar and the Unforgiving Servant. We must not be discouraged if we cannot quickly enter, or even see, God's kingdom. Instead we must remember how patient God himself has been so far. That is taught by the Sower, the Growing Seed, the Weeds, the Mustard Seed, the Yeast, the Unfruitful Fig Tree, the Fishermen's Net, the Man Absent from Home, the Burglar, the Watchful Servants, the Three Servants with Coins and the Ten Girls with Lamps. As we wait, we must serve one another in a completely practical way, learning from the Sheep and the Goats. And we must pray, as encouraged by the Father Asked for an Egg, the Friend Asked for Bread and the Judge Asked for Justice. Even if not all these parables originated with Jesus in something like the words in which we have them, the cumulative message would seem to be reasonably clear.

8. Exercising his personal authority, Jesus summoned and sent out messengers to Israel; and the message he gave them was potentially for the whole human race

All the evidence agrees that Jesus spoke and acted with authority, and that the authority which he claimed was more than that expected in a teacher or prophet.

There is uncertainty about exactly what he claimed about himself, but it is clear that one way in which he showed his authority was by choosing his followers (whereas the rabbis' pupils applied to them) and demanding that they should give up literally everything – wives, children, jobs, possessions, opinions – in order to be with him. He did not urge this on everyone. According to Mark, one man whom he had cured offered to follow him and was told to go home (5:18,19). But with those he wanted, he was ruthless in his demands. At a time when the literature of Early Catholicism was stressing how good Christianity was for family life, the gently humane Luke attributed to Jesus the saying that if "anyone comes to me"' he must "hate his father and mother, wife and children, brothers and sisters, even his own life" (14:26).

It lies beyond doubt that Jesus associated others intimately with his work. It is also clear that Jesus expected others to share his glory. Not only do all the gospels say so repeatedly. It is inconceivable that Jesus thought of a reward for himself alone, since the whole emphasis of the Old Testament and of the Jewish religion, from first to last, was on the people of God and its future. All the mysterious figures symbolizing the Jewish experience and hope – Messiah, Servant, Son of Man – were related to the people of God. The Bible knows no such thing as a solitary Christ. On the contrary, Paul and the Synoptic gospels say that Jesus had twelve special disciples. Luke and Matthew have lists of names slightly different from Mark's (3:13–19), but always there are twelve. The number is important because it is a sign that the mission was directed to the twelve tribes of Israel. It is so important that Paul seems to forget that there were only eleven apostles to witness the resurrection (1 Corinthians 15:5).

One of the most striking features of the Synoptic gospels is their admission that the historical Jesus was a thorough Jew, who for all his unorthodoxy thought as a Jew and worked only among fellow members of the twelve tribes. It must have been tempting for Mark and Luke to pretend that Jesus was at heart a Gentile, transcending all the limitations of his surroundings. Matthew, too, writing for Jews when disaster had overtaken the Jewish nation, must have been tempted to present a Jesus who from the first had had his eyes set on "all nations" (28:19). The gospel-writers do not make that pretence, any more than Paul appeals to the teaching of Jesus to justify the inclusion of the Gentiles on equal terms.

However, if God's offer was as Jesus said it was, it could not be confined for ever to Jews. The restriction of the mission of Jesus and his apostles to Israel resulted from the limitations of time and energy; it was not a matter of profound and permanent principle. Q and the later gospel-writers all mention individual Gentiles who were included in the mission. Even more significant is the willingness of the Jewish Christian community to allow the Gentile mission although it so deeply disturbed their own conservatism.

Why, then, was there such controversy about the terms on which Gentiles might be baptized into the Church? The most likely explanation is that what little Jesus said about any future appeal to the Gentiles imagined the Gentiles going to Jerusalem. They would go in repentance and faith when they saw the glory in Israel at the End. That imagery is found in the Hebrew prophetic books (for example, in Isaiah 60:1-6) and also in Q. A vast mission to the Gentiles, beginning in Jerusalem, was not in mind. On the other hand, the use of this imagery did not rule out any possibility of such a mission. In the time of Jesus orthodox Jews conducted extensive missionary activities among Gentiles. As Matthew has it: "You travel over sea and land to win one convert" (23:15).

9. Jesus disclaimed knowledge of the exact date of the End and foretold great suffering for himself, his followers and his people
All the evidence agrees that Jesus and the early Christians hoped passionately that the end of the world they knew

would come quickly. But also deeply embedded in the early Christian tradition – in all the evidence which we have considered, for example in Mark 13:32 – is the denial of knowledge exactly when the End would come. All the enthusiasm about the near End always included this reserve. Some passages are sometimes quoted as evidence against that – for example, "the present generation will live to see it all" (Mark 13:30). But such sayings are known to us only because they are reported by gospel-writers who knew that the End had not come within the lifetime of Jesus' first hearers; a person aged twenty in AD 30 would probably be dead by AD 50. It seems that the gospel-writers put any such sayings in the context of a controlling disclaimer of knowledge about the date of the End. Otherwise they would not have written as they did about the wisdom of Jesus.

It was an age keenly interested in "apocalyptic" prophecies, and material collected in all three Synoptic gospels (specially Mark 13, Matthew 24, and Luke 12 and 21), in the Revelation of John and in letters such as 2 Thessalonians, shows how fascinated the Christians were by signs of the coming End. But it is almost certain that such collections of signs were revised to take account of events like the attempt of the emperor Caligula to install a statue of himself in the Jerusalem temple in AD 40 (this seems to have been the "abomination of desolation" which the reader of Mark 13:14 is told to understand), or the fall of Jerusalem thirty years later. It is impossible to be sure what, if anything, in these passages goes back to Jesus. However, the main thrust of the Christian teaching was that when the End really came its signs would be clear enough. As is said in several places, it would come suddenly and unmistakably, like an eagle swooping from the sky or like a thief in the night. That may well be what Jesus emphasized most strongly.

This evidence of caution and reverence is what we should

expect of devout Jews. It reserved knowledge of the date of
the End to God alone, even if it meant admitting that here
Jesus was himself ignorant. The heirs of the piety of the
Hebrew Scriptures would have abhorred as blasphemous
any suggestion that they should force God's hand into acting
in the way they wanted. Always God was to be left with his
sovereignty. The theory that by seeking crucifixion Jesus
hoped to force God into establishing his kingdom is for this
reason psychologically improbable.

Another theme is clear in many reports of what Jesus
expected. He foretold suffering for himself, his followers and
his people, before the End. No doubt the reports which we
have in the gospels have been phrased in the knowledge of
what took place, but we have no good reason to reject them
entirely. It needed only common sense to see that a man
liable to be called "King of the Jews" was liable to be
crucified in first-century Palestine; and that even if they
escaped with their lives his followers were liable to face
unpopularity, despair and actual punishment after his
execution. It also needed only common sense to see that the
pride of the Jews was such that rebellion against Rome was
inevitable, and that rebellion would bring catastrophe. And
such expectations fitted in well with the general Jewish belief
of the time that the coming glories of the messianic age
would be preceded by a time of sufferings, the "birthpangs
of the Messiah". One of the most moving passages in the
Hebrew Scriptures communicated the vision that the servant
of God had to suffer (Isaiah 49:14–53:12).

It is certain that Jesus' hopes about the End arose out
of belief in God's supremacy, thoroughly Jewish although
exceptionally intense, passionate, personally decisive and
also infectious. People who do not share that belief naturally
ask: why was his hope so intense that his Father's will would
soon be done as perfectly in the towns and villages of Galilee

and Judea as in heaven? Why did he teach his followers to hope with a similar passion, even if it meant that they were to be punished by a disappointment as bitter as his own? Surely the answer is that he was a man. In order to be human he had to belong to some group whose own world-view he would accept in parts and reject in parts, according to his education and experience – and the group where he lived was the Jewish, and in particular the Galilean, people at a time when passionate hopes of liberation and the coming kingdom of God (or of Israel) were many. And we may guess that, even had he been born into a community without those particular hopes, a man with such an overwhelming vision of God would always experience in the depths of his soul the hope that in his time this loving Father would triumph. To him, belief in God would be no comfortable convention but a light by which to walk in darkness. He would hope that the light would soon shine fully on him and on all. Because the world, made so lovely by God, had been so thoroughly polluted by the crimes and follies of mankind, he would wish to purify it as if by fire, even if in order to do so he himself had to be burned.

If Jesus the Jew accepted or used the titles which Christians were to use about him, he did so because they were titles in common use – but always he understood them in his own special sense. He did not wish to be treated as the Messiah or Son of David who would defeat all Israel's enemies, although the manner of his last formal entry into Jerusalem, and of his demonstration in the temple, was bound to encourage talk about him in this role. That talk led to his execution. Despite the claims in John's gospel, it is probable that he did not refer to himself as the Son of God except in the sense that he felt that he had a unique insight into the character and will of God his Father, and had a unique role to fulfil in his Father's purposes. ("Son of God" was a phrase used widely about royal, great or holy men, as in Psalm 2:7.) It is more likely that he referred to himself as the Son of Man.

In Q that phrase occurs twelve times, in Mark's gospel thirteen; it is also prominent in the special material of Luke, Matthew and John. It was remembered by the earliest Christians: it did not need to be explained in their gospels. In Acts 7:56 Stephen cries out that he sees "the heavens opened and the Son of Man standing". But that is the only use of the title outside the reports of the teaching of Jesus, and the explanation seems to be that it sounded too odd in Greek. In a Jewish setting it could be used solemnly, with reference to Daniel 7:13 where an exalted being "like a son of man" represents "the holy people of the Most High" (the faithful Jews) as he comes "with the clouds of heaven" to God "the Ancient in Years". "Son of Man" is used in that sense in some Jewish documents surviving from the first century AD, including the Similitudes of Enoch, thought sufficiently important to be quoted in the New Testament (Jude 14,15). That is a sense in which the title can be used in Q (as in Luke 18:8) and by Mark (as in 8:31,38 and 13:24,25), supremely in the report of Jesus' reply to the High Priest: "you will see the Son of Man seated at the right hand of the Almighty and coming with the clouds of heaven" (Mark 14:62). It is clear that the gospel-writers thought that the title applied to Jesus himself. They provide no evidence for the improbable suggestion that he expected another to be Son of Man. (A saying such as Luke 12:8, which may seem to refer to another, is an "I" saying in Matthew 10:32.) But the evidence agrees that Jesus "began to teach them that the Son of Man had to endure great sufferings" (8:31) – as, indeed, "the holy people of the Most High" had done when the book of Daniel was written. And the term "son of man" could also be used as a way of referring to oneself

(like our "one") or to humanity (like our "Man"). The
prophet Ezekiel often says that God addressed him as "son
of man", and in Psalm 8:4 "son of man" means "Man". It
seems likely that Jesus used the phrase partly because it
could have this modest sense, stressing his humanity. But
even if the phrase referred to Daniel's vision, it referred to
triumph after human suffering: "the Son of Man had to
undergo great sufferings" (Mark 8:31). For the Son of Man
was the servant of God.

*10. Jesus believed that his death lay within the good purposes of
God*
The fact that Jesus was betrayed by one of his twelve chosen
apostles is often repeated in the gospels, and there is no
good reason to doubt it. The story was no advertisement
either for the apostles or for their training. Exactly what
secret Judas Iscariot betrayed, and precisely why he did it,
we cannot tell. The gospels suggest that he betrayed the
secret of when Jesus could be arrested quietly, and did it
for money, yet was stricken with remorse and hanged himself. Many have looked for a deeper explanation. Did Judas
betray the secret that Jesus would now admit to claiming
the Messiahship? If he was a rebel (*sicarius*), did he attempt
to force his Master's hand into launching a rebellion in order
to escape death? Did his plot go terribly wrong? All these
are speculations. All we can know is that, if Judas ended up
as a suicide who chose self-murder as an escape, the character indicated in all the evidence about Jesus was not of that
kind.

The gospels which we have considered never explain at
any length why Jesus laid down his life. But Paul, as we
have seen, teaches what he had been taught – that the death
brought about the forgiveness of sins. Mark, as we have
seen, says that the death was the price paid to liberate

"many" and to seal a new "covenant" between God and Man. And he provides another clue in the shape of the story of the preparatory "transfiguration" of Jesus (9:9–13). It is a story which is mysterious and may have been embroidered in the telling. But essentially it rings true, for it is a record of a mystical experience in which Jesus felt that he was talking with Moses, with Elijah and ultimately with God himself, about his own coming death. This took place "up a high mountain", presumably Mount Hermon, and Jesus was accompanied by Peter, John and James, who were somehow affected by the intense experience of their Master. At the end "only Jesus was with them" – a Jesus strengthened in the faith that his death was in accordance with the teaching of the Old Testament and the will of God.

The story of the last supper of Jesus with his disciples is another such clue. It seems certain that Jesus did then link his death with the coming of the kingdom of God. The saying in Mark's gospel must have puzzled those who read it in the first century, as it has puzzled Christians since: "Never again shall I drink from the fruit of the vine until the day I drink the new wine in the kingdom of God"(14:25). That is an argument for the substantial authenticity of the saying. Mark also records the saying over the bread, repeated countless times by Christians in the first century as in every later age: "Take this; this is my body" (14:22). Such a saying is so obviously liable to lead to a rumour of cannibalism (as it certainly did) that it is hard to believe that extremely devout Christians with a Jewish training, such as Paul or Mark, could have invented it. As the loaf of bread was broken and given, so the life of Jesus was being broken and given; and Jesus said so.

The third highly relevant story is of the distress of Jesus before his death. The Letter to the Hebrews says that "he offered prayers and petitions, with loud cries and tears, to

God who was able to deliver him from death" (5:7). Mark
gives us a picture of Jesus praying in "horror and anguish"
during the night before he was tortured to death: "*Abba*,
Father! All things are possible for you; take this cup away
from me. Yet not my will but yours" (14:32–26). Virtually
the same picture of the Lord Jesus in weakness is given by
Matthew and Luke, and it is not a picture the early Christians would have cared to invent.

All the evidence in the Synoptic gospels points to a man
who was careful not to fall into the hands of his enemies –
until he deliberately and publicly went to Jerusalem at the
time of the Passover feast. He could easily have remained
in comparative safety, outside the city where his enemies
and the Roman soldiers could be expected to gather at that
time. If he had merely wished to worship in the temple, he
could have done so without allowing a provocative demonstration and without issuing his own public challenges in
his teaching. He risked death. He almost courted it. A man
so devout and so shrewd would never have done so except
after self-searching prayer. It therefore seems certain that
after a struggle Jesus believed in the depths of his being that
it was his Father's will that he should accept the cross.

So he was scourged and hung up to die. The best attested
cry from the cross is the one which causes the most pain in
any Christian who records it: "My God, my God, why have
you forsaken me?" (Mark 15:34, also in Matthew). That is
a cry of human anguish. It is a quotation from Psalm 22,
where the despair moves into faith. Whether or not Jesus
before he died experienced and voiced a calm faith as Luke
and John report, we do know that Mark and Matthew, who
preserved only this cry of despair, believed passionately that
the despair was not ultimate, for they believed that the
crucified had been crowned as the Messiah and as the Son
of God. They were already on the road which led Luke and

John in their gospels to present this horrible death, accepted in faith and in love for others, as itself part of the glory of the divine love. So these gospels of Luke and John give us the deeply moving and even joy-making features of the full Christian tradition about the "passion of Jesus". They proclaim the death as it releases forgiveness, gives the assurance of Paradise, perfectly sums up a life of trust in the Father, binds all Christians together in a new family, and finishes the revelation of the light that shines on all.

11. Followers of Jesus believed that he had been raised from the dead

Some modern writers, seeking to explain the reports that Jesus was seen alive after his crucifixion, have speculated that he was not dead when taken down from the cross. They imagine him reviving, and being nursed back into some sort of existence in hiding. But it is extremely unlikely that Roman soldiers would have left an execution uncompleted, even if they had had any motive to do so. Such a lapse from duty would certainly have meant death to them, when discovered.

Other modern writers have suggested that the corpse was taken to the common criminals' grave in the Valley of Hinnom (that nauseating rubbish dump which provided the imagery of hell), not to a private tomb provided by Joseph of Arimathea as reported in the gospels. That is the most likely alternative to the Christian claim about the resurrection. But if the story of the private burial is a Christian invention it is strange that the name of Joseph of Arimathea is given by all the gospels with such confidence. It therefore seems reasonable (although not necessary for the historian) to accept the tradition that Jesus was buried in a private tomb whose ownership was known to some of his despairing ex-followers. It has been suggested that his followers were not clear exactly where the tomb was, and that the women who later went to embalm the body went to the wrong tomb, which was empty. But it is worth remembering that when Matthew mentioned the official Jewish story it was that the followers of Jesus went to the right tomb – and stole his body. There are difficulties in the stories of the gospels, but there are also difficulties in stories which suggest carelessness or sustained deception on the part of the disciples.

The mental agony of Jesus, expressed in the prayer in Gethsemane and in the cry that God had abandoned him, was so great that many modern students of the gospels find it impossible to accept completely their statement that Jesus was sure that he would be raised from death after a short interval. Equally, the bewilderment and despair of the disciples – to be expected after the horror of the crucifixion, and clearly reflected in the gospels – persuade many modern students that the resurrection of Jesus on the third day was not expected and therefore had not been predicted as precisely as the gospels say. The phrasing of the predictions which we find in the gospels – including "rise again three days afterwards" at Mark 8:31 – may well have been coloured by the Church's reflection on the prophecy made about a conquered Israel in the book of Hosea (6:2):

> After two days he will revive us,
> on the third day he will raise us
> to live in his presence.

But what is psychologically possible, and in keeping with all the evidence we have, can be put quite simply. Jesus trusted that he would be vindicated by God at the End; but since he disclaimed knowledge of when or how the End would come, he died on the Friday without knowing when or how his victory would be declared.

One of the features of the End, as expected by many, was the physical resurrection of the dead. We find this belief stated in the book of Daniel, written almost a century and a half before the death of Jesus:

Many of those who sleep in the dust of the earth will awake, some to everlasting life
and some to the reproach of everlasting abhorrence (12:2).

At that time many Jews had been put to death because they had refused to renounce the peculiarities of their religion, at a time when great pressure had been applied by the political rulers to fit Judaism into the culture of the Greek world. The cause of Jewish separation had then triumphed temporarily through the rebellion led by the Maccabees, but there had been a cost in lives. The conviction had grown among many Jews that the martyrs would be rewarded and their persecutors punished – and the only way in which such rewards and punishments would be effective had been thought to be the resurrection of their dead bodies by the divine Judge. In the time of Jesus the Pharisees held this belief strongly, and in the Acts of the Apostles Paul is said to have defended himself on this ground: "My brothers, I am a Pharisee, a Pharisee born and bred; and the issue in this trial is our hope of the resurrection of the dead" (23:6). But the Pharisees were themselves the products of the religious crisis in the days of the Maccabees, and the belief was rejected by more conservative Jews who regarded as authoritative only the first five books in their Scriptures. According to Mark (12:18–27) these conservatives included the Sadducees, who were said by Jesus to be "very far from the truth".

Obviously nowadays this belief in a physical resurrection – the revival of corpses – strikes most people as incredible. We can glimpse the scepticism which often greeted such a belief, even in the ancient world, in the account in the Acts of the Apostles of reactions in Athens when Paul was preaching about "Jesus and the Resurrection"; they had admired much in Paul's preaching but when they heard about the raising of the dead, some scoffed (17:18,32). In our time many people who call themselves Christians are among those who share that Athenian scepticism. To this, many believers reply that it is possible for God to perform miracles; that this was supremely appropriate after the death of Jesus; that, indeed, the raising of Jesus from the dead was (as Paul believed) the beginning of a "new creation". And the debate continues.

The truth that can be established by historical methods is that after his death the followers of Jesus became convinced that God had raised him from the dead. That was why they acclaimed him as "Messiah" and "Son of Man" where these Jewish terms meant much, and as "Lord" and "Son of God" where they did not. We have seen that this and this acclamation can be heard in all the gospels which we have considered. Something must have happened to change the disciples from the despair surrounding the crucifixion to this new joy capable of producing the glad courage of martyrs. It is thought-provoking that the early Christians remembered the death of Jesus joyfully in the Eucharist – and met for their own worship not on the Jewish Sabbath but on the first day of the week (then beginning on Saturday evening) when the resurrection was believed to have occurred. Something happened – but it is impossible to establish by historical methods exactly what this "something" was, whether it was a series of visions, or was a physical resurrection, or was utterly unique.

Reports of "appearances" by the risen Lord are, so far as we know, earlier than stories about the empty tomb but they do not enable us to be sure whether the "body" said to have

been encountered was physical or not. We are told that Jews
such as Jesus who believed in "resurrection" could also
believe that it led to a radically new life, when the dead
become "like angels in heaven" (Mark 12:18–25). Paul
writes that "flesh and blood can never possess the kingdom
of God, the perishable cannot possess the imperishable" (1
Corinthians 15:50). Even the gospels' stories about the
empty tomb and subsequent appearances are ambiguous.
For all that we can *know*, they may all be legends. Within
their own terms, mystery is signalled when angels appear –
one in Mark if the "young man wearing a white robe" is an
angel, "two men in dazzling garments" in Luke, one "angel"
in Matthew, two in John. The mystery does not disappear
when the women come, for they and their experiences are
described variously. It is impossible to construct a neat time-
table of the events. And the body which they and others
meet in their stories has both everyday and supernatural
moments: it wears clothes like a gardener's but is not recognized, it eats fish but enters a room through locked doors.
When the New Testament is so unclear, it is not possible to
be more precise almost two thousand years later unless our
religious faith makes us more precise.

12. Jesus entrusted his message not to a book but to a community
The contrast between Christianity and Islam, a religion
based on a book believed to have been dictated by an angel,
is very great. Jesus was a communicator, but only once in
the gospels is he described as writing. The incident occurs
in a passage missing from many ancient copies of John's
gospel: Jesus bent down and wrote with his finger on the
ground (8:6). We are not told what he wrote. But we are
told that he devoted much time and skill to teaching his
disciples, and that even in his lifetime he sent them out to
spread his message. This report is likely to be true about a

man consumed by his sense of being on a mission; and the probability of its truth becomes all the greater when we notice how seldom the tradition about the teaching of Jesus includes words such as Spirit and Church which became supremely important to the Christians.

The New Testament demonstrates that after his death more organized communities told his story and spread his message. Out of the faith and preaching of these communities arose the eight "gospels" which we have studied. As we saw, they presented him as the fulfilment of the great Jewish tradition; as the crucified and risen Lord and Saviour of Paul's Gentile congregations; as the Christ of Early Catholicism; as the unique teacher of the Q material; as the Son of God who was martyred and who called martyrs to follow him; as the healing and liberating friend of the marginalized; as the preacher of a heroic morality; as the Word of God made flesh. These gospels gave a common witness to the historical Jesus at a number of important points, although much longer volumes of a very different kind would have been needed to provide anything like a modern biography. A vast literature has grown about the different interpretations of Jesus presented in these gospels, and about the subsequent theologies. At least it can be agreed that these eight gospels all left much out. "If it were all to be recorded in detail," John wrote, "I suppose that the world could not hold the books that would be written" (21:25). Since his day the idea of a library about Jesus larger than the world has become more realistic.

But who is Christ for us today?

Christ For Us

THE name Jesus has reached us through Latin from the Greek Iesous, which came from the Hebrew or Aramaic Yeshua. The fact that it has been translated implies a claim that the man still deserves our attention. When "Christ" as a title abbreviates the Greek translation of the Hebrew or Aramaic for "Anointed", it may be used with a conscious reference to Jewish hopes about the Messiah, but in most uses that origin has been more or less forgotten. Virtually "Christ" has come to mean what the name Yeshua originally meant: "God saves". The name and title together announce that Jesus Christ is the One through whom God saves – or the two words would mean that, were they not so often used without thought. Here can be an answer to the question asked of every generation and every individual: "And you, who do you say I am?" (Mark 8:29).

The fact that the New Testament contains at least eight different traditions which I have called "gospels" points to the fact that Jesus of Nazareth becomes "Christ" for Christians without turning them into robots programmed to copy him exactly. Never in the teachings of the masters of the spiritual life does the "imitation of Christ" substitute his personality for ours. Paul was different from Jesus; so was

Francis; so was Luther; so was Ignatius; so was John Wesley. Women following Christ have always had to follow their own way of discipleship, and never on any large scale since the first Christian century has it been thought necessary for every Christian to become a Jew, or to remain unmarried, or to be penniless, or to teach or heal with no deviation from the styles shown in the New Testament. Christ's call to us has been heard both as a call to be Christlike and as a call to be ourselves. Paul grasped the paradox in his second letter to the unruly Corinthians. "We are being transformed into his likeness with ever-increasing glory", he assured them – but he had just written: "where the Spirit of the Lord is, there is liberty" (3:17,18).

Unfortunately this insistence that we are not to be robots programmed by Jesus of Nazareth has often been debased. Jesus Christ has become our own duplicate – a totem around which our group can dance, a mascot we can follow as we march in a direction we choose. He has been treated as a supporter of a congregation or denomination, even as a pillar of a particular church building. Alternatively he has been a harmless idealist – in the eighteenth century a teller of charming stories to illustrate the precepts of a rational morality, in the nineteenth century a romantic figure who advocated middle-class love, in the twentieth century the Invisible President of the United Nations. He has also been a perfectionist having little contact with humanity's world – in the Catholic tradition a monk who confines his approval to the sexless and spineless, in Protestantism a holy Saviour who saves only those who are steadily respectable. He has been worshipped as supporting the successors of the Pharisees and Sadducees – as a preacher who demands the repression or persecution of those who make him nervous, or as a priest preoccupied with the status and privileges of his profession. He has been seen as blessing the transfer of the privileges of Caesar to the successors of Peter. He has been acclaimed as supporting the successors of Pontius Pilate – as the senior colleague of the Byzantine emperor or as the junior colleague of the heroes of Socialism. He has been followed as a supporter of Pilate's enemies; he has become the inspiration of terrorists. Or it has been denied that the meek Christ could ever give trouble to anyone. This endlessly elastic Christ has become a popular chaplain among colonialists or nationalists, or a highly paid American salesman who on TV is willing to share with the dollar-sending public the secrets of health, prosperity and happiness. He has perhaps been at his worst as the patron of antisemitism and apartheid. In brief, "Christ" has become an idol, and silly or wicked people have danced around him.

All these Christs have been condemned by almost all Christians (often after a considerable delay) as false Christs. My descriptions can of course be attacked as oversimplifications of what (it may be claimed) were pictures of Christ dear to sincere Christians and valuable in those Christians' circumstances. But I believe that the negative verdicts reached in the end by almost all Christians were broadly right because these Christs bore too little resemblance to the Jesus Christ who was crucified and who steps out of the pages of the New Testament. And I believe that it is not necessary to have a false Christ in order to have a relevant Christ. In the twentieth century, when Christian life and thought have been at least as vigorous as ever before, new understandings of Christ have been prolific – and some have been legitimate interpretations of the historical Jesus.

In a century when the poor, the colonized and the women, who constitute all but a small minority of the human race, have won at least the right to vote in political elections, and have begun to struggle for more substantial freedoms, the image of Jesus Christ the Liberator has become the most widely powerful of all Christian images, by no means confined to Latin America. The image of his mother has also changed, to become the divinely liberated woman rejoicing over the vindication of the poor. These images have been criticized as being too political or too feminist, but in comparison with previously popular images (for example, the dead Christ upheld by the sorrowful mother) they affirm human life and human dignity – and they are far closer to the New Testament, where the poor and the women are lifted out of many centuries of contempt, and Christ is the living Lord.

In Africa the understanding of Jesus Christ as the Great Ancestor is in tune with a very long tradition of venerating both the founders of a tribe who are celebrated mythologically and the "living dead" who are remembered personally. Many traditional beliefs and practices were concerned with the need (often anxious) to secure the blessing of the ancestors, whose nearness seemed to be a daily reality. In most African tribal traditions, all this was under the presidency of the Creator-Father, who is now distant but who can be sought with awe. When Africans become Christians it is not difficult to form an image of Jesus as the founder of a new tribe embracing all peoples. The Living Dead One is remembered – but more: he is spiritually able to lead and teach in a new way of life. And because the continuing life of Jesus has brought him close, the Creator-Father who was remote is now near to all Christians who may sing, clap and dance to a new drum-beat.

In India the understanding of Jesus Christ as the One Avatara connects with the immensely ancient and fertile Hindu tradition of worshipping human or animal figures, originating in history or mythology, as incarnations of the Unlimited and Undescribable Divine. The intention has been that every Hindu should find and love an embodiment of God, a Lord or Isvara, matching the spiritual life of the area, the caste or (less often) the individual. When Hindus become Christians the belief that the Avatara of the one true God in Christ was unique, decisive and authoritative is a new belief which changes many things. In a change which is momentous for many converts, the new Christian caste excludes no one. But in the basic change there is also a continuity, for it is not difficult to greet the living Lord Jesus with devotion (*bhakti*) as the unique Avatara, the human name and face of the God who is holy love, displacing all images of the divine which are less than human, less than loving or less than supreme.

In the many Asian lands where Buddhism has been profoundly influential the image of Jesus Christ as the Enlightened One is no stranger. The southern (Therevada) school of Buddhist thought has venerated Gautama as the One who showed the way to the ultimate peace of Nirvana by the discipline of all the passions – and Nirvana has been the contradiction of all trivial or local images of Transcendence. The northern (Mahayana) school, while retaining the idea of Emptiness or Sunyata as ultimate, has moved away from the austerity of this religion by developing a mythology of many divine or semi-divine beings. These Bodhisattvas not only postponed their entries into the glorious Nirvana in order to guide and help troubled mortals, but have also been open and responsive to prayers addressed to them in Nirvana for the kind of help which in the Christian tradition has been called "grace". This form of Buddhism has often been reckoned as the non-Jewish religion nearest to Christianity. Certainly it has not proved difficult for Christians coming from a Buddhist background to think of the Jesus who is very much alive as the Enlightened One. He leads sinners, however passionate or troubled, to a heaven which is very much more than the peaceful extinction of the ego.

There, individuality is not denied but fulfilled; so here, life is accepted not as a punishment for past misdeeds but as a preparatory gift.

Islam has proved to be the world religion which is most resistant to Christian approaches. This is partly because so many of the approaches have been made with sword or gun in hand, but another reason for the solidarity of Islam has been that here is a community with a clear self-definition achieved by the discipline of sacred customs and also with a prayerful sense of the living God. (Allah is also the name for God used by Arabic-speaking Christians and connected with El, a divine name in the Hebrew Bible.) God is held to be revealed, and in a sense incarnate, in the words of a book, the Quran. The Prophet is honoured with an intense love and veneration, keeping him as a figure of history but ranking him with, and above, earlier and later prophets, including Jesus. But the Christian belief is that Jesus Christ is the Word of God, once made flesh and now alive, near and strong to save. That belief can grow for Muslims (as it did for the first Christians) out of the conviction that he is the greatest of all the prophets because the most God-filled. And the way to the belief that "God was in Christ" may be through the Christian experience of defeat and death. Jesus was not successful in the eyes of the world, as the Prophet of Islam was in life and later. He was "crucified, dead and buried" (ugly facts which the Quran is usually understood as denying). But according to Christian faith he was raised from the dead by the power of God. That great act affirmed the crucified prophet to be more than a prophet. It began the experience of meeting Jesus as the living Word of God, better than any book.

Those recognitions of Jesus as the Liberator, the Great Ancestor, the One Avatara, the Enlightened One and the Word of God have been made after non-Western experiences

– as the original Jewish recognition of him as Messiah was made. I offered a study of them in *The Futures of Christianity*. I shall now attempt to say what Jesus Christ can mean after experiences, and within heritages, such as my own. Inevitably this attempt will depend on what I have experienced for myself and on what I have appropriated from my heritage. It will also depend on how I read and assess the New Testament. But I hope I shall never use the title "Christ" in a way that has little or no connection with Jesus of Nazareth. For I believe that each of the statements which are reasonably certain to be true about the historical Jesus, set out in the last chapter, can be connected with a statement about "Christ" which has been approved – sometimes after a tragic delay – by multitudes of Christians who have been interrupted, mystified, fascinated, rebuked and not let go, as I have been.

1. Today as surely as on the day when he was crucified as a rebel against Rome, Jesus challenges every form of injustice and calls his followers to right wrongs wherever possible, but his message is mainly spiritual, not political

In every generation Christians have legitimately derived from their Lord an inspiration to advocate, and (so far as was open to them) to struggle for, a society in which no man, woman or child would be treated unjustly. The understanding of what is just and of what is possible has varied greatly from time to time. Already within the New Testament there is a contrast between two chapters (both chapters 13). Writing to the Romans, Paul urges obedience to the emperor Nero, who is in his own sphere God's servant; but writing to the churches of Asia Minor a little later, John the Divine sees the Roman empire as evil and doomed like the old empire of Babylon. However, the Lord and Judge of Christians has always been seen as demanding righteousness in society, as the Hebrew prophets did before him. Many Christians have accepted great suffering in order to echo this demand and make it one that unjust authorities could not escape. And many have believed that particular movements in politics have served the cause of justice and so have done what Jesus, in common with the prophets of Ancient Israel, commanded. Whether or not they have disobeyed earthly rulers, Christians have always asserted that "there is a rival king, Jesus" (Acts 17:7). That has caused endless trouble to the authorities.

But when disillusionment has followed a change in politics, and even when a political movement has been at the height of its moral prestige, many Christians have also affirmed that the government which Jesus Christ proclaimed and served in life and death under Pontius Pilate was and is different from political movements including rebellions. It uses the weapons not of coercion but of charity. It offers as a reward not prosperity but eternity. Again and again in the history of the Christian understanding of Christ, the reply to Pilate in John's gospel is repeated: "My kingdom does not belong to this world. If it did, my followers would be fighting . . . " (18:35–36). And the reward is understood: "Even when a man has more than enough, his possessions do not give him life" (Luke 12:15).

2. In our society as in ancient Galilee, Jesus Christ sets before Christians standards in morality so high that they seem to be impossible for human nature; yet in ethics his chief commandment is that we should forgive and love one another

The positive attitude to the Jewish religions and moral tradition taken in parts of the New Testament suggests that Christ blesses all the goodness in all the religious and ethical traditions of humanity. He says "do that and you will live" (Luke 10:28) to the non-Christian who loves God and neighbour. He admires the person who is "not far from the kingdom of God" (Mark 12:34) because he or she is sincerely doing what seems to be best within that non-Christian tradition and situation. But he is unlike most other moralists. He goes beyond the conventions, challenging the person to greater moral heroism, so that the code of a society becomes internalized in sternly self-critical conscience, and the standards of a society become a vision of the perfect life which is made possible by God's grace. Paul's exposition of this process is unmatched in eloquence about the psychology of conversion but it does not stand completely isolated in the New Testament or in later Christian experience. For Jesus in Matthew's gospel, for example, the one standard by which human goodness must be judged is this: "there must be no limit to your goodness, as your heavenly Father's goodness knows no bounds" (5:48). In John's gospel the goodness of Jesus is itself a challenge shattering all our satisfaction with ourselves, for "I give you a new commandment: love one another; as I have loved you, so you are to love one another" (13:34).

Christian ethics is therefore something like judging all music by Beethoven at his most sublime while not rejecting pop. This pressure of Christ has been felt in the worship which has spoken of heaven amid the materialism of a Roman or Communist empire, or in a silent meeting of pacifists amid a society which loves violence as entertainment. But it has also been felt in moments which are secret – in the struggles of a business chief to form policies not directed towards profits alone, or of a general to make war a little less unjust, or of a politician to take the next least bad step although it will disappoint supporters, or of an excited lover to remember the difference between love and lust, or of a parent to conquer tired impatience.

Often Christ takes a respectable person and asks that a saint should be allowed to break out – and often the power of Christ has made that impossibility possible. But Christ will have nothing to do with the self-righteousness or sheer hypocrisy that so often makes the morally improved complacent. Nor does he ever endorse the pride that makes the very good feel superior to the less good. He condemns the good who refuse to get their hands soiled by involvement in the messy problems of their neighbours. He who surprisingly criticized ritually pure priests and Pharisees is surprising still, for in all such cases he regards human goodness as a barrier erected against the all-loving graciousness of God. He teaches that all human beings are sinful and can receive God's pardon only to the extent that they are willing to forgive their fellow sinners: the barrier that excludes the neighbour from the heart also excludes the Father. Therefore no Christian saint is aloof from the rest of humanity. As a Jew needed a Samaritan as a neighbour, so the holiest Christian needs to find an equivalent to the Master's dangerous table-fellowship with prostitutes and traitors.

3. Jesus Christ teaches about God as the loving Father but he is more than a teacher. His whole life embodies God's love
The teaching of Christ about God is summed up in the formula repeated in John's letters: "God is love." Even shorter is the word *Abba* which began the Lord's Prayer and, as we saw, was quoted twice in Aramaic in Paul's surviving letters. But what is "love" or "fatherhood" in this context? Everyone is aware that human "love" can be a camouflage for the desire to possess. In practice it may mean domination, lust or sadism. In the ancient world fathers had immense rights over wives and children, and it has proved possible to twist what Jesus says about God (in Matthew's gospel, for example) into a nightmare about an all-powerful bully and torturer, a monster who has hell as his unending playground. It is because human fatherhood has sometimes

been perverted so as to come close to this nightmare that the image of God the Father can be repulsive. And everyone is aware that, at the other extreme, what is called "love" may be a sentimentality which indulges every whim however disastrous the long-term consequences. It can be thought that in modern societies parents are more likely to be guilty of that irresponsible weakness than of a cruel brutality. Here may be another reason why the image of the Father is discredited: it may seem to have as much connection with reality as Father Christmas.

However, according to all the gospels both severity and mercy are characteristics of the God about whom Jesus spoke. These characteristics are not contradictory. Drawing on happier human experience, it can be seen that true love seeks the best both for the lover and for the beloved – and under its influence the best does grow. The reality that disciples need discipline accounts for much in the stern passages in the teaching of Jesus according to the gospels, although no doubt some of the severity here results from the bitterness of the divorce between Church and Synagogue in the period when the gospels were being written. But always the motivation of the Father of Jesus is said to be a holy love. Whenever Jesus Christ summons his followers to resemble God, it is in this respect, not in any mere wish to control or punish. And he teaches this more clearly and effectively by his life and death than by his words, unforget-table as those are. His life, summed up in his willingness to die, was the unfolding of a love which was neither possessive nor sentimental but was directed to the welfare of others with the practicality of a physical and spiritual healer. This love was derived not from his own idealism but from the indwelling of the spirit of his Father: so he said, with a life and a death that bore witness to the truth and strength of what he said. That is why Christians have rightly commented that in spiritual reality his life was the fruit of divine not sexual love, when God loved the world even more than Joseph loved Mary. And Christians have rightly confessed that they would never have been released to love in Christ's way, had not the divine love spoken the liberating word to them in Christ – not only in their conversion but also in daily experience of help.

It does not seem essential for Christians to agree about exactly how the divine and the human have been mingled in the life of Jesus. As we have seen, there is no agreement in the New Testament. The earliest belief appears to have been that Jesus had been the unique agent of the Father he worshipped. He was declared to be the Messiah at his resurrection and would soon show himself to have the Messiah's victorious power. Then the belief grew that he must have been Messiah and Son of God from his birth, or from eternity. Using a style which was devotional rather than accurate, Luke and Matthew told of the birth of Jesus the Messiah after a virginal conception, but they made no mention of the glory of the Son of God before conception. Although he included no account of the birth in his gospel, John believed that Jesus had been born to "bear witness to the truth" (18:36), and for him the truth was that Jesus was the Word of God, glorious "before the world began". Paul and his successors, who also left behind no account of the birth, seem to have based their vision of the eternal Christ as the agent "through" whom "God" had created the universe on the picture of Wisdom in a late part of the Hebrew Bible; and before the New Testament closes Christ can himself be called "God", although infrequently and without explanation. Where the New Testament disagrees, the lack of unanimity among more recent Christians ought to come as no surprise. When in the fourth and fifth centuries Christians were free and able to develop more systematic doctrines about Christ, they used philosophical terms which do not appear in the New Testament. Modern Christians have used other terms.

4. Jesus Christ brings healing of body and spirit, with forgiveness, in our time as he did among the sick in Palestine. If faith is strong then miracles are possible. A new life, a "new creation", can begin Jesus would not have had the character emerging from all the gospels had he not been willing to use the power in him to heal the sick who surrounded him, by methods within the tradition which he shared with them. Although some or many of the stories may have grown in the telling, they often have clearly understandable features in common. The healing was of the spirit as the spirit affected the body, and it depended on faith, whether in the patient, in the patient's family or friends or in the healer himself, for the power was believed to come through faith from God. The healing was valued not only for its own sake but as proof that God was able to inaugurate his reign on earth in what felt like a new creation. In traditional words, the "miracles" were "signs" of the "kingdom" of God. Some Christians have understood these miracles to suggest that the slow growth of scientific medicine has been an inferior activity. They have believed – or have given the impression of believing – that only cures which cannot be explained scientifically are signs of God's power, and therefore "Christian healing". Others have despised all claims about healing which infringe the mono- poly claimed by hospitals, doctors, psychiatrists and drugs. They have believed – or have given the impression of believ- ing – that Jesus was an amateur in a field where the pro- fessionals (perhaps encouraged by his example) have been more useful. But despite all the stupidities of Christians, the steady influence of Jesus Christ the healer has supported every kind of effective healing. In particular it has supported the teaching that many ills require most basically the healing of the spirit by the acceptance of God's love.

Where such faith has been strong enough to create hope, there is reliable evidence of unusual events which may be called miracles. Some of these "miracles" show how the mind can cure the body. Usually this is the patient's mind – which is strange but not totally surprising, for it is a well-known truth at the basis of scientific medicine that many ailments are cured by the brain ordering the repair of the rest of the body. Sometimes the faith seems to be communicated to the believer by those who pray for a recovery – which is even more mysterious but again not completely bewildering, for it is well known that the "atmosphere" in a sick room or hospital can quicken or delay a cure. And the influence of Christ has also persuaded countless Christians to practise, support or simply accept with gratitude scientific medicine which to the eye of the believer is one long marvel and one colossal gift from God. That influence of Christ has also persuaded most Christians that when a person cannot be cured either by "scientific" or by "spiritual" healing, the sickness need not be God's punishment of sin. Some illnesses and deaths are caused by lives or actions which almost all Christians would regard as sinful; for example, deaths after heavy smoking or careless driving. But the Christ who was crucified can teach that when the body is inescapably subject to defects or decay, the body's failure can be used by God gloriously. It can be a blessing.

Often healing is associated with forgiveness. It remains a common human experience that a believer in God can be damaged in body as well as spirit when it is also believed that God is hostile. Almost everyone stores in the memory and the conscience enough reasons to condemn oneself, and when God is thought to be both real and holy, he can easily be thought of as the hostile judge: memory and conscience

reach the verdict of guilty, and a God full of wrath pronounces the sentence which allows no appeal. Christ himself
can be pictured as divine in that way (perhaps needing his
mother to make him less hostile and angry). The actual
message of Christ, heard even among the screeching voices
of human guilt, is that God is always ready to forgive. When
it is added that God forgives after man's repentance, the
essential meaning seems to be that humanity needs to turn
towards God's cleansing and healing power. Once that turn
is made, we discover that God's forgiveness is unconditional.
It is of course often very difficult for humanity to be humble
enough, or confident enough, to turn. We need to be persuaded, taught, encouraged, supported. According to a
Christianity which is based on the New Testament, that is
why God our Father has provided the life and death of
Christ (however we may understand them) as the great act
of reconciliation, the "at-one-ment" of sinners.

When it remembers the teaching of Jesus, Christianity
always says that it is necessary for sinners to forgive each
other as they receive God's forgiveness. That insistence is
in contrast with the normal human practice. Even if we are
religiously minded, often we sinners do not feel at the deepest
level of our personalities that what has gone wrong in our
lives is sin against the Creator who loves us. We prefer to
think that our offences have been against other people or
ourselves: that is less terrifying. But when we confess that
we have sinned against God, and need his forgiveness for
our peace, we see that other people are in almost exactly
the same condition; there is a human solidarity in evil as
real as the solidarity of being born. And when we begin to
try to look on ourselves and other people as if we could look
through the eyes of Christ, we see that no one fully intends
to do evil – the insight which comes with supreme clarity
when we read Luke's story that Jesus kept on praying for

his executioners as they drove nails through his wrists. We are accustomed to make excuses for ourselves; we now learn to make excuses for any who have wronged us. We did not know that evil was evil. We did not know what would be its consequences. If we did know, we were unable to avoid evil because we are the creatures of our circumstances, trapped by what we have inherited, immobilized by our surroundings. When we see that others are like us in our weakness but that God stands ready to forgive all, we also find ourselves ready to forgive. It is a gift that comes from God with the gift of our own forgiveness. Other people may, or may not, be willing to enter into a new relationship with us, a relationship of mutual forgiveness, but if we are willing to do so we find that even as we accept the other's decision, which may be not to be reconciled, we have been freed from the worst poisons of bitterness and hatred. We have escaped self-destruction.

In these ways we find in our own experience that Christ who brings the assurance of God's forgiveness of all brings a new life. We enter a new world. Those are old Christian phrases, but they become new when they are true for us.

5. Jesus Christ blesses moral and religious traditions which prepare for his message but now, as when confronting his fellow Jews, he refuses to let his followers be imprisoned by life-denying rules and rituals

A strong moral or religious tradition brings great advantages and great dangers. It can give the individual security and dignity, a sense of profoundly belonging and a sense of being capable of spiritual greatness, because the individual lives in the company of heroic ancestors. That is part of what Christians celebrate when they speak of the "communion of saints" – a fellowship which reaches back, and up, to Jesus Christ himself. But a tradition can also deny the individual's

God-given right to be Christlike and Godlike in his or her
own way. Or a tradition can ask an individual to be satisfied
with something less than the highest. Or it can make an
individual feel the agony of perpetual guilt, dissatisfied by
failure to be perfect even at the level recommended by the
tradition. To such an imprisoned or tormented individual
the Christ of the Sermon on the Mount or of Paul's letters
speaks, protesting that no rule or ritual is important in
comparison with the direct encounter of the human spirit
with the holy God who demands, forgives and empowers.
No moral rule is anything more than an attempt to apply
the one law which is valid in all situations, the law of love.
As Paul wrote, "the whole law is summed up in a single
commandment: 'Love your neighbour as yourself' " (Galatians 5:14). No ritual matters except as an aid to the life
of the spirit in love. In that sense Christ is the perpetual
Protestant.

6. *Today, as when he had meals with prostitutes and swindling
traitors, Jesus Christ specializes in loving and liberating those who
are despised by the powerful and the respectable*
Luke's gospel celebrates the revolution with a special beauty
but all the story of Christianity has this plot, overriding the
reactionary attempts of Christians. One of the signs of the
influence of Christ in an society at any time has been the
raising of the status of women, both in their own eyes and
in the eyes of men. This influence has often been defied by
women's low self-esteem or by the blindness of male arrogance (present within the Bible). But the Jesus who welcomed women into the circle of his disciples with a radical
and highly controversial courage has become the Christ who
has been an influence making for women's liberation in
many times and places. It can be said that the mother who
rejoiced at his birth made all women "blessed", and that

the women who announced his resurrection inaugurated their half of humanity's rise to equality. This influence ending many centuries of subordination has been stronger than ever in the twentieth century, although the idea that women may be called to be leaders and priests in the Church still awaits reception in the consciences of many Christians.

Similarly, the influence of Jesus Christ has been on the side of the children, the uneducated and the poor. The blessing which the privileged have received has been in this form: "When I was hungry, you gave me food; when thirsty, you gave me drink; when I was a stranger, you took me into your home; when naked, you clothed me; when I was ill, you came to my help; when in prison, you visited me" (Matthew 25:35–36). That degree of solidarity with the poor has inspired the only truly Christian crusades in history – the wars against poverty, whether poverty has been caused by injustice in the arrangements of a society or by inefficiency in handling the rich resources of Earth or by poor education. Innumerable Christians who have refused to be shut in, or sheltered, by the conventions of comfortable respectability have been strengthened by the memory that Jesus was criticized for his compassion for the "people of the land". In the twentieth century Christ's influence on the side of the poor has grown as the numbers of the poor in the world and in the worldwide Church have grown.

7. Now, as when he told parables, Jesus Christ shows that living under God's government brings great joy but demands both courage and patience
The parables of Jesus could have as sequels innumerable stories about Christians finding how happy and how hard it is to accept his invitation to enter the kingdom of his Father. Any Christian who at the deepest level of his or her personality accepts the invitation comes to believe with Paul

that "there is nothing in life or death . . . nothing in all creation that can separate us from the love of God in Christ Jesus our Lord" (Romans 8:38,39). Many forms of suffering have proved weaker than this conviction, partly because they are believed to be less significant than life after death. But the hardness of Christian faith and life is almost always also real. When Luke, the happiest of the evangelists, writes of the Christian's cross being taken up "day after day" (9:23) he writes about Christian experience life after life, time after time. The experience has become no less painful with the virtual disappearance of crucifixion as a form of torture and execution; and it can be no less agonising when the suffering is mental rather than physical. This explains the petition in the Lord's Prayer not to be broken by being tested.

8. Jesus Christ's invitation to live under that government is for all races, nations and classes. His influence can break down the biggest barriers dividing humanity, now as in the past
Nothing in Paul's vision of Christ has proved more influential in recent times than his acknowledgement of the unity "in Christ" of Jew, Greek and barbarian, slave and free. Nothing in the vision of Early Catholicism has been more attractive than its insight that the Church is for everyone everywhere. Increasingly in modern times it has been realized that the inter-racial, international and classless nature of the Church is essential because the Christian Church is meant to be a model to the whole human race. This conviction runs against the whole tendency of human nature to identify with one group in opposition to another, and many Christians have refused to believe that this acceptance of other groups was a necessary consequence of their acceptance of Christ. Indeed, Christian history has been full of blind prejudice and cruel violence invoking the name of

Christ. But Jesus is seen in all the gospels as moving out from the circle into which he was born, and his influence as Christ has frequently disturbed the prejudices and hatreds of his followers. The twentieth century has produced conflicts more destructive than any before because modern weapons have been wielded by ancient evils. The century has also failed to achieve a Christian unity which would be a clear sign to the world. But Christ has been seen more clearly than ever before as the One who rises above all human divisions and who crosses (which is an appropriate verb) over all the minefields separating group from group. One good legacy which will be bequeathed by our bloodstained age is the knowledge that to be Christian is to be inclusive.

9. Any title used about the living Jesus must be used with the knowledge that what interests him most is our willingness to share his struggle and his suffering as he serves God's government

From the first Christian century comes the piercing question of Jesus: "Why do you call me 'Lord, Lord' – and never do what I tell you?" (Luke 6:46). From the twentieth century comes a shamefaced but profoundly Christian agreement that it is not enough to echo the tributes paid to Jesus in the words of former generations: we are asked to give our lives. To call Jesus "Messiah" never meant thinking about him as a victorious general: it always meant taking part in the victory of the cross. If in our time Jesus Christ is called "God", or is called anything less with the wish to honour him, there must be the wish to surrender unconditionally to his moral commands, in accordance with the warning: "Not everyone who says to me 'Lord, Lord' will enter the kingdom of Heaven, but only those who do the will of my heavenly Father" (Matthew 7:21). And it is one of the redeeming features of our tragic time that the Christian conscience has grown impatient with talk, however orthodox, which is not matched by Christlike action or patience. Such a time, for all its evil, has drawn closer to the Teacher who is reported to have left behind a test for spotting the genuine ones: "you will recognize them by their fruit" (Matthew 7:20).

10. Jesus Christ died for us. However we understand the significance of his death, we need to see it as supremely significant for us, for it has enabled God and Man to be at one

The death was no mere incident in his life. The death was the climax and its impact has been even greater than the influence of the spoken teaching, for the death has demonstrated that Jesus was genuine: he practised what he preached. The way in which he first accepted and then endured his very painful, and isolated, execution proved the sincerity of his message and the depth of his commitment to those to whom he tried to deliver it. His refusal to escape into obscurity proved that he was completely the servant and son of God, the mysterious Father to whom he had prayed in the agony of Gethsemane. Stripped, tortured, deserted and doomed, he gave not less than everything. The pouring out of such love has converted countless Christians and has reached many more hearts. Medically he choked to death. Spiritually he has addressed the world. It is therefore appropriate that the central image of Christianity should still be the sign of the cross. But we have seen that in the New Testament no clear doctrine of "atonement" or "justification" is worked out. In particular, no full explanation of why he came to believe that he must sacrifice his life is given in the gospels which present the teaching of Jesus. A doctrine has therefore never been agreed by all Christians.

In modern times some interpretations or images found in the New Testament have been felt by many (not all) Christians to have lost much of their power to convey the transforming significance of the cross. To compare the death of Jesus with the sacrifice of a lamb or other animal meant much when such sacrifices could be seen daily not only in Jerusalem but also in pagan temples or shrines all over the world. But many people do not find the comparison very helpful in a time when the sacrifice of animals for religious purposes has been abandoned – or when not abandoned has been greatly reduced in importance. The temple in Jerusalem must have had the sounds and smells of a slaughterhouse despite the use of incense, and were it to be reconstructed in modern Jerusalem it would arouse disgust. Equally disgusting to the modern conscience is the belief that a sacrifice could change God's mind, appeasing his wrath, bribing him in order to earn his favour. In the Hebrew Scriptures the prophets often denounced such a misunderstanding of the sacrifices which God was still believed to have commanded. In our time it has been realized even more fully how spiritually dangerous it is to attribute to God behaviour which, if practised by a parent towards children, would arouse universal condemnation. Therefore many conservative Christians avoid that insult to the All-Holy, stressing rather that the sacrifice of the cross is provided by God's love so that Man may have something worthy to offer; but it is still easy to slip into the old misunderstanding when the old language of animal sacrifice is used. It seems safer to use the idea, also found in the Jewish tradition, that the death of a martyr can atone for sins. The supreme biblical expression of the idea comes in the Song of the Suffering Servant (Isaiah 53:4,5,10). Even this idea, however, is nowadays unfamiliar. It is never said that their casualties in battle have atoned for the sins of modern nations.

To describe the death of Jesus as a ransom paid to free

us from our sins meant much in an age when every one of many millions of slaves dreamed of being freed by a payment to his or her owner. But in our time the use of this metaphor not only has less meaning but has also raised acutely the old question: to whom was the ransom paid by Jesus? Was it to God? If so, why did God need payment? Was he a hostage-taker? Or was it to the Devil? If so, why did the Devil have rights? To describe the death of Jesus as the conquest of evil spirits meant much in societies (such as the one he knew) where it was widely believed that such spirits, imagined as invisible people, exercised a terrifying power. Devil-frightened societies exist in parts of the twentieth-century world, but for many people such talk now seems mythological, trivializing the human experience of evil, when it is not despised as mere "primitive" superstition. To describe the death of Jesus as the acceptance by an innocent man of the punishment we deserved, thus preserving the rigour of God's justice, meant much when justice was rough. Provided that crimes were punished in the appropriate quantity as a deterrent to criminals and a restoration of the ruler's honour, no great fuss was made if an individual who had not committed that particular crime was made to suffer. But nowadays very few people think that the punishment of the innocent can be an exhibition of true justice: it makes people agitate in furious protests, not give thanks.

Fortunately much twentieth-century experience has shown that it is unnecessary to insist on the prominent use of such interpretations or images. This century of many wars has witnessed the willingness of many fighting men or civilians to make the supreme sacrifice for the sake of causes which they thought just. This century of many persecutions has witnessed the willingness of many martyrs to sacrifice their freedom or their lives. The image of Christ the mar-tyred soldier of God speaks directly to the heart of such an age – speaking not of a death to satisfy God, but of a death which is the price of a better future in a world spoiled by Man. So does the image of Christ the liberator, in an age when there have been many costly struggles which have won freedom from many evils. And even in an age when the health services have had astounding successes in the reduction of physical suffering, every child has continued to enter the world through the undeserved, bloody, pain of a mother. This has been a time for the spread of the image (found in some medieval writers) of Christ the mother. That image is a focus for the light which the cross throws on the patient and suffering love of God for all.

II. Jesus Christ rose from the dead and has always been the contemporary of passing generations. We can know that he is alive for us today and in his resurrection we can glimpse our own eternal life

The posthumous influence of Jesus Christ has been unique in history. In age after age, individual after individual has experienced the living presence of Christ and in response has changed a whole life. That has been more than the mere recalling of a memory about a dead teacher, and it has been more than the mere realization of the presence of God. It seems to be an experience open to anyone who sincerely wants it. It has been the innermost secret of the continuing vitality of the Christian tradition. It began in experiences which reversed the first disciples' feelings of despair and shame about the execution of their Master and their own failures to understand him or to be loyal to him. In the twentieth century this encounter with the risen Lord has continued with all the old psychological consequences, but with a difference. Modern study of the New Testament has opened many eyes to the uncertainty about details in the narratives of the resurrection and the subsequent appearances. Modern knowledge of the process of bodily death has increased scepticism about the possibility that the resurrection of Jesus was physical. Modern reflection about the possibility of life after death for ourselves has strengthened the conviction that any "bodies" which our personalities may have after death will not be within the categories of this universe of space and time.

The question is therefore whether it is necessary for church leaders and theologians to insist on a physical interpretation of the resurrection. Many Christians continue to believe that it is necessary. They hold that if a modern intellect rejects the possibility of a physical resurrection, the intellect must be sacrificed. I am, however, one of those who are often persuaded that Jesus rose from the dead physically, but at other times are less confident. To such Christians, reports that the risen Jesus was clothed with a physical body are as strange as reports that he was clothed with ordinary garments (reports about which there has been almost no discussion). Equally strange is the proposition that in order to become a Christian one must move away from that position of uncertainty, for in that position one does not see how the uncertainty about the history can be settled finally by argument about what took place one night in AD 30 or 33. If there is confidence about the physical resurrection, it is because the argument has been settled by religious, not historical, considerations. However, those considerations are themselves questionable by Christians who are extremely reluctant to believe in any event which science declares impossible.

Uncertainty about the history therefore appears to be the lot of many people who would call themselves Christians whether or not they welcome it. Is this a total disaster? Experience has shown that it is possible to live with such uncertainty – and, many add, to live as a Christian. Multitudes of Christians have learned (as I have) that the beating heart of the Easter faith is not found in arguments about history or science; that one conviction only is necessary. It is the conviction that Jesus Christ lives, lasts longer than all the tragedies and is able to end our worst fears. Faith in the resurrection occurs whenever the heart and the life are changed, so that it is as if a voice had been heard saying to me in my prison: "Do not be afraid. I am the first and the last, and I am the living One; I was dead and now I am alive for evermore . . . ' (Revelation 1:17–18).

12. Now, as when he called the first Christians, Jesus Christ wants us to belong to a community which will continue his work and spread the message

Jesus did not "found the Church" if by that statement is implied any claim that he laid down rules to decide its organization or its theology. All the many claims which have been made on behalf of denominations or theological movements to be uniquely favoured by Jesus of Nazareth can be falsified by any examination of the New Testament. He keeps his distance from all the churches. The freedom which is given to each individual Christian, to become Christlike in his or her own way, or to make his or her own mistakes, is therefore given to every Christian group. But as is shown by the New Testament which is the Church's book, Jesus left behind him a body of disciples whom he had brought together and trained. Despite their continuing weaknesses they became in a profound sense his continuing body – his feet, hands, brain and voice. He asked them to repeat his last meal, assuring them that the bread and the wine would now mean his life. He promised that the spirit or energy of his Father would be their best guide. And after his death he communicated to them an instruction to carry on the mission he had begun. Christians have obeyed that instruction as after long hesitations they have gone "to all nations beginning from Jerusalem" (Luke 24:47). And the message that Jesus is Christ has made more converts in the twentieth century than in any previous age.

CHRIST IN THREE CONTROVERSIES

As a result of my own experience as well as the Christian tradition, I have maintained that the impact of Jesus who is Christ reaches not only my brain but my whole existence, and I respond to it by a style of living and dying. (It is "existential".) But I should never wish to deny that Jesus Christ also asks us to think about him. Some of those Christians who can think rigorously ought to become amateur (or even professional) theologians. Therefore I shall mention three controversies which mark epochs in the history of theology – intellectual controversies about how Christ is "for us".

1. No sooner had the fourth-century Church emerged victorious from the persecutions inflicted on it by the Roman empire's emperors, magistrates or mobs than it suffered under fierce debates between its theologians supported by rival political forces. These debates were about Christology. How should the Church's faith in Jesus Christ be expressed using the language of Greek-speaking Neoplatonic philosophers? One climax (although not the conclusion) of these conferences came when, on 25th October in the year 451, 462 bishops meeting in Chalcedon (near the modern Istanbul) rejected various theologians' suggestions as heretical. Stimulated by pressure from the political authorities whose priority was unity in the empire, they reached agreement about "our Lord Jesus Christ, at once perfect in Godhead and in manhood, truly God and truly man, and consisting of a reasonable soul and body; of one substance (*ousia*) with

the Father as regards his Godhead, and at the same time of one substance with us as regards his manhood; in all respects like us, apart from sin, as regards his Godhead begotten of his Father before all ages, but as regards his manhood – on account of us and our salvation – begotten in these recent days of Mary the Virgin, bearer of God; one and the same Christ, Son, Lord, Only-begotten, to be acknowledged in two natures, without confusion, without change, without division, without separation; the distinction of the two natures being in no way destroyed on account of the union, but rather the peculiar property of each nature being preserved and concurring in one person and one subsistence (*hupostasis*) – not as though parted or divided into two persons, but one and the same Son and Only-begotten God, Word, Lord, Jesus Christ."

It is clear from the end of this Chalcedonian Definition that the bishops intended to be loyal to the teachings of Jesus himself, of the Old and New Testaments and of "the Creed of the Fathers" in the Church before their day. Without treating Jesus as a god in the pagan style, or as a being half way between God and Man, they wished to affirm that he was "truly God" because of the "salvation" which they had received through him. They also clung to the affirmation of his humanity, partly because they believed that when he had "assumed" humanity he had "saved" it. Using the philosophical language of their time they thought it necessary to affirm that he had two natures after his birth, divine and human, while remaining one person. But it is also clear that the Council of Chalcedon underestimated the extent to which their language was different from the Bible's or the earlier Church's. As we have seen, the writers of the New Testament became sure that the power of Jesus was in deepest reality the power of the God known to the Hebrews. But they were reluctant to call Jesus "God" and in the few passages where they did this they did it without any philosophical explanation. All the evidence about him shows that Jesus thought of himself as uniquely God's son, servant and messenger, but never as "God"; he prayed to God. Even in John's gospel "Jesus" is distinct from "God" and less than him (14:28), although as the Word or Son of God he is intimately united with God (10:30). So the doctrinal material on which the Council of Chalcedon drew was comparatively recent.

It is clear, too, that the language of their definition is not easy for modern people to understand. Puzzled questions are inevitable. How can a human being, limited as all human beings must be, be "perfect in Godhead"? What is this "substance" which he shares with the divine Father? What does it mean to say that the Son was "begotten before all ages"? Does talk about his two "natures" have any meaning if the two natures cannot be separated in his case? Should it have inspired the later talk about his two "wills", which sounds like schizophrenia?

Many attempts have been made to answer such questions while preserving the Chalcedonian Definition as fully authoritative, but I share the widespread view that they have not been successful, for the claim of Chalcedon to define the divine mystery and the mystery of Jesus authoritatively was itself an error. I am also one of those Christians who share the concern of Jews, Muslims and other monotheists about some possible implications of talk about Jesus Christ as one of the three "persons" who are God the Holy Trinity. For such language can lapse into talk about the Trinity as a society of three people, and can produce much speculation about their relationships with each other, thus confirmimg the suspicion that Christians have departed from the most basic revelation given to the Hebrews, the revelation that God is One. I gladly acknowledge that when theology about the "social" Trinity has been done by orthodox Christians there has always been an insistence on the basic unity of the "persons" and on the Father as the sole source of the divinity of the Son and the Spirit, but pictures of the Trinity used for teaching purposes have often been pictures of three people and the very word "person" has come to mean "centre of consciousness and will". There is danger there.

The extensive modern discussion of ancient Christology (which I studied, however inadequately, in *Tradition and Truth*) seems to point to a simple conclusion. It seems right for me to pray to Jesus as "My Lord and my God!" (John 20:28) because the living Jesus is the Lord of my life. He is the expression of God's love for me and for everyone else, in a human life which has changed mine and the world's. Beyond that I cannot go, being human and therefore ignorant as well as sinful. I cannot go beyond what is experienced and reasonably interpreted if I hope to talk (or think) sense. What is "experienced and reasonably interpreted" is to the believer "revelation" coming from God. So I have to ask whether the doctrines about Christ and about the Holy Trinity which were declared orthodox by councils of the Church in the fourth and fifth centuries were the sole reasonable interpretations of revelatory experience. I think they were not. They were not among the interpretations given in the New Testament, as we have seen, although texts from that source could be quoted in favour of the development (particularly texts selected from John's gospel and understood as the words of the historical Jesus). They do not appear to be necessary interpretations of later experience. What seems necessary is to say that Christians have experienced encounters with the power of God's love still touching human lives in the risen Christ, as in the days of the historical Jesus. Many denials of the traditional doctrines have involved denying either the great experience itself or this awestruck but simple interpretation of it. But we need not make these denials. The experience of meeting God in Christ can be affirmed fully without claiming that it enables us to understand the nature or natures of the historical Jesus, a knowledge hidden from him and from the writers of the New Testament; and without claiming that it enables us to understand the relationship between God the Father and Jesus in eternity. While it may well be thought (and it is my own opinion) the ancient councils of the Church were right to prefer the phrases which they accepted to other phrases on offer at the time, in the twentieth century as in the New Testament less ambitious theology is an alternative which is legitimate.

I now offer some brief responses to claims which have been made in support of the conviction that the definition of Christ's divinity decreed by the Church's ancient councils ought still to be regarded as authoritative for all Christians, albeit after some explanations and minor revisions. It is claimed that since Christian experience of God the Father is distinct from experience of God the Son, there must be two equally divine "persons" co-existing in eternity; and clearly meeting God in the wide world is different from meeting God in Christ. But I submit that Christian experience may also be interpreted by saying that the one God is now known both through his self-disclosure in the created world and through the continuing impact of the life of Jesus. "God as Creator" and "God as Saviour" are two modes of the true God's being, as truly known to us. It is claimed that since some parts of the life of the historical Jesus were obviously divine (for example, his miracles) and some parts divinely human (for example, his suffering), he must have had two "natures'. But I submit that his story may also be interpreted as a whole mysterious blend of the divine and the human. When he healed miraculously he was human;

when he forgave sins he did it by God's authority given to him as "Son of Man"; when he suffered and died he enfleshed the love of God for sinners; when he taught it was the Word of God speaking, but he had to use the knowledge, language and imagery he had acquired in Nazareth. It is claimed that since human nature cannot have been "healed" without being "assumed" by God the Son, that "incarnation" was necessary for our salvation. But I submit that in Christ God has saved, and does save, people one by one, "human nature" being an abstraction.

It is claimed that since Jesus is felt by Christians to be alive after death, and is prayed to, he must be divine in the sense decided by the councils. But I submit that the continuing life of Jesus Christ may also be interpreted by saying that this man has been raised from the dead by God, as other people are or will be, although also in a unique and supreme way, declaring him to be "the Son of God" – which is what the New Testament says. This resurrection is unique because in his "risen" or "spiritual" life, as in his "earthly" or "physical" life, he is still transparently open to God as "*Abba*, Father" and thus still able to communicate the Father's loving presence and saving power. He represents God and embodies God in this human life which has never ended. What God was and is in order to communicate with his creation, this embodied "Word" was and is. What God did and does to teach and save humanity, this "Son" did and does. Jesus is, so to speak, a miniature of God, scaled down so that we can begin to understand; or a mirror reflecting the light of God which would blind anyone seeing it directly; or a lens through which the light of God is brought together and sets us ablaze. As such he ought to be worshipped, although normally Christian prayer is addressed to the "God and Father of Jesus Christ" as his own prayer was while on Earth. He can be talked to and

listened to in prayer; and as we listen we hear the command-
ing voice of God, so that "Christ for us" is for practical
purposes "God for us". Am I denying the experience of
definitely Christian prayer? No, enabling definitely Christian
prayer to take place is my full-time job. I reckon that any
representative collection of Christian prayers or hymns,
ancient or modern, demands a theology no more elaborate
than the one I have just outlined: it is mainly prayer to the
Father through the Son in the Spirit, and it ascribes glory
to the one God revealed in three ways. Am I saying that
"Jesus is only a man"? Yes, what I believe may be understood in that way by anyone who thinks that a wedding ring
is only a piece of metal, or a Rembrandt only a daubed
canvas, or a symphony only a noise.

Towards the end of the twentieth century, some Christians
still find it honest to treat as authoritative the definitions of
Christ reached by the Church's councils in the fourth and
fifth centuries. Other Christians think that those definitions
need quite drastic interpretation but would not think that
an account such as mine is adequate. Other Christians
would find their own interpretations close to mine. And
others – surely, the majority – carry on without much or
any knowledge of the councils' decrees. Christians in the
last two categories may be called "heretics" by their fellow
Christians. But only professional theologians really understand the meaning of the words of 451 translated as "substance", "nature" and "person" – and they often agree
that the splits between Churches, Chalcedonian or non-
Chalcedonian, which occurred with very damaging consequences for Christianity, were not necessary and should
now be ended. A far simpler creed, far closer to the New
Testament, seems to be enough for people to pray and live
as Christians.

2. No sooner had the fifteenth-century Western Church

emerged united from its divisions under two or three Popes than the seeds were sown of the divisions which were to produce the harvests of the Protestant Reformation and Catholic Counter-Reformation. In these disputes the theologians were again supported by rival political forces: this was the beginning of the age of nationalism in Europe. And behind the debates were questions about the power and pay of priests and preachers. The intellectual debate, however, involved theological questions which arose out of utterly genuine, and quite often agonizing, religious feelings. For a Christian to be "saved", was it sufficient to have faith in Christ and his perfect sacrifice to the Father? Was this the Gospel to be preached? Or was it necessary for this faith to be expressed in good works, including faithful and obedient participation in the life and worship of the Church, where every Mass was in some sense a sacrifice? Did God the Father "justify" the sinner, declaring him or her righteous, only for Christ's sake? Or did the sinner still need to be made righteous before being accepted into heaven – righteousness being in practice defined and achieved by the Church?

Here as in the disputes about Christology, definitions were developed in opposition to each other and provided, it was thought, some sort of justification for Churches splitting from each other and persecuting each other. Clearly the different definitions appealed to different temperaments: otherwise passionate religious lives, Protestant or Catholic, would not have been fed by them. But here as in the disputes about Christology, it is possible for a Christian not to be satisfied by any old definition. To be sure, the Christian is said by the Bible, and is known by experience, to be entirely dependent on the grace of God operative through Christ. No human being can "save" himself or herself if "save" means reaching anywhere near God's level of life. Faith in God is needed if God's grace is to be believed in and received. But faith is not "faith" as the New Testament recommends it if it means nothing more than an intellectual assent or a conventional agreement. Faith in Christ must show that it is real by producing love for God and the neighbour. According to Jesus, the sinner is accepted by God before he or she is righteous – but he or she cannot receive this acceptance unless there is willingness to sin no more because sin hurts God's love. In the twentieth century the divisions of Churches split in the time of the Reformation persist tragically. But increasingly the theologians agree that they were not necessary for intellectual reasons, and most Christians do not see their own spiritual struggles and discoveries in the terms used either by the Catholics or by the Protestants in that distant age.

3. No sooner had the twentieth-century ecumenical movement begun to heal the divisions between the Churches than a fresh controversy arose. This dispute is about the "wider ecumenism" – the growing contacts, unprecedented in history, between the Christians and the adherents of other religions. Once again political factors are mixed with the theological debates: in our time more power is being gained by the majority of humankind, non-white as well as non-Christian. But theologically the key question has often been put like this. Is Jesus Christ the world's only Saviour? Is Christianity the world's only "true religion" because it alone names the Saviour? Is it true in relation to other religions that "there is no salvation through anyone else; in all the world no other name has been granted to mankind by which we can be saved" (Acts 4:12)? Was Cyprian in the fourth century right to teach that "outside the Church there is no salvation"? Or do other religions teach much truth and encourage much goodness which God rewards with eternal life? Is it true in relation to other religions that, as Peter is said to have believed, "in every nation those who are god-

fearing and do what is right are acceptable to him" (Acts 10:34)? Should the praise which Jesus bestowed on the goodness he observed in his fellow Jews be extended to the goodness in the non-Christians of our own day? If the second position is correct, what does it mean to call Jesus Christ "the Saviour" and what is the right motive for the Christian mission to the world?

This controversy may grow as contacts between the religions grow. It may become as disruptive as the two earlier controversies. But the debate so far (which as an amateur I explored in *Tradition and Truth*) has led me and many others to another simple conclusion.

I know that Jesus Christ is my Saviour because I know how, and from what, he has saved me. I also know that no other teachers in the whole history of religion has done what he has done for many millions. Judaism has no human Saviour. The Prophet of Islam is not said by Muslims to be the Saviour. The rich mythology of Indian religion contains no figure like Jesus Christ, as many modern Indians have observed. Gautama the Buddha denied that any person except the individual concerned could do what was needed to enter Nirvana. I observe that the uniqueness of Jesus as Saviour is declared not by Christian dogma but by history. But I know, too, that Jesus taught that all goodness comes from God. I must conclude that the goodness in the religion which educated Jesus himself is from God; that the sense of Muslims that the holy God must be obeyed is from God; that the Indian or African sense that God is mysterious yet very near is from God; that the Buddhist sense that escape from illusions requires self-disciplining is from God; that non-Christian terms from Allah and Brahman to Yoga and Zen refer to parts of the general self-revelation of God to humanity. And as I read the stories in the gospels, I meet a Jesus who knows that human nature is a mixture of good and evil. "He knew them all" (John 2:24) – and so he knew that the "non-Christian" scene was not all darkness (whatever John's gospel says). I read that in the world where he lived – a world of fields and roads, kitchens and markets – he admired in his neighbours a sharp eye for the weather and for profit, but most of all he admired people's care for children and animals. He praised a Samaritan's mercy. He was moved by a Syrian woman's anxiety about her daughter, and by a Jewish widow's generosity in the temple. He pictured Lazarus, a beggar not known for correct theology or conspicuous piety, with Abraham in heaven. His heart went out in love to a young man who said that he had kept all ten commandments. When being crucified he said that his executioners did not know what they were doing. The constant theme of his parables was that his hearers, being neither entirely stupid nor entirely wicked, ought to have the intelligence to see that God was even more loving than they were. That seems to be the Saviour's verdict on so-called "Christian" doctrines which have claimed that the Father is considerably less compassionate than the average parent.

If God is the loving Father of all as Jesus proclaimed, it seems to most Christians in our time simply incredible that he should have created the innumerable millions of non-Christians alive, either today or in past ages, knowing that they had no likelihood of being "saved". Non-Christian ways of faith, morality and life must be the ordinary means of salvation for the bulk of humanity. To see this, however, is not to deny that the power of Jesus Christ to save from the darkness is extraordinary. He is the Saviour.

One of the profound changes which has come over Christianity, mainly during the twentieth century, is the decline of the belief in hell. The traditional images of hell either terrified previous Christian generations or tempted them into pride by the thought that this destiny was not to be theirs although it was to be the fate of almost everyone else. Modern Christians have increasingly seen that these images of torturing devils, never-ending fires and never-dying worms cannot be literally true. They are poetic images of horror, used to describe the state of being cut off from the love, and therefore from the life, of God. Modern Christians have also seen increasingly that great theologians such as Augustine and Calvin were wrong to speculate that God "predestined" people to hell. If God is love then he cannot be willing that any human being – let alone the vast majority of humanity – should be for ever excluded from his love and life. In the time of the making of the Acts of the Apostles Christians had, for all their virtues, a very limited understanding of the extent of the non-Christian world needing to be "saved". The Peter whose two (apparently contradictory) statements as given in Acts are so often quoted in the modern debate was no authority on "non-Christian" religions. He must have been ignorant of the very existence of most of Asia and Africa and of all of the Americas and the Pacific islands. It seems clear from the gospels that Jesus used the traditional imagery of hell to brand the imagination with the urgent warning: "Fear him who, after he has killed, has authority to cast into hell" (Luke 12:5, a Q passage). For many modern Christians, under (it is believed) Christ's influence, these images warn of the eternal consequences of profound and persistent rejection of God's self-revelation, taken to its extreme. It seems that the ultimate compliment which God pays to Man is to declare everyone free to reject his offer of love, even to reject it finally, thus rejecting life itself. God values our freedom that much. A modern Christian belief, therefore, is not that the universal salvation of humanity is inevitable. It is that a universal salvation is the will of God and is possible. That belief develops Paul's hope that finally "all" will be saved and John's unexpectedly generous vision of "all" being drawn to the crucified Christ.

I do not pretend that all Christians agree about the solutions of the problems raised in these three controversies, and I certainly do not claim that all ought to agree with my own views. Here again I am convinced that Christian diversity has existed, does exist and is desirable. But I think I can say what many Christians know to be the tasks ahead of honest theological thinking in the next century, showing why the message about Christ deserves to be believed and spread. It will be necessary to speak of the self-sacrifice of Jesus in terms of the noble way in which people still sacrifice themselves; and to speak of the resurrection of Jesus as the decisive beginning of a transforming encounter with the living Teacher. "Messiah" and "Son of Man" will be translated by words such as "Liberator" and "the peak of humanity", and the One rightly worshipped in the past as "Lord" will be presented as the director and manager of free lives. The "Word of God" made "flesh" will be seen as a man who is the clue to the meaning of God's creation of our mind-staggering universe. The "Son of God" or "God the Son" will be obeyed as the Creator's self-revelation and self-expression in a human life, when "God was in Christ reconciling the world to himself" (2 Corinthians 5:19). Words will have to be limited by what can be said out of the experience of being reached by God in Christ, and it may follow that much less can be said than used to be thought right about Jesus before his human birth or after his human death. The strength of the words that have meaning will depend on the strength of an experience which, being profoundly Christian, is profoundly in the realm of the spirit – of the spirit flooded by the Spirit.

IN THE POWER OF THE SPIRIT

The impact of the living Jesus Christ on the Christian and the Church, producing this experience, is a spiritual impact. In the New Testament that is often described as the work of "the Spirit". Although the treatment of the Spirit, both in prominence and in content, is different in each of the eight "gospels" which we briefly studied in chapter 2, it is surely significant that in the church behind Matthew's gospel (12:19), some fifty years after the death of Jesus, baptism was "in the name of the Father and the Son and the Holy Spirit". As Christian theology developed, the Spirit was believed to be a distinct "person" in the Holy Trinity, like the Father and the Son. During the twentieth century Christians of many different kinds have emphasized the importance of the Holy Spirit in fresh ways because of their fresh experiences of this power, in contrast with the pressures coming to them from a largely non-Christian world (even in lands traditionally regarded as Christian). Understandably there have been many claims, often made by "charismatic" Christians whose experience of this power in their own lives has been intense, that every first-class Christian should undergo "baptism in the Spirit" – a crisis which is believed to include the gifts of "tongue-speaking", "prophecy" and "healing".

It is also understandable that there have been many claims, often made by Eastern Orthodox Christians and others who feel close to the Fathers who created traditional theology, that every faithful Christian ought to accept traditional language about the distinct existence in eternity and the distinct activity on Earth of the Holy Spirit as the third divine "person" in the Trinity. For such Christians, it is not enough to compare the Spirit with wind and fire, as is done in the Acts of the Apostles (2:23), or with a dove, since the dove was traditionally regarded as a messenger of God's forgiveness and love (Mark 1:10 connects with Genesis 8:8–11), or with a modern phenomeon such as electricity, causing a shock and bringing light and power. The Spirit, no less than the Father and the Son, must be regarded as an eternally existing "person" (meaning, at least in modern times, a centre of consciousness and will), and direct prayer to him (or occasionally to "her") ought to be encouraged. The development of this doctrine owed much to the development of the understanding of Jesus Christ as the "Second Person in the Godhead" but it never received a similar elaboration. Controversy in this field was given as a reason for the split between Eastern Orthodoxy and the Western Church which became final in 1054 (did the Spirit "proceed" from the Son as well as Father?), but it never aroused the passion of the disputes about Christology.

What came to be regarded as orthodoxy in East and West alike was not created by theologians in a vacuum; it arose out of the experience of the power of the Spirit. It did not intend to assert the existence of a third, independent, god; in heaven the Spirit "proceeds from" the Father, somewhat as the Son is "begotten by" the Father. (The difference between these two origins has, however, never been described satisfactorily, and in the divisive *filioque* controversy the problem about whether the Spirit proceeds from the Father "and the Son" or "through the Son" was indeed hard to solve except by different appeals to authority.) By using the word "person" about the Spirit the doctrine did not intend to make a complete comparison of the Holy Spirit with a human person. While the description of the Spirit as the "co-beloved" of the Father and the Son has often been preferred (and the Trinity has even been compared with a family of father, mother and child), the Spirit has also often been spoken of as the "bond of love" between the Father

and the Son: a bond is not a person. And the doctrine was
not separated from the practicalities of Christian behaviour.
On the contrary, it has been taught that the relationships
of persons-in-community on Earth ought to be modelled
on the selfless love between the three divine "persons" in
heaven.

I believe, however, that there is an alternative to the
claims which I have outlined – an alternative which represents what most Christians now believe about God the
Holy Spirit.

I do not wish to deny either the reality or the value of the
ability to speak or sing or pray in ecstasy without using
ordinary words, to have an uncanny insight into what is
going on and is likely to go on, and to heal through the
influence of spiritual power over physical disease. In the
New Testament and later, these are parts of the experience
of Christians. But these gifts of God have not been given to
every Christian, and it seems wrong to make an emphasis
on them as part of the faith on which every Christian can
be expected to agree. Writing to the early Christians
(specially in chapters 12–14 of his first letter to Corinth and
in chapter 12 of his letter to Rome), Paul wisely taught that
these were only some of the gifts which God had poured
into the hearts and lives of the new community. This has
also been the teaching of the wisest leaders of the twentieth-
century "charismatic" renewal of Christianity.

I do not wish to deny either the reality or the value of
any of the experiences of God which have led to the worship
of God the Father, God the Son and God the Holy Spirit.
They are my own experiences. But they are not experiences
of the relationships of three divine people in heaven. Therefore it is, I fear, impossible to talk sense about those relationships. The New Testament does not make that mistake, for
even those theologians who have been most eager to turn

its teachings into a system have never been able to show that it distinguishes between "God" and "the Spirit of God", or between "Christ" and "the Spirit of Christ", or between "the Spirit of God" and "the Spirit of Christ". No more did the Hebrew Bible intend to say that when "the spirit of God hovered over the face of the water" in the beginning of the creation, that was not the Creator (Genesis 1:2) – or that when Yahweh the God of Israel filled Bezalel the craftsman "with the spirit of God, making him skilful and ingenious", that spirit was somehow distinct from Yahweh (Exodus 35:31).

What the New Testament proclaims, because of what Christians have experienced, is this. As "Spirit" – that is, very powerfully – God took control of Jesus at his baptism (Mark 1:10–12), inspired him to offer himself as the perfect sacrifice (Hebrews 9:14) and raised him from the dead (Romans 1:4). As Spirit, God has enabled Christians to say sincerely "Jesus is Lord!" and has given them nothing less than "the mind of Christ" (1 Corinthians 2:16;12:3). John believes out of rich experience that the Father has "sent" the Spirit to stand alongside Christians as their advocate, to witness to Christ, to guide them into all the truth about Christ and to teach them what is sin and what is not (14:16;15:26;16:13;20:22). But the whole of his gospel makes it clear that this "Spirit" is not independent of the Jesus who promises his perpetual and intimate presence in the Christian community, any more that the Spirit is independent of the Father: "he will speak only what he hears" (16:13). The New Testament's language indicates an overwhelming spiritual experience, and at the peak of his theology (Romans 8) Paul uses this experience as the decisive clue to the whole future. The gift of the Spirit, he writes elsewhere, is so great that it is a "pledge" guaranteeing the glory which is the Christian's destiny (2 Corinthians 5:5).

CHRIST FOR US   191

But never is it a gift which may be detached from God's gift of his Son. Indeed, John (7:39) goes so far as to say that before Jesus was "glorified" the Spirit was not "given". The early Christians differed from each other in many perceptions, as we have noted. But never did they deviate from the insistence that God is one, active in the creation, active in the Son and active in the Spirit. They worshipped the One whom they called "God" through Jesus Christ and in the power of the Spirit. As Paul reminded the Christians in Corinth soon after AD 50, they knew God's love through Christ's grace in the fellowship made by the Spirit.

That is the faith in the New Testament and it does not seem necessary to add to it if we want a creed on which all Christians should agree. But I turn now to the challenges which have been raised by discoveries and thoughts which are not present, or at any rate not prominent, in the Bible. I turn in the belief that the work of God as Spirit has not ceased.

CHAPTER
FIVE

God's Reality

THE CHALLENGE OF MODERN ATHEISM

THE modern question has been whether God is real in a universe fifteen billion (thousand million) years old and observably fifteen billion light-years wide (with light travelling at 186,283 miles a second). But the Bible and most of the Christian tradition belong to a world, little in time and space, where it was taken for granted that God or gods existed and ruled. Jesus belonged wholeheartedly to that world.

Most people in the 1990s still belong to it with parts of their minds. In most countries modern enough to have public opinion polls God gets the majority's vote, whether "God" is described as "personal" or as "Reality" or "Something", although this is often not reflected in regular public worship. In most traditional societies people tend not to have their own views but to take part in the religious practices of the communities to which they belong, although the practices may not be frequent. Few Africans, for example, are atheists. Few Indians are. The whole world of Islam affirms that Allah is great. But it would be foolish for religious people to take too much comfort from this continuing world of faith. It often seems that a belief in science and its material

benefits is the modern religion, and that consequently scepticism is likely to be the post-modern creed. For whole peoples
or for influential élites, traditional religion is being eroded
by an educational process which (perhaps only through the
media or conversations) challenges belief in God in the name
of science. The overwhelming secularization of China under
Communism is the largest example of what may follow.
Already the central religious question for the modern, mod-
ernizing or post-modern world is whether any belief in God
or gods is compatible with science – and, if so, what kind
of belief. In Psalms 14 and 53 it was "the fool" who said in
his heart: "There is no God." But what is folly now?

Only a few sentences in the teaching ascribed to Jesus
contain faint suggestions of the problems on which modern
atheists and agnostics have fastened. All the sources show
Jesus as accepting pre-scientific theories about the universe
as well as pre-critical ideas about the Hebrew Bible. When
Mark (10:6) presents him as saying that "in the beginning,
at the creation, 'God made them male or female' ", no
hesitation about the accuracy of the myths which begin
Genesis is implied. When Matthew (5:34,35) reports a reference to heaven as God's throne and earth as his footstool,
he does not add any caution that the picture of the Creator
as seated above the earth is mythological. Jesus is said to
have accepted without question the idea that God directly
controls, or at least permits, all events in the universe,
including the death of a single sparrow (Matthew 10:29).
He would never have asked the urban Paul's question: "Do
you suppose God's concern is with oxen?" (1 Corinthians
9:9). Through nature God feeds the birds and his human
children; through nature God teaches a lesson by making
the wild lilies of Galilee which "do not work or spin" more
splendid than King Solomon (Matthew 5:25,33). His reverence for nature as a devout countryman was such that he

did not think it ridiculous to compare the coming of the
kingdom of God with the growth of a mustard plant (Mark
4:31). But being a true countryman, he was not a naïve
romanticist about nature. He noticed weeds growing and
lilies dying. His parables were full of the cares and labours
of people who lived close to the soil and to poverty, and who
knew well how "each day has troubles enough of its own"
(Matthew 6:34). According to Luke, he did not think that
eighteen people killed by a collapsing tower were specially
sinful (13:4), and Matthew tells us that he did not believe
that God distributes sunshine and rain according to people's
moral condition (5:45). His parables showed how closely he
had watched the processes of nature in the fields, although
it is said in the gospels that he shared the common beliefs
that seeds died in the ground (John 12:24) and could be
sown successfully in unploughed ground (Mark 4:3–9).

Some passages in the tradition suggest a naïve belief that
all prayers, or at least all "in the name" of Jesus, will be
answered favourably. But "in the name" meant "in the
nature": the prayers which the Father will "hear" are prayers such as Jesus makes. We therefore ought to look at the
tradition about how Jesus prayed if we would understand
passages such as "Ask and you will receive; seek, and you
will find; knock and the door will be opened to you"
(Matthew 7:7). We read of intercessions, the lifting up of
others to the God of love in prayers which may be disappointed. An example is "I have prayed for you, Simon, that
your faith may not fail" (Luke 22:32) – before Simon Peter's
faith did fail. But the tradition was that Jesus had been very
far from regarding prayer as a list of demands which must
be satisfied by magic. Whether long or short, prayer in the
style of Jesus is a personal, self-purifying, communion with
the divine Father. From time to time he would withdraw to
remote places for such prayer and might spend the night in

prayer (Luke 5:16; 6:12). Matthew's gospel includes the teaching: "When you pray, go into a room by yourself, shut the door, and pray to your Father who is in secret . . . Do not go babbling on like the heathen, who imagine that the more they say the more likely they are to be heard" (6:6,7). Two parables retold by Luke teach that prayer must be humble and persistent: the widow who keeps on bothering a judge is praised, the Pharisee who thanks God that he is not like the rest of mankind is condemned (18:1–14). The Letter to Hebrews records the cost of the obedience which such prayer expressed and increased: "In the course of his earthly life he offered up prayers and petitions, with loud cries and tears" (5:7). His own model prayer taught his disciples to concentrate not on themselves but on the God who is both intimately approachable as *Abba* and awesomely transcendent as "hallowed". Their prayer must be that the heavenly Father's kingdom may come and his will be done on Earth – and that was his prayer also, facing death in Gethsemane, where his heart was "ready to break with grief" (Mark 14:34) and "his sweat was like drops of blood falling to the ground" (Luke 22:44). From such prayer his disciples were to gain the humility needed to forgive others and to know that their own strength was still fragile. So there is nothing in these traditions about the prayers of Jesus which cannot be prayed in the age of science.

But that does not dispose of the modern event called "the death of God". In the story of the crucifixion Mark's gospel gives, as the only words from the cross, the cry: "My God, my God, why have you forsaken me?" (15:34). That cry of dereliction makes Jesus the brother of all who have felt, often in great anguish, the absence or unreality of the God in whom they had trusted. A man dying under torture in what is felt as complete failure and utter isolation experiences the question, even though he still takes it for granted that God exists. A modern person may undergo mental torture through the feeling that science reveals a pitiless universe where the fates of all beings are decided not by a God who counts the sparrows but by a combination of blind chance with necessity as decreed by the laws of cause and effect. After the modern question it may not seem possible to continue to pray as Jesus did to "my God, my God".

I admit that during the twentieth century people who have ceased, or always refused, to believe in the reality of God have often become more comfortable in that position. Their relaxation may be contrasted with the agonies which often accompanied a "loss of faith" in the nineteenth century. To thoroughly secularized people religion now often seems remote, uninteresting or comic. If taken more seriously, religion may seem a phenomenon of history or current affairs and nothing more – to be studied in the spirit in which a Christian scholar studies the religion of Ancient Egypt or of a "primitive" tribe in a tropical jungle. It is difficult to exaggerate the contrast between such attitudes and the prestige of religion in most societies in history. I also admit that religious believers may cease to be in conflict with the scientific world of thought which surrounds them by ceasing to be in contact with it. In its small ghetto religion then becomes little more than a game played for one's amusement or comfort, a ritual creating the cosy illusions of childish make-believe, questions about unpleasant reality being forgotten. Or science can be dismissed as not worthy of respect. The misuse of science for military or commercial purpose has played a large part in the sorrows of the twentieth century, and science itself may be blamed. And I admit that there are religious believers who accept science, and in many cases practise it (sometimes with high distinction), without being troubled in their religious faith. This may be because they have thought things through for themselves so successfully that they have forgotten the questions which disturb ordinary people. Or it may be because any branch of advanced science means specialization, so that general questions are no longer considered at any depth. Or it may be because it is possible to draw from the vast mass of scientific facts support for one's religious faith, without taking into account the reasons why science and religion have so often been felt to be incompatible. Or scientifically-minded people may be happy to be also religiously-minded because the two activities are kept in separate compartments of the mind.

Actually, however, the impact of science on religion has produced changes in human feeling and thinking so great that the phrase "the death of God" is not completely silly. Obviously it is not a phrase which belongs to good philosophy, for if God has ever lived he cannot die. But it dramatizes the psychological and social fact that belief in God can die. Modern science has challenged traditional religion by being more successful in its ability to explain what happens in the world, by its greater powers of prediction and by its more obvious achievements in transforming the world. It has also been more impressive (many people think) because more humble. It is constantly self-critical. It is not afraid to say when it does not know – and not afraid to test, and if necessary abandon, a great teacher's honoured theory which may no longer fit the known facts. These features of science have led many to conclude that its power will grow in the centuries to come, while the authority given to religion diminishes. And this victory of science is being achieved by the use of methods which deliberately exclude the possibility that God or gods may have acted. Individual scientists may or may not believe in a few or many divine interventions in the course of nature or in the course of history, but such interventions are never discussed scientifically. The only subject within the scope of science or science-influenced history is the human belief that miracles have occurred – a belief which is usually dismissed. Laplace's famous reply to Napoleon's question about where he put God in his system ("Sir, I had no need of that hypothesis") spoke permanently for science, although Laplace's version of science has since been discredited and replaced. There is a very great difference between this worldview and the beliefs that every part of nature is under God's control, that every part of human life ought to be submitted to that control, and that the most important events in history were miracles making that control firm and clear.

Some lines which have often been taken by recent defenders of religion have, I think, only a limited truthfulness. It is, for example, true that Marxism, which has often inspired attacks on religion, is not truly scientific as an analysis of history or as a theory of economics. It is also true that in most countries Marxism is now more or less dead – more dead than God. But that does not dispose of the charge that religious claims may also be untrue in the light of science. Indeed, the truth of religion may be questioned more destructively when religion is no longer given prestige as one of the forces resisting the obvious evil of a Marxist regime.

It is true that recent developments in sociology and psychology, and in the study of history, have discredited the idea that the disciplined understanding of Man-in-society can safely ignore the role of religion. Religion, it is clear, has often dominated and integrated both personalities and societies. On the other hand, these reconsiderations have not completely invalidated the critical approach to religion taken by modern intellectual giants of the height of Marx, Durkheim and Freud. They pointed to ugly truths – that religion has often been not a way of holiness but a way in which a society has expressed and strengthened its own togetherness; that it has often been controlled in the interests of a society's more powerful members, as "opium for the people"; that many religious beliefs have been the illusions of people seeking escapes from realities – "opium" taken willingly; and that the realities which drive people to behave as they do, in religion as in other spheres of life, are often far more like the sexual and predatory drives we observe in other animals than most religious believers have liked to think. While recent "social" scientists and " scientific" historians have tended to accept the prominence of religion in history, many have continued to accept the devastating modern criticisms of religion. They refuse to place this highly questionable human activity on a level with the knowledge attainable through science. To them, religion can be significant psychologically and historically without being either admirable or true.

It is true that modern science has made its advances by narrowing its attention to small and preferably non-personal bits of reality. Scientists find results easier to get when they are reductionists – when they study not a person but the chemistry of a toenail; not a rain forest but the physics of a tree. Many trends in post-modern thinking are much broader. They can be called "holistic" because they attempt to study wholes, specially living wholes. A linkage is found between every thing and every person – and it is often found not so much by "objective" study, for example the dissection of a frog on a laboratory table, as by participation in life, sympathetically watching the frog move. Yet holistic talk about wholes may have a considerable defect: it may be nonsense, more inflated than any frog and much less useful. Science as it describes objects one by one, as objectively as possible, has at least one obvious merit: it contributes to human knowledge.

It is true that by its patient investigation of small realities modern science has helped to end beliefs which had a long run as rivals to belief in one God (monotheism). Many traditional societies have believed in a supreme God, the ultimate Creator, but they have concentrated on the worship and appeasement of lesser gods believed to control human affairs (polytheism), and have also believed in powerful spirits inhabiting animals or natural objects (animism). The sun was often worshipped as divine. Such beliefs could produce a religion where the most frequent emotion was fear. That was why sacrifices to feed the gods or spirits seemed vitally necessary, and could include the sacrifice of human beings. Some more sophisticated societies or individuals have been attracted instead to the belief that all nature is divine without a creator (pantheism). Modern science has, however, explained the phenomena which previously caused people to worship many gods or spirits, and has treated nature as far from divine: nature has often been explored or exploited without inhibitions. In the modern world all this has cleared the ground for belief in the one Creator. But modern science has also raised insistently the question which believers have to consider. Is "God" – for example, the God named El or Yahweh by the Hebrews or Allah by the Arabs and the non-Arab Muslims – any more real than the gods or spirits of pagan mythology? If the sun or the universe is not truly divine, is God? Is the God of high religion anything more than the projection of the fears and hopes in the ignorant mind of a child?

It is true that modern science, fearless in experimental research and prolific in its applications to technology, made its breakthrough in a Europe which had been saturated by centuries of the dominance of the Christian religion. That is true despite very impressive advances of mathematics and scientific thought and invention in other societies, including

Ancient Greece, China and Islam. Almost all the great names in the early history of modern science regarded themselves as devout Christians whatever the clergy thought – and some great scientists were priests. Such men viewed nature as "God's book" to be studied alongside the Holy Scriptures, and they were confident that it would respond to reasoning enquiries because its Creator was an orderly God who could also be understood (at least up to a point) by the exercise of reason. Nature, it seemed, deserved this study because it was the solid work of the all-wise God; it was not illusory or contemptible. But it was also material suitable to be probed by the human mind in detailed experiments because it was not divine. Indeed, according to Genesis, the Creator had intended Adam (Man) to "fill the earth and subdue it" and to "have dominion over . . . every living thing" (1:28) and had invited him to "name" each living creature (2:19). These religious beliefs, accepted with enthusiasm by many of modern science's early practitioners and propagandists, had shaped a Europe which was favourable to the rise of modern science, and it seemed clear that the new power, given by scientific knowledge, inherited the old divine blessings on dominant Adam. Although economic and social factors were no less indispensable, and although the official custodians of the religious tradition often discouraged and sometimes persecuted individual scientists thought to be heretical, the psychological origins of modern science in Christian Europe were facts. The facts have been expounded by many recent historians and deserve to be more widely known. Yet modern science's challenge to religion cannot be silenced by telling this story of its origins, for it is possible that those religious authorities who tried to censor its development were right to see it as a threat to religion itself as well as to their own privileged positions. And it is certain that, although some scientists have continued to be Christian believers, on the whole the effect of science's growing influence on society has been to discredit religion. Theology has been deprived of its old privileges as "the queen of the sciences", and often the public has been left with the impression that faith has been in intellectual retreat. Science has become first independent and then widely victorious.

It is also true that with the growth of scientific knowledge the recognition has grown that the universe remains mysterious. It has proved impossible to begin science at a point further back than the existence of the "singularity" which became a fireball in the "Big Bang". Much – it seems, most – of the matter in the universe has so far been beyond the reach of the scientists' instruments and theories: it remains "dark". Scientists have so far found it equally impossible to predict whether the universe will expand infinitely or will one day contract by gravitation into another ball of unimaginably hot matter resembling matter's earliest known state ("the Big Crunch"). Already these questions are being explored scientifically. But light from the regions farthest from us cannot reach this planet since it takes too long to travel here; so the universe may well be very much larger than the immensity which we can observe. And it seems impossible for science to tell us whether or not this is the only universe there has been or is. The suggestion is logically possible that ours may be the smallest of all the universes that exist. There is, it seems, no way of knowing whether or not life exists on other planets, despite all the science fiction. Above all no scientist, as scientist, can tell what is the purpose of the development of a universe of such dimensions, with so much of its fantastically long history so strangely determined in the first few minutes or seconds of the Big Bang. No scientist, as scientist, can tell why the evolution of life on this planet has been so astoundingly possible and so astoundingly creative. The scientist discusses the "how" – not the "why".

But religion should be careful before making propaganda out of these reminders that the universe is still mysterious. Scientific cosmology may well progress in the years to come, solving problems which at present seem to be insoluble mysteries. Already science has made advances which have consigned all the old pictures of the universe, even those enshrined in holy scriptures, to museums. Humanity unaided by science could imagine with the Hebrews that rain came from waters above the "firmament of heaven", and that the sun took a daily journey across the sky, moving above the flat Earth like a bridegroom who rejoices as he moves towards consummating the marriage (as in Psalm 19:5). The more observant Greeks (such as Ptolemy in about AD 150) could imagine that Earth was a ball around which the sun and the stars rotated in perfect circles. The clergy of the Roman Inquisition who condemned Galileo in 1633 imagined that a combination of these pictures – a combination which could not be explained – had to be compulsory if the authority of the Church and its Bible was to be preserved. If we ask what is the truth which we glimpse, we have to answer that much about our mysterious universe is not known and much can never be known. But what is really known scientifically is known reliably, unlike much that the spokesmen of religion teach or used to teach. Galileo is said to have defied his persecutors by his observation about Earth: "it moves". The human mind also moves. It moves away from the belief that religion has the right to contradict science.

It is true that the advance of physics has discredited the picture, dear to earlier scientists, of the elementary particles of matter as solid objects banging into each other like billiard balls and moving under iron laws which allowed no exemptions. Since 1926 it has been known by physicists that the elementary particles move in "indeterminate" patterns which cannot be predicted except as probabilities, and that it is impossible to measure simultaneously to a high precision both the position of a particle and the speed at which it moves. At its simplest, matter can thus be pictured as a dance, rather than as a machine. It has both the properties of particles and also the properties of waves. More complex systems of matter also have in them an "indeterminate" element; for example, as a wave crashes in the sea the fall of the water cannot be predicted precisely. These discoveries of turbulence have fed the "chaos theory" in mathematics. But they have only a limited significance for our understanding of matter as it impinges on our daily lives. Despite the miracles described in the Bible, a staff still does not become a snake, and iron still does not float in a river. Many more important old stories of miracles – the Easter stories, for example – are still very difficult for anyone influenced by science to accept with the old confidence, and the inclusion of a story in the Bible is no longer thought by most people to decide whether or not it is literally true. That makes a profound difference to people's understanding of the authority of religious scriptures and officials. The Christian battles for the Bible which have defended its "infallible" or "inerrant" authority – and which still continue in some minds – have not been fought so passionately about nothing. Similar battles waged by Muslims (for example) in defence of the perfection of the Quran are well known to be a major feature of the modern world. Many people do find it very difficult to see how scriptures can be true in any sense if they are not completely true.

It is true that the advance of biology has changed the picture associated with the (much more cautious) scientific work of Darwin – a picture of evolution resulting from "natural selection" as the prize of survival went to the victors in a struggle for food between competitors who somewhat resembled Victorian or American capitalists. Later scientists have seen more fully that evolution is a process with its own energy, often developing in spurts between long periods of equilibrium, always building up more complex forms and filling up any vacant niche in nature. They have also seen more clearly the advantages which come from social behaviour in birds or animals, for example in the care of the young. Thus biology may be said to have become "post-Darwinian". But the difficulties for the religious vision of the world as God's careful creation have been increased by another development in science. The discovery that microscopically tiny genes give the instructions for physical growth has been followed by proof that the mutations in these genes are caused by chemical changes. These mutations may sometimes be "advantageous" (assisting behaviour adapted to a particular environment and therefore helpful for the individual's survival and for the survival and multiplication of offspring), but they are always "random" (they are not intentionally related to the environment). Indeed, mutations are usually "regressive" (producing handicapped "freaks").

Unimaginably immense tracts of time are often required for such random mutations to be combined in bodies adapted to environments and to be spread by breeding, but some species, including *homo sapiens*, have flourished quite quickly in a way for which there is as yet no agreed scientific explanation. It is understandable that many people have at first refused to believe that evolution was the origin of the species in nature, and it is certain that the contrast with the old religious picture, where each living creature was purposefully designed by the Creator, is very sharp. And the discovery of the number of surviving species (more than two million) has combined with informed guesses about the number of species now extinct (perhaps about 500 million) to show how evolution, whether "blind" or not, has been productive on a scale which in human estimation amounts to fantastic waste. In nature many of the numbers are bewildering. A single oyster may lay several hundred million eggs in a four-month season, and the relatively infertile codfish produces an annual average of fifteen million eggs, of which all except about a dozen get eaten as part of the plankton of the sea. Fortunately death or destruction takes care of such numbers. In fish and insects, normal losses among eggs and among the immature are said to exceed 999 in every thousand. Among wild birds, three-quarters of the young die before breeding. Most animals die before they have produced any offspring, while most of the rest die before they have borne as many offspring as was biologically possible. Few animals die of old age. Perhaps about a thousand million million million stars with their planets look down on this littered battlefield.

It is true that the knowledge of these processes that has been gained by modern science is a very striking example of the achievements of the human brain. *Homo sapiens* has turned out to be clever enough to understand his physical environment to an extent thought impossible until very recently – and has only just begun the history of science. This triumph is a new advertisement for human dignity, freshly demonstrating that the mind of Man need not be totally baffled by the spectacle of nature. But even as we celebrate the victories of science we are made religiously uneasy by the reminders of human weakness which science inflicts on our pride. We now know that our ancestors "behaved like animals", for they were animals and, before that, the humble predecessors of animals in the very long and down-to-earth story of evolution. We know that the

notorious misuses of science for purposes of violence or commercial greed spring out of human habits which were formed
in the ages when our ancestors were hunting apes, or ape-like
hominids, or half-starving human beings who used stones to
kill their fellow animals. We know that however sophisticated we may be, we who are human embody the legacies of
evolution in body and mind, being driven by urges which
remain more powerful than reason or the conscience. Whatever may be our cleverness or our idealism, our actual
behaviour is frequently degrading and disastrous. Thus a
city as rich and sophisticated as New York can be a violent
hell at street level; a cause as idealistic as Communism can
be murder; shrewd and ambitious men can jeopardize or
sacrifice their marriages or careers when struck by the physical charms of a woman (or man); the news, like history, is
full of the crimes and follies of humanity. And so we ask
whether such pitiable animals as we are can qualify as
teachers of religion. Could we ever form reliable ideas about
the purpose behind our own emergence out of the universe
– or about any reality said to be bigger and more permanent
than everything we can see? Charles Darwin, for example,
found his respect for religion diminishing because he asked
himself this humiliating question rather than because of his
detailed discoveries.

FAITH IN THE AGE OF SCIENCE

So reflection seems to show that the significance for religion
of recent advances in science has been ambiguous. This is
in keeping with the fact, known to the clearsighted in many
generations, that nature itself gives an ambiguous reply if
asked about the reality of its maker. Some aspects of nature
support faith; others do not. God may be seen everywhere
– or nowhere. The decision really to believe and trust in

God is always essentially a personal response to personal religious experience (although of course the religious beliefs of parents, teachers and friends, and of the public at large, greatly influence the personal decision). But that does not necessarily discredit religion, any more than it discredits agnosticism or atheism. Many human activities proceed after a leap of faith which affirms that they are worthwhile. Modern science is somewhat like religion, because it has depended on its own faith that its tradition of reasoning will unlock the secrets of nature because nature has patterns and processes which human powers of reason may discover.

Religion has depended on what are believed to be the discoveries of ancestors, particularly on what are believed to be revelations communicated by the founders of the world's great faiths. These teachings are conveyed to new generations within a community of believers. The Hebrew Scriptures include classic examples of this process. The belief that the one God, known to Israel as Yahweh, had created the whole universe had to struggle over a long period with the belief that every nation had its own god or gods, with whom Yahweh had to compete. The belief in Yahweh as the sole Creator received decisive boosts from what were believed to be displays of supreme power in history, particularly in the rescue of the Israelites from the Egyptians and of a remnant of the Jews from the Babylonians. Israel's history lay behind (for example) Psalm 19, which celebrated the creation together with the liberated community's law. Other scriptures celebrated the exodus from Egypt with an enthusiasm which saw little difference between the retreating waters of that sea and the retreating waters of primal chaos. Israel's history inspired the celebration of a new exodus, the return from exile in Babylon by the anonymous prophet known as Second Isaiah (in chapters 40–55); and he was the man who, more emphatically than anyone else in the

Hebrew Scriptures, believed in one Creator – because he believed that Yahweh had done this new thing. But here again science may be compared with religion up to a point. Scientists rely on discoveries made by their predecessors, and in comparatively few cases do they verify or falsify these by their own experiments or theoretical work. Like religion, science is practised within a community which depends largely on its history. It is a community of faith which has to take largely on trust the discoveries made by ancestors.

Religion has also depended on the aesthetic sense and on the powers of the imagination. Belief in the Creator has often been connected with an appreciation of the beauty of the creation, and statements about God or gods have been made more effectively by the creation of new beauty in art or music or dance than by spoken or written words. Most words used to teach religion have been used in myths – stories told about God or gods as if about human beings. Many religious myths have been legends: the events related in them never took place, although the stories may illuminate what actually exists or happens. Almost all religious statements include words which are "mythological" in a broader sense, for in order to talk about God or gods in terms which begin to make sense, believers have to use terms derived from human activities such as making, ruling, fighting or parenting. Indeed, any comparison between God and a person is a myth or at least a metaphor, since if God is real God, who creates persons, must be more than personal. But religion often treats God (or gods) as at least personal because religion believes that it has experienced God (or gods) communicating with it in a way which is like the way in which persons communicate with each other – and if God is the Source of human personalities, that Source cannot be inferior to personality. It is also the case that scientists depend on the aesthetic sense and on the powers of the imagination. They tend to think that a theory is more likely to be true if it is elegant, appealing to their sense of beauty – and the history of science has shown repeatedly that they are right to think so. And for their practical purposes they need to use their imaginations. For example, at its most basic, matter may usefully be called either a particle or a wave. Metaphors abound in science. So do the systems of metaphors which may be called models. And often scientists speak of natural processes such as evolution as if the process were a person planning and struggling, succeeding or failing. They speak of "Nature" in this way because the power of nature, and particularly of evolution in nature, can best be imagined if it is compared with the power of a person.

Thus in their different ways both religion and science depend on faith, on a community's history and on words or images which are beautiful and suggestive rather than accurate. This fact ought to help Christians to admit finally that the pictures of the Creator and the creation given in the Bible are metaphorical or mythological. The frequent comparison between God and a craftsman suggests much, but it does not prove that he had material ready to his hand when he began to create. God is a bit like a king, but he also judges kings; a bit like a warrior, but he also makes peace. The image of God as a father suggests much, but it does not say that he is male in anatomy, and it is better if it is accompanied by the biblical comparison with "a woman in labour, panting and gasping" (Isaiah 42:14). God is always something more, and the biblical phrase "holy, holy, holy" could also be translated "different, different, different". In the twelfth century Anselm well defined God as "Something than which nothing greater can be thought".

Modern critical scholarship has shown that the stories about the creation given in the first two chapters of Genesis come from two different sources. These myths are in many ways legendary. In the age of science it is known that the creation was not complete within six days, light and plants were not created before the sun, rain was not stored above the vault of the heavens, *homo sapiens* was not made of dust and was not immortal, the first woman was not made from a man's rib, evil did not begin by eating fruit, God did not walk in a garden "at the time of the evening breeze" . . . But these stories were told for some purposes which modern scholars have begun to understand. The earlier myth was told in order to portray Adam (Man) as a mixture of earthiness and "the breath of life"; in order to deny that Man may decide for himself what is good or evil; in order to affirm the mutual dependence and the shared sinfulness of a man and a woman (Eve means "life"); in order to say that human innocence has been lost, but not the presence of God; and in order to add that human life is now hard but not impossible. The later myth (Genesis 1:1–2:4) was told after the exposure of exiles to Babylonian religion, in order to deny that anything other than the will of the one God brought about the creation; in order to reduce the sun and moon, often worshipped, to the status of "signs both for festivals and for seasons and years"; in order to honour human beings, often enslaved, as Godlike; in order to proclaim that the whole of the creation, often thought to be the battleground of good and evil, is "very good"; and in order to encourage the Jews to absorb all these truths (denied in the surrounding society) by celebrating the one Creator's goodness as they rested and worshipped on the Sabbath.

These are, however, not the only biblical myths about the creation. The peaceful beauty of the world is said to have resulted from God's victory over the sea-monsters Leviathan (Psalm 74:14) and Rahab (Psalm 89:10), because to the Hebrews the sea meant chaos and danger (as in Job

38:8–11). That was not very different from the Babylonian myth that the world was formed out of the body of a murdered goddess, Tiamat. It is tragic as well as ludicrous that Christians who did not "believe in" Rahab and Leviathan any more than in Tiamat thought themselves obliged to defend Adam and Eve as historical characters – and, when Genesis was no longer thought to be literally true, to insist that humanity must have descended from a single couple of perfect and immortal parents who sinned. But it is equally tragic when Christians think that they have nothing to learn from the myth of Adam and Eve – or from the story, more or less contemporary, of the sin of David and Bathsheba, the lovers who became the parents of King Solomon. The Bible is perpetually eloquent about the human condition under the stars and under God.

The great question mark put by experience against faith in God has been the fact of suffering. Countless people have asked: if God is good, why does he allow so much suffering? Modern knowledge of nature has increased our knowledge that all that lives must suffer (although less than humanity) if only because it must die – and must devour other creatures because it must eat if it is not to die. In the Bible the book of Job is the classic dramatization of the religious problem of human suffering, and at first sight it is very strange that the climax of this poem should be the presentation not of something pretty but of the wonders of the stars, the sea, the dawn, the snow, the storm, the hunting lioness, the mountain goat, the wild ass or ox, the ostrich, the horse, the hawk, the vulture, the whale, the crocodile. Is that the answer to Job? Surprisingly it is, because the feeling at the heart of religion can be inspired through magnificently beautiful animals and birds. It is the feeling of being confronted by "things too wonderful for me to know" (42:3). Here is wonder that anything exists rather than nothing –

and from this wonder arise the philosophers' words that God is "Being" itself, the "Source and Ground" of all that merely exists. No alternative that begins to make sense has ever been offered as the beginning of an explanation of the mystery of sheer existence. And religion grows as wonder grows that what exists is so beautiful.

In beautiful words Job is invited to admire the beauty of the creation which he cannot understand. The animals and birds which eat their fellow creatures do so in order that they may survive beautifully – and often they kill beautifully. Confronted by this beauty, which is not of his making and is beyond his understanding, Man feels obliged to increase the beauty in his surroundings. He begins to worship the Creator of it all and, sensing that the Creator is at least beautiful, worships by creating yet more beauty. These seem to be deep instincts in humanity. They are strong in "primitive" peoples. They can also be strong in many artists or musicians who distance themselves from organized religion. Such instincts respond with awe to the picture in a Hebrew psalm:

> You bring darkness, and it is night,
> when all the beasts of the forest go prowling;
> the young lions roar for prey,
> seeking their good food from God (104:20,21).

What is beautiful may not be thought to be morally good; indeed, it may have to be called cruel. Accordingly the Creator of nature may be thought to be amoral, "beyond good and evil" as in some Indian thought, and life may seem to be a dance from birth to death where morality is irrelevant. But the moral sense, no less than the aesthetic sense, fertilizes the religious sense. The book of Job explores the connection with a unique eloquence. Job knows the difference between right and wrong, whether he thinks of himself as innocent or as needing to repent in dust and ashes; and he demands that life ought to be fair because it is the creation of the God who is just. He persists in this protest against life's injustice although patronized, mocked and contradicted by his "friends". In the end, when the suffering against which he rebels has strangely purified him, he is vindicated by that God. The book has moved so many because it speaks about the human conscience as a pointer towards a pattern in life's mysteries.

Many teachers in the history of religion have attempted to supply answers to the problems of evil which are more philosophical than the drama and poetry of the book of Job. Many modern philosophers and theologians have examined the arguments used. In so far as I understand things (which is not very far), the debate leads to a few simple conclusions. Any creation distinct from the perfect Creator must be less than perfect, but the question here is whether the creation which we experience is so full of evil that it would have been better – better morally – if this planet had never been created and evolution never allowed to end up with us. Not many people would say that. If the creation seems to us on balance "good" we can see that features which seem to us "bad" may in fact be needed in order that good may result. Thus earthquakes, floods and hurricanes seem to be needed if Earth is to be what it is, so constituted that it can sustain life. The deaths which are parts of nature seem to be needed if life is to be what it is, needing to be fed, to be limited in numbers and to be replaced when worn out. Pain seems to be the price paid for the development of a complex nervous system and for the receipt of stern warnings against worst damage. Suffering seems to be the price paid for our own moral improvement: so often we can look back on suffering and see that enduring it made us braver, wiser, both more confident and more sympathetic. And if we feel that the evils which we experience are more than we need, we can reflect that many of the evils result from human failures, as when people fail to admit how dangerous living near a volcano, or using a bomb, motor car or cigarette, can be. Such thoughts do not solve the problem of evil. But they reduce it and they encourage a religiously minded person to ask whether, despite all the evil in it, the mysterious world around us is created by God with a good purpose.

These considerations arising from the aesthetic and moral senses are not proofs of God's reality despite the claims of some theologians or philosophers before science showed what proofs really are. But to many minds they remain pointers to God's reality. The argument against relying on them is that in fact they may point only to human feelings about beauty and goodness. Nature, it may be said (and said by extremely well-informed and sensitive people), is indifferent to the ideals and dreams of *homo sapiens*, because no less than all the other species *homo sapiens* is an accident in evolution, produced by blind chance, serving no purpose other than survival for a time. Steven Weinberg's interpretation of his knowledge as a physicist has become famous: "The more the universe seems comprehensible, the more it also seems pointless." But this feeling that *homo sapiens*, with all his finer feelings, is no more than a freak may itself be no more than a feeling.

This universe, for all its bewildering mystery, is where matter, life, consciousness and conscience emerged from earlier levels of reality. Modern science has revealed how marvellous it is that in its first three minutes the Big Bang started the processes which had this result. At point after point the processes could have been very slightly different, and if so would have made the result which we know – the result which means that we exist – impossible. This "anthropic principle" (so called because the end is the appearance of *anthropos* or Man) explains nothing and predicts nothing within the scope of science, and it proves nothing religiously. The whole process may have been nothing but a series of accidents brought together by regularities which have nothing to do with any divine will or plan or with any hope that we might emerge. But in all its stupendous size and mystery the process may also seem to be something like "fine tuning" in order to manufacture us in the end. The wonder remains and grows – not only wonder that anything exists rather than nothing, but wonder that we exist in a universe which is our home, together with wonder that we have the ability to understand our surroundings to an amazing extent and to view what seems beautiful or good as the most significant features in our surroundings. And when we wonder about these things, it may seem reasonable to treat our sense of being at home here, and our aesthetic and moral senses, as telescopes through which we can glimpse our infinitely mysterious Source. The conviction that we really do belong in the universe, and that the "ultimate reality" which we encounter is beautiful and good (as well as much more), has been experienced most intensely by the mystics. But many people – it may be, almost all – have this conviction to some degree because of their own feebler experience. "I am not here because of a process which is nothing but an accident. I belong and what I belong to is good." That simple conviction is deep in many people who may not have heard of the mystics, and who certainly do not intend to contribute to the literature of mysticism.

That may be called "religious" experience and it is widespread in the modern age of science, as in previous ages. One reason why it does not always lead to a confident belief in God the Creator is this: honest modern people know that there is a vast amount of chance in nature and history, crucially in the genetic mutations which move evolution forward. That often seems incompatible with the existence of God. It is asked how a God who is at least "beautiful" should cause or permit so much disorder, and how a God who is at least "good" should cause or permit so much damage, by causing or permitting so much chance. Inevitably much in the old argument for belief in God from the appearance of the world as having been "designed" in every detail is no longer convincing. But without pretending to be able to justify or understand every instance of disorder or damage, we can be helped by modern science to see that there is no alternative to a big role for dangerous chance if God is to create out of love.

The universe, and particularly humanity in it, must have a degree of independence and freedom if it is to be the worthy object of God's love. A love which dictates is no love. A perfect love which immediately reproduced perfection would have nothing to love because nothing would be different. But Christianity claims that God loves the free. Since for such a God control in every detail is ruled out, there is no alternative to a big role for chance if there is to be genuine novelty to improve the creation. Novelty emerges out of the chance of chemical changes such as those which cause mutations in genes. And novelty comes out of chance combinations of materials already existing: the more complex systems thus produced has new properties. When the genes of parents are joined by sexual intercourse in a manner which cannot be either controlled or predicted, an individual is born who combines the parents' identities but who is also new. However, it is unscientific to say that chance rules everywhere. Indeed, the process by which a new individual is formed is an astounding example of the regularity in nature, for the information stored at the moment of conception decides the whole of the new individual's physical growth on the stable basis of the parents' combined genes. Here is a very wonderful combination of chance and regularity – and it is a combination which, on the whole, works marvellously well. Religious believers ought to be grateful that God's method of creating novelty, previously unthinkable, has been made known by modern science.

I conclude that although a religious faith is somewhat like science (in that it depends on personal decisions, is influenced greatly by a community and has to use myths, models and metaphors which never fully match the reality it is trying to describe), it is also very unlike science. Its theories cannot be verified or falsified by precise observations and experiments. Religious faith is based on religious experience. It arises out of wonder at the sheer fact of existence. It marvels at the mysterious beauty of what exists, and it asks whether what exists can be admired in the exercise of the human sense of right and wrong. It is open to a "revelation" which is unlike a scientific observation or experiment. When after its experience it takes the leap of faith into a decision that God exists (or gods or a non-personal ultimate reality), and when it takes the further leap into the faith that the Creator is good, the wisdom of that decision cannot be proved or disproved – at least, not before death. The personal factor in a religious decision is much more important than in science. So is the influence of the opinions of other people. Unlike science, therefore, a faith cannot reasonably demand that everyone sufficiently interested and intelligent should accept its tested conclusions as the best accounts available of what is really there. A faith will appeal to some and not to others. Religion itself will seem natural to some and nonsense to others.

In the context of challenges by science I have to repeat that different styles of belief are inevitable if there is to be any religious faith. Christians (for example) will prefer different forms of Christianity. Within many agreements they will believe and spread different "gospels". In responding to scientific knowledge, one Christian will believe that the Creator has been revealed with considerable clarity in nature – but another will be much more suspicious of "natural theology", thinking that a special revelation must be granted by God if the enigma of nature is ever to be understood. One Christian will feel strengthened by science to love and admire nature as God's handiwork – but another, more akin to Job or Lear, will feel burdened by the mystery of suffering in the good God's creation, will ponder suggested answers and will be somewhat comforted by the hope of getting an answer after death. One Christian in the age of science will hear the story of the emergence and development of life in this universe without much surprise. Our whole planet will seem to be a kind of organism itself, producing, sustaining and developing life (the old Greek name Gaia has been applied to Earth so pictured). But another Christian will be amazed by the improbability of it all, bewildered by what seems to be supercolossal waste, astonished that novelty often emerges out of chance not design, reluctant to believe that the Creator has a detailed control. Basically there would seem to be differences of temperament, somewhat like the differences in the New Testament between those who saw continuities between Judaism and Christianity and those who found the only light in the One who had been crucified and crowned; or somewhat like the differences between the sunny and dark gospels of Luke and Mark.

Since that seems to be the intellectual situation for Christians who take modern science seriously, I now offer in outline one "gospel" as one possible way of thinking as a Christian within this situation.

A GOSPEL FOR THE AGE OF SCIENCE

If we decide to believe in God because of the evidence which has revealed him to us (although it is not proof), is it possible to have a deeper understanding of God because of what is revealed in Christ? I believe that it is. For me and for many others, the supreme moment of the Christian revelation is the crucifixion of Jesus. Is it possible to understand that moment better if we consider what is revealed by modern science? I believe that it is. The thought that the cross and the creation are connected is not original. Mark's gospel (15:33) says that at the time of the crucifixion "there was darkness over the whole land", Matthew's (27:51) that "the earth shook and the rocks were split". These touches in the story seem to be myths, which for us can carry the meaning that the life of Jesus now reaching its climax in death is significant for our whole understanding of nature, just as the picture of the sacred curtain in the temple being "torn in two, from top to bottom" seems to be a myth meaning that this death is a new beginning for religion. But I believe that the creation can also illuminate the cross. So I want to explore the possibility of a gospel which is expressed in a way that makes sense to the age of science. As once the Christian message was communicated to the audiences of the New Testament, so those who now carry the message have the duty as well as the right to speak in a language which may be understood today.

I have found that the key is the insight that God is involved as much in the creation as in the cross. The insight which was strengthened for many people by John Robinson's *Honest to God* was the vision of God as the "Ground of Being" and the source of the world we can see and touch – not as an old man in the sky. (In the history of theology this is known as panentheism: "God is in everything".) Of course in serious religious thought the image of God as "above" the world has always meant chiefly that God, being all-holy, must be spiritually and morally superior to the world, worthy to be worshipped "in spirit and truth" and in holiness. That image points to perfection – and the world is not perfect. The history of religion shows that it is less dangerous than the image of the fertility goddess, Mother Earth, the source of crops through rain and of children through sex. She is asked for her favours without much regard for what the Hebrew prophets and their heirs would teach as morality (sexual orgies could seem religious). But the history of religion also shows that very often the more spiritual and moral image of God as "above" nature has meant picturing him (it is a masculine image) as being above the sky, detached from Earth, aloof from human anxiety and suffering. This popular picture of God has been translated into philosophy (with some refinement) as the idea of the "unmoved Mover" or "First Cause". In the eighteenth century this idea developed into Deism, a movement which continues whenever it is believed that God caused the universe but then retired from activity. That is the image which is destroyed when it is believed that a man being crucified after a life of active love is the Son or Word of God.

A crucifixion is a very physical event: flesh is nailed down, lungs are paralysed. The world revealed by modern science is also very physical. It has no place for life or mind, spirit or soul, as a ghost-like substance existing with little or no connection with the soil or the body. Dispelling these illusions which have haunted human thought, science tells the true story. It is staggering. From a beginning which is thought to have been smaller than an atom to a universe which is known to be too vast to measure or imagine, from the sub-atomic particles to the mental and spiritual powers of genius in *homo sapiens*, the subsequent story is a continuous whole.

In the first three minutes of the universe's history after the "Big Bang" some fifteen billion years ago, the gases we call hydrogen and helium were formed. After half a million years or so, the universe was cool enough to allow atoms to form. A billion years later the force of gravity condensed clumps of matter into stars in their galaxies. Inside stars nuclear furnaces started up which made the remaining ninety chemical elements. Our own galaxy, the Milky Way, which contains about ten billion stars, formed. Old stars died and about five billion years ago our sun gathered carbon-rich debris flung from a dying star (a supernova) although almost all of it consists of the ferocious energy produced as hydrogen is converted into helium: it may be compared (very feebly) with a hydrogen bomb. About 4,500 million years ago our planet flew off the disc of molecules which formed around our sun's helium; it is related in size to the sun as a grain of sand is related to an orange. It ended up the right distance away, and the right size, to have an atmosphere which made its later history possible (unlike all the sun's other planets and our own satellite, the moon). On Earth iron, rock, water, sand, organisms, soil, plants and oxygen emerged. The elements of Earth's surface and its early methane-rich atmosphere combined to yield amino acids, which in their turn built up complex replicating molecules, leading to the proteins and to the nucleic acids, DNA and RNA, which control the proteins.

It was now a planet pregnant with life and about three billion years ago life was born in chemical events sheltered in soup-like water as energy beat down from the surrounding universe. The first living cells contained single filaments of DNA molecules arranged as genes, but they were able to function independently. A cell lives when it metabolizes, using energy to draw in elements from its environment, organizing those elements to maintain itself, discarding what is surplus and so producing more energy, dividing when it reaches a certain size and so reproducing its life. Emerging between a thousand and 700 million years ago, the first complex living being was a combination of cells that was capable of movement in water. Fishes developed backbones, jaws and fins. Coming out of the water perhaps 375 million years ago, an amphibious fish survived and its remote descendants began walking and flying. The reproduction of life by sex became more complex, and the higher forms of life, including birds, reptiles and (about 180 million years ago) mammals, were conceived when two cells each containing genes which carried instructions for hereditary characteristics fused as the male sperm entered the female egg (human life being male when one of the forty-six chromosomes is "Y"). This form of reproduction made possible another novelty – differences between individuals. The evolution of some apes (the Australopitheci) about four million years ago, probably in East Africa, led to the making of axes and fires perhaps a million years ago, and to the appearance of *homo sapiens* probably between 400 and 300 thousand years ago, although before fossilized skulls less than 50,000 years old can be studied even the experts disagree widely about dates. That is the picture which modern science sets alongside the biblical picture that Adam was made from dust. It is a picture no less marvellous than the myths of Genesis. If one believes in a God who reveals anything, one may say that this picture of Man as animated stardust was revealed.

But the crucifixion of Jesus was not only a physical event. Here was a man dying by choice, with courage, out of love. It was an act of the mental and spiritual powers. These powers, including self-consciousness, the ability to converse in verbal languages, ever-growing technical ability and ultimately the power of abstract thought, grew slowly as the ancestors of *homo sapiens* developed brains extraordinarily large in relation to their bodies. To people who have inherited such brains with such powers, that still mysterious development is what matters most in the whole story of evolution. And to Christians, what matters most in human history is the life of Jesus, made possible by the whole of what had gone before. So we can move towards a modern Christian interpretation of the ancient mythological picture that a woman called Wisdom (in the Hebrew Scriptures) or a person called the Son (in the New Testament) was God's agent in the creation. For a modern Christian, what was actually present from the start was the Creator's intention that the creation would one day produce a life which would express his wisdom and father-like love. A Christian who accepts science may say that the man who hung on the cross had taken about fifteen billion years to be formed and was the supreme point of a universe which observably is fifteen billion light-years wide.

A crucifixion results in a death. To the eye and to medical science, what is left is a stiffening corpse which will rot if not burned. To religious insight, however, another reality which is left is the mental or spiritual product of the life – the personality which can be taken into the spaceless and timeless condition called eternity. The personality which is capable of eternal life and which is called the "soul" in religious language can be known to others in this life only through the movement of the body. Even in self-consciousness, what we call the "mind" can be known only as the mental activity of our brains which are physical. Yet most of humanity has the constant conviction that our personalities are more than our bodies and more than our brains. That cannot be proved if others, or we ourselves, are sceptical, but it certainly can be felt and human life would be very different if that were not the case. Science, which has done much to demonstrate the physical basis of humanity, has also done something to show that the difference between physical, mental and spiritual levels of existence remains – and remains mysterious.

This mysterious relationship between the human being and the human body seems to be a clue to the relation of God and the world in the religious thought which takes full account of science. In our experience God cannot be separated from the world, for he cannot be known except through the world and its inhabitants. But the old and often revived image of "the world" as "God's body" has its dangers, for "God" is not another name for nature. From the fact that God cannot be known by us except through his creation, it does not follow that the world should be worshipped. All stars and planets will eventually be burned as their energy is exhausted. But the word "God" voices belief in a transcendent and eternal reality, whose existence, glorious beyond all that we normally call "existence", we can share. To that reality, a dying man can say: "Father, into your hands I commit my spirit" (Luke 23:46).

A crucifixion limits a man's freedom even before death. In fact physical freedom is almost completely ended as the nails are hammered in. The world revealed by science is a world in relation to which God (if he is real) has limited his power. Regularities in the created order may be compared with human laws and if God is real then he established them. The drama of nature includes a big role for chance: if God is real, this is the strange play where he is director. He made these decisions, it seems, because he wanted a creation which he could love and which could produce novelty, but they must prevent him from interfering in a way which would reverse his decisions. We do not understand all the regularities, let alone all the chances, so that it would be arrogant to rule out the possibility of every event which could be called a "miracle". A miracle occurs when a fresh decision by God, not chance, makes an event differ from the regularities of nature.

Clearly it is far easier for the influence of God to be exerted through the regularities of nature and through influence on human minds and spirits, and many modern religious thinkers have drawn the conclusion that this is the only power which God exerts. But at the foundations of the Christian Church lie the very strange events after the death of Jesus – events which led to the conviction that God had acted in a new way. The whole life of Jesus came to be seen as a new act of God. The central message of Jesus, that God would act in a new way so that his kingdom would "come", has been believed. And in the universe-sized background to the life of Jesus Christians have observed novelty emerging in evolution. It has emerged often and (after all the scientific explanations) often mysteriously. Moreover, looking back over their own lives many Christians would agree with Paul that "in everything God co-operates for good for those who love God and are called according to his purpose" (Romans 8:28). In Christian faith, such experiences should be allowed their value alongside the value of insisting on the regularities in a good creation. It seems wisest to preserve a sense of mystery when thinking about the work of God. Such a religious awe would not be out of keeping with the humility of true science. However, it can be agreed that the biggest *miraculum* (which is Latin for "object of wonder") is that the combination of regularity and chance in the universe has produced human beings who can love their Creator. The price of that miracle, Christians believe, has been the Creator's self-limitation, the sacrifice of his own freedom for the sake of the freedom of his creatures.

The crucifixion of Jesus was the self-sacrifice of a man

who became convinced that the cause of God demanded nothing less. The world as known before science, but as known in much greater detail after the revelation given through science, is a world which depends on sacrifices. Many people (including scientists) have often had to sacrifice themselves for the sake of what they think is true or right. Many people have had to sacrifice themselves if the regularities in nature were to be maintained for the ultimate good of humanity: processes under the soil cannot be altered so as to spare the people the effects of earthquakes, and a motor car out of control cannot be halted so as to save the life of a child. At the height of his vision of glory Paul reminds the Christians in Rome that they, too, are not rescued by miracles. They can be "treated like sheep for slaughter" as they experience affliction, hardship, persecution, hunger, nakedness, danger and the sword (8:35,36). Sheep being slaughtered are not the only living creatures that have had to sacrifice themselves in order to provide food for each other: the food-chain ("eat or be eaten") binds many creatures together. And ultimately all that lives has to pay a price for living: the mortality rate is a hundred per cent. Consequently this is a world of loss and pain. For many, the quantity and quality of loss and pain would make belief in the goodness of the Creator very difficult, if not impossible, were it not for the thought that God is involved in the suffering. The crucifixion of Jesus reveals not only the love of that man for his friends but also the love for us of the Creator whose love was embodied in him. The cross is like a placard which announces that the Creator is neither aloof nor immune from a world of suffering.

God's love is suffering love. That is not a thought which is expounded at any length in the New Testament, but it is at least implicit in the very frequent comparison between God's love and a parent's; and it has grown in modern times along with modern knowledge of the world's pain. It has come to seem the only answer big enough to match the pain. Here, many have found, is the only alternative to the conclusion that the world is full of pain because the world is empty of meaning. For many, it has become both possible and necessary to think of God the Father as the fellow-sufferer and as the One who suffers worst, although divine suffering must of course be different from all the pains we know. God has things done to him which he does not want and which frustrate his intentions. These things include very great tragedies. Therefore he can sympathize with us. That vision has a long history, partly in the Bible, although it first dawned clearly over the battlefields of the First World War, sometimes as a blood-red dawn rose over a shattered wayside crucifix. It is the only vision that can begin to illuminate Auschwitz, Hiroshima or the killing fields of Cambodia. In the age of the Napoleonic wars William Blake saw it:

> He doth give His joy to all;
> He becomes an infant small;
> He becomes a man of woe;
> He doth feel the sorrow too.

> Think not thou canst sigh a sigh,
> And thy Maker is not by;
> Think not thou canst weep a tear,
> And thy Maker is not near.

> O! He gives to us His Joy
> That our grief he may destroy,
> Till our grief is fled and gone
> He doth sit by us and moan.

The crucifixion of Jesus was apparently the waste of a life. His followers were (to put it mildly) disappointed. His enemies were triumphant. Science has done much to reveal the apparent waste in nature. Believers in God are (to put it mildly) puzzled. But that "waste" of a life made possible a victory for Jesus which would have been impossible without his union with the defeated and the dead. Looking back in the knowledge of that victory, John could see that the crucifixion was itself glorious, the time when God's work was "accomplished" (19:30). In this light, the claim of Christianity is not to explain everything in nature or in human history. It is to have grounds for the hope that in the end it will be seen that it was better to have had existence, with all its mysterious ingredient of suffering, than to have had nothing (no creation) at all. Even the "waste" will be seen to be justified by being seen as contributions to the accomplishment of God's purpose – the accomplishment which in the New Testament has the image of the kingdom of God. The truth of Paul's short history of the universe will then become clear: "the whole created universe in all its parts groans as if in the pangs of childbirth" (Romans 8:22).

The crucifixion of Jesus was intended by him not as a stimulus to theological or philosophical speculation but as a challenge to his followers to "take up" their own crosses in order to enter that kingdom. The world as known before science, but as known much more fully in the light of science, is a world full of practical and very urgent challenges to the whole of humanity. These challenges amount to nothing less than a summons to all human beings to be co-creators with God, not only taking care of the creation entrusted to us but also improving it. In that sense the humblest worker is God's colleague, given authority as a world-manager. But in our time the co-creators face a crisis which cannot be ignored or escaped. It is true (no less true for having been repeated so often) that after some fifteen billion years of evolution in this universe, the technology of the millennium about to begin could create something like a paradise; yet suddenly we see that it is possible that war and pollution will wreck the higher forms of life on the only planet where life is known to us. If the history of the universe is to be represented by a book of about 3,500 pages, the whole of recorded human history is included on the last page within the last two or three letters, and if the history of the planet Earth be represented by forty-eight hours, the ape-like ancestor of *homo sapiens* has stood on his feet within the last minute, and the science-based industrial revolution has occurred within the last second. The possibility of a last-letter, last-second, Man-made catastrophe is the crisis. A response to God's love, supremely revealed by the crucifixion of Jesus, must be action to serve, not the trends which move towards that catastrophe, but God's government of Earth. In some ancient manuscripts of Matthew's gospel (16:3) the question is asked: "You know how to interpret the appearance of the sky; can you not interpret the signs of the times?" In Luke's gospel (23:28) Jesus on his way to his crucifixion warns: "Daughters of Jerusalem, do not weep for me; weep for yourselves and your children."

God's Government

THE QUESTION OF THE KINGDOM

THE diversity which we have observed in Christianity from
New Testament times onwards has arisen partly because
the central message of Jesus of Nazareth has always seemed
to need interpretation. It was about the "kingdom" of God.
The phrase was wide open to misunderstanding even as
Jesus used it. Heard as an actual or potential call to rebellion
against Rome in Jerusalem, it so alarmed the colonial
authorities that he was executed. So he paid for it with his
life. After his death its continued use still caused trouble,
for it was still easy to associate it with the hope that the
glorious "kingdom of David" might be re-established after
the political liberation of the Jews. Luke's gospel begins with
a pious circle expressing that hope in connection with the
births of John the Baptist and Jesus, and the Acts of the
Apostles begins with the question: "Lord, is this the time
when you are to restore the sovereignty of Israel?" (1:6).
The phrase was so easily misunderstood that the two greatest thinkers in first-century Christianity, Paul and John,
made little use of it.

It kept a place in the vocabulary of the early Christian

movement, however; the readers or hearers of the written gospels were expected to understand it, at least to some extent. It was retained because it indicated a hope. This hope was not that the Jews would recover their political sovereignty. It was that the whole of the world was about to be transformed, when Jesus the Messiah would return in royal power and glory. As we have seen, this was the hope which inspired the mother church in Jerusalem even as it continued to be thoroughly Jewish. The hope equally excited the church in Thessalonica, and Paul's earliest surviving letters were written in order to instruct the new Christians not to be so absorbed in the hope that they stopped working. But we have also watched the excitement dying down as the triumphant return of Jesus, in Greek *parousia*, was delayed. Some Christians came to believe that "the Day of the Lord is already here" (2 Thessalonians 2:2), but that did not conceal the disappointment. As generation has succeeded generation in the history of the Christian Church, this problem of the non-appearance of the kingdom has obviously increased, despite many moments of renewed excitement that the promise at the end of the Revelation of John, "Yes, I am coming soon!', was about to be fulfilled. In modern or post-modern days honest Christians have to face the question whether the hope needs to be revised drastically and openly.

Part of the growing problem has been the incredibility of the traditional imagery of the kingdom. At the beginning of the Revelation of John, this imagery is neatly assembled: "Look, he is coming with the clouds; everyone shall see him, including those who pierced him; and all the peoples of the world shall lament in remorse. So it shall be" (1:7). But increasingly it has been felt, by Christians among others, that so it cannot be. The imagery depends for its effectiveness on the picture of heaven above the clouds, with Earth small and flat so that it might be imagined that a glorified man descending to it could be seen by everyone. That picture was finally shattered when space travel began. Even in its smashed condition it remains on the wall of the Church (so to speak) because it remains in the Bible and in traditional hymns and prayers, but few modern Christians are as excited by it as the Thessalonians were in Paul's day. And many modern people are frankly contemptuous. Like the traditional imagery of hell, this picture of the Second Coming has ceased to terrify sinners. It has caused some amusement.

In the background to the traditional imagery has been the picture of a universe physically glorified. Those Christians who have taken literally the hope of the Revelation of John (20:1–6) that Christ and the saints would reign on Earth for a thousand years have often formed "millennarian" movements in anticipation of that glory. Other Christians have been fascinated by Paul's hope that "the universe itself is to be freed from the shackles of mortality and is to enter upon the glorious liberty of the children of God" (Romans 8:21). Probably most modern Christians have not been literalist in their hopes for "a new heaven and a new earth" when "the first heaven and the first earth had vanished" (Revelation 21:1), but it has still been difficult to fit the picture of a glorified universe into the predictions of science.

Scientists' predictions have to some extent confirmed the expectation of the Second Letter of Peter that the End "will set the heavens ablaze until they fall apart, and will melt the universe in flames" (3:12), for our planet is expected to be absorbed one day by gravitation back into the fiery sun which will then be about fifty times larger ("a red giant"). But science with its "law" of entropy has added the prediction that ultimately the sun will itself cease to be luminous, its energy exhausted, ending ignominiously as a "black dwarf". Eventually all the stars will burn themselves out although it seems possible that new stars, similarly mortal, will be formed in an infinite succession – if the expectation is wrong that the entire universe will one day implode in the "Big Crunch". The early Christian document just quoted assured its readers: "Relying on his promise we look forward to a new heaven and a new earth, in which justice will be established" (3:13). But probably few modern Christians rely on the future appearance of a universe where the permanent glory will be physical.

It is understandable that the gap left in the Christian imagination and enthusiasm has been filled with a variety of substitutes for the New Testament's kingdom. Within the New Testament it was said that the kingdom which was still expected to come speedily on Earth was already flourishing in heaven, and that entry into the kingdom on Earth was in spiritual reality entry into eternal life. We have already found that both Paul and John taught that. So, in a less exciting way, did the Early Catholics. The development was encouraged when later generations took Matthew's use of the term "kingdom of Heaven" – a term originating in the Jewish feeling that it was irreverent to refer too directly to God – to mean that the kingdom was confined to heaven, meaning eternity. But at that point the development went too far to be loyal to the teaching of Jesus, for as we have seen, the New Testament shows that Jesus taught about a kingdom to come on Earth as in heaven – not one which only the dead could enter.

There have been many attempts to translate the idea of the "kingdom of God" into hopes about life on Earth. The Christian Church has itself often been claimed to be the kingdom for all practical purposes, despite the clear teaching of its Lord and despite its own far from perfect record. When

Christians have acknowledged that the message of Jesus concerned a wider kingdom more than the Church, and have also faced up to the Church's frequent misbehaviour, they have often transferred imagination and enthusiasm to movements in society. The emperor Charlemagne propagated the dream that the Holy Roman Empire would fulfil the Bible's promises. The Byzantine emperors tried to keep alive the world-dominating dream of the first Christian emperor, Constantine. When medieval Christendom disintegrated, similar propaganda surrounded the nation states and in particular their colonial enterprises. When colonies achieved independence it was often amid dreams of a new age, beginning in the USA as eighteenth-century optimism adapted the hopes of the Puritans. "Nation building" in the twentieth-century Third World has been supported by many Christians with a similar enthusiasm – as has been "the building of socialism". Even capitalism has had its Christian devotees. There was a time when Fascism recruited Christians. But as the twentieth century ends it is hard to find Christians who still nurse such illusions. The performances of the political and social movements which have offered themselves as substitutes for the New Testament's kingdom have been too savage or too sordid.

The question therefore remains: how is the twenty-first Christian century to interpret the central message of Jesus of Nazareth, about the kingdom of God? What are the permanent essentials of that message? If there can be an answer, presumably it will supply a message which the Christians of the future can share with the world – and will provide dynamite to set the Christians' own lives moving in the direction to which Christian faith points. We are not looking for information about exactly when and how the persistent dream of glory is to come true. As we saw, Jesus himself disclaimed knowledge of the date of the End, with a modesty

which not all Christians have copied; and his vision of the
kingdom was expressed with imagery which now seems to
us antique. But we are looking for a kingdom to which
people can be asked to sacrifice much, without hesitation or
pretence, as the parables of Jesus urged.

A BANQUET IN A LAND

The idea of the kingdom of God begins with the promise of
a better land. That promise goes back to the Hebrew Bible,
which tells the story of the entry of the tribes of Israel into
the land of Canaan (Palestine) as promised to the ancestors,
Abraham, Isaac and Jacob, and to the Liberator, Moses. A
vision of Canaan in Deuteronomy (8:7–9) has remained
famous. It is the poetry of physical delight: "Your God is
bringing you into a good land, a land with streams, springs
and underground waters gushing out in valley and hill, a
land of wheat and barley, vines, fig trees and pomegranates,
a land with olive oil and honey. It is a land where you will
never suffer any scarcity of food to eat, nor want for anything, a land whose stones are iron ore and from whose hills
you will mine copper." A farmer's creed is preserved in
Deuteronomy (26:5–10) which celebrates the deeds of the
God of Israel who brought the tribes "out of Egypt with a
strong hand". That creed still conveys the delight of Israel
that it was no longer a "homeless small company". Many
modern scholars, however, add a commentary on it: they
believe that the exodus from Egypt through the "Reed Sea"
(originally not the Red Sea) was made possible by a wind
temporarily drying a marsh, and that the naming of the
tribes, and their solemn federation, took place within
Canaan when the Hebrews had taken over much of the land
with considerably less violence than was suggested in their
boastful folk-tales.

In that land the tribes settled. In their more expansive moments they dreamed of a wider territory, and one promise ascribed to God, almost certainly in the time of the Israelites' short-lived unity and prosperity under King Solomon, covers all the land from the Nile to the Euphrates (Genesis 15:18). But in their tragic history the Israelites were not able to keep even their own land. The northern kingdom fell to the Assyrians, the southern to the Babylonians. Archaeological evidence suggests that even while the Israelites were independent the influences on them of the Egyptians, the Canaanites and the Philistines were far stronger than they liked to record in their heroic literature. Eventually a remnant returned from exile in the Babylonian empire, and after many delays a little state was constructed around the temple in Jerusalem, only to be subject first to Hellenistic attempts to stamp out the old-fashioned religion and then to Roman conquest and destruction. It was in reaction to these tragedies that the hope of a "kingdom of God" was born, to console and to inspire. Much of the "apocalyptic" literature which communicated this hope did so by elaborating the picture of a good land, miraculously better than Canaan itself. In the kingdom which the God of Israel would at last create and govern, wine would flow instead of water, milk and honey would be inexhaustible, gold would replace iron and copper.

That tradition was taken into the teaching of Jesus through the image of the banquet. One change then made has separated Christianity from the belief of religiously minded Zionists that the biblical prophecies were mainly fulfilled by the establishment of the state of Israel in 1948. The change is indicated by the prophecy that occurs in the thoroughly Jewish gospel of Matthew (8:11): "Many will come from east and west to sit with Abraham, Isaac and Jacob at the banquet in the kingdom of heaven." Elsewhere it is stressed that the "many" include women. In accordance

with the startling new habits of table-fellowship practised
by Jesus, they are no longer to be only cooks and waitresses.
And the "many" include foreigners who remain foreign, in
a no less revolutionary development of the Jewish hope that
Gentiles would come as respectful pilgrims to Jerusalem in
the great day when Israel would be vindicated. Before long
it was seen to be in keeping with the spirit of Jesus that
Gentiles should be admitted to the Church without becoming Jews, because they would be admitted to God's kingdom.
In the end the most discerning Christians have seen that
each nation's history is its own Old Testament, with its own
exodus from slavery – as was glimpsed in the Hebrew Bible
when the story was told of Jonah's indignant discovery of
God's love and care for the Assyrian capital Nineveh, or
when Amos (9:7) heard God asking:

> Did I not bring Israel up from Egypt,
> and the Philistines from Caphtor, the Aramaeans
>   from Kir?

The image of the banquet is of course both physical and
corporate: food and drink are consumed by bodies with
pleasure and in company. It is strange that although this
image is so prominent in the parables and sayings in the
gospels – and is lifted up in the Easter stories of Luke and
John when the risen Jesus appears at meals in Emmaus, in
Jerusalem and on the shore by the lake – in the history of
Christian spirituality other images have been preferred. The
Christian life has been imagined as a climb up a ladder
away from earth and flesh, or as an arduous and lonely
journey (Bunyan's *Pilgrim's Progress*, for example), or as a
battle against "the world, the flesh and the Devil". Such a
life ends in the solitary escape of a soul from the body. Of
course there is value in those images also; they will always

mean much to those for whom life is a struggle. But the twentieth century, although often thought of as a totally degenerate age so far as Christianity is concerned, has moved back to the main emphasis of Jesus. The spiritual teachers most representative of the best in our time have seen that God who created the human body and the human community on this planet did not make a mistake. Indeed, he began the programme of his government by blessing those physical and corporate realities. This growing emphasis in teaching about the Christian life ("creation spirituality") has been one of the inspirations of the return to the centrality of the Eucharist in Christian worship. There, the disciples of Jesus come together, as he commanded, in order to "eat and drink at my table" in anticipation of the greater party "when the kingdom of God comes" (Luke 22:18,30).

This emphasis on the physical and the corporate in the kingdom of God still seems essential if the idea is to be realistic about human life. But precisely because of the need for realism, it does not seem essential for Christians to take literally all the Bible's pictures of the coming glory. A Christian agreement ought to concentrate on what can be believed by all Christians, including those who are not fundamentalists. Let me suggest an outline of this.

The twentieth century is bequeathing many problems to its successor, but at least it leaves behind a Christian vision which strongly affirms that the body and the planet are the gifts of God, not smaller and larger prisons. For many twentieth-century people, a firm "yes" to the body and to Earth has become spiritually necessary, because everyday work has exercised the mind rather than the body and everyday surroundings have been urban rather than rural. Modern life had been in obvious danger of being cut off from its physical roots, and the modern spirit has begun to wither in the condition often analysed as stress or anxiety.

But Christians, in addition to sharing in the widespread alarm about modernity's alienation from nature, have had a special motive for their own "yes" to the body and the planet. This has been inherited through Jesus from the main tradition in Judaism, which has always refused to join those religions and philosophies which advocate an escape from the physical. In Genesis (9:6) are words about the dignity of the human body which, it seems, were recited when a murderer was executed:

> Anyone who sheds human blood,
> for that human being his blood will be shed;
> because in the image of God
> has God made human beings.

But the idea behind those words has also encouraged the abolition of capital punishment. This chant is quickly followed in Genesis by God's agreement with Noah and his sons. "I am now establishing my covenant with you and with your descendants after you, and with every living creature that is with you, all birds and cattle, all the animals with you on Earth . . ." (9:13,14). In psalms such as 65 or 104 (and elsewhere) scriptural expression is given on a magnificent scale to the celebration of nature. And in the Song of Songs scriptural approval is given to the joy of sex, the beauties of human bodies seen through the eyes of love and compared in sensuous detail with those beauties of nature. A long and entirely healthy-minded Jewish tradition supports the lifestyle of Jesus, the mystic who closely observed his fellow villagers, the prophet who was criticized as "a glutton and a drinker" and the celibate who was the friend of women with a strong sexuality (Luke 7:34).

The recovery of this positive attitude, so sadly forgotten by much that has been negative in Christianity, will give the next century's Christians a starting point. They will share the human movement into man-made towns and cities but they will start in a world which is seen by its Creator as good.

Genesis, which clearly affirms all that in its first chapter, also knows how great was "the wickedness of human beings on earth, and how their every thought and inclination were always wicked" (6:5). Jesus did not need to be reminded of this continuing reality as he rose from table to go to his cross. The celebration of the creation in much twentieth-century Christian spirituality would be unrealistic if it had not been accompanied by many struggles against the century's notorious misuse of the creation. Most Christians, seeing the effects of modern war, have ceased to take wars for granted. When the century opened it was widely taught and believed in the churches that a nation which declared war had an automatic and sacred right to the support or acquiescence of its citizens. When the European nations went to war in 1914 pacifism crumbled quickly. As the century closes pacifism has not become the position of the majority of Christians. It is still believed that Christians may rightly be among those making the agonizing decision that a war against an aggressor, waged with an international mandate and with the minimum necessary use of force, may be the lesser of two evils. What has changed profoundly has been the end of the old acceptance of war. Similarly, it is still widely believed that Christians may be among those choosing, as the last resort, to reply to unjust oppressors who use violence by using violence in a rebellion. But the use of non-violent civil disobedience is seen to be preferable wherever that has a real chance of ending the tyranny.

Most Christians have also become aware of peacetime scandals such as the fact that some 500 million human beings began the 1990s seriously undernourished, while many other millions were dangerously overweight. Many Christians have involved themselves in struggles to end that obscenity. Christians have been troubled as deeply as anyone else by the new form of mass suicide (appealing to the privileged as well as to the desperately poor), drug abuse. Indeed, for many young Christians around the world *not* to be "on drugs" has been the chief affirmation that life is not a bore and the chief declaration of discipleship. Christians have learned fresh reasons for maintaining their fights against addiction to alcohol and addiction to gambling – addictions which have become compulsive for many millions. By other tragedies of our time Christians have learned about the penalties attached to heavy smoking in the age of cancer, and to the lust for speed in the age of murder on the roads. Many eyes have been opened to the evils of such behaviour which destroys the body which is the creation's crown. And many consciences have been awakened to see the human destruction of the environment. Non-Christians have of course been active in all these concerns, but Christians have had a special motive for responsibility. According to this faith, to touch the body or this planet is to touch the fragile work of God – the work through which the Creator has embodied or "made incarnate" his love. To take care of the human body by proper food, exercise and rest is to take care of something in which God takes pride. And to understand the marvellous ecosystems of nature, so vast yet so intricate, is to understand something of the Creator's work. It is to worship.

In Genesis (1:28) Adam is given "dominion over the fish in the sea, the birds of the air and every living thing that moves on the earth". In a psalm (8:5,6) God is praised for sharing his own dominion with "a frail mortal":

You have made him little less than a god,

crowning his head with glory and honour.
You make him master over all that you have made,
putting everything in subjection under his feet . . .

In its early days modern science was celebrated as a new gift of God, a new way of achieving that biblically promised dominion over nature. Such ideas have recently been attacked as endorsing the rape of nature, and it is a fact that even before the industrial revolution and the application of science to agriculture, "dominion" often meant destruction. Readers of the Bible will recall the glories of the cedars of Lebanon, almost all of which have been cut down without being replaced. Innumerable trees met the same fate, as in Europe or China. Deserts spread, as in North Africa. Species were destroyed, as by hunters in North America. But the danger was not on anything like the scale which has now rightly alarmed all thoughtful people, including Christians. Now people watch with horror the poisoning of earth, water and air and the destruction of forest and ozone. Now people ask whether carbon dioxide could make Earth uninhabitable – and can be told of the thick yellow clouds of that gas which surround the planet Venus, Earth's nearest neighbour.

In this unprecedented crisis, proposals for abdication from human "dominion" – "leaving nature alone" – are understandable. But as is often pointed out in the Third World, this ultra-green vision appeals only to those who can afford the luxury of sentimentality, for it ignores the problem of feeding the billions. To be realistic, *homo sapiens* has to increase his dominion by increasing his knowledge of nature and his technical, organizational and financial capacity to repair the damage done to nature, and to develop sustainable sources of energy, food and materials with full knowledge of the ecological consequences. Obviously in this new crisis much of the response must be new – for example, in the infant science of biotechnology. Many Christians would add that new contraceptive pills or devices must be used if the human population is to be kept at a size which can be fed. But the ancient idea of the kingdom of God is not irrelevant to the modern or post-modern world as it works out new ways of "dominion". To acknowledge the Creator's right to govern is to acknowledge limits to humanity's right to use the creation. To acknowledge humanity's need of God's control is to acknowledge the wickedness present, if not dominant, in every human thought and inclination. To acknowledge God's invitation to humanity to enjoy the blessings of his government is to acknowledge that humanity is not doomed to destroy what God has made through the processes of nature. And to acknowledge the gentle character of God's government, shown by the almost unbelievable patience of his non-interference with those processes, is to acknowledge that humanity must learn to be very sensitive and cautious if it does interfere. Dominion exercised under the government of God would do no harm to God's good creation, for it would not be a brutally selfish domination.

A banquet needs to be cooked. Even the simplest meal is the work of human hands: at every Eucharistic meal of bread and wine that ought to be remembered, as twentieth-century Christians have increasingly known. But for most of history it has been very difficult to persuade the men and women who have done most of the world's work that their work was more than a burden. In Genesis (3:16–19) work is seen as a curse. Eve the housewife is cursed in that she both desires and serves her husband. Childbearing brings "great labour" and so does child rearing. Adam is cursed in that he must win his bread by the sweat of his brow amid thorns and thistles. It has seemed unrealistic to talk about work as co-creation and therefore a worthy expression of the dignity of

humanity as the image of God. Only for some of the time
have some people who have enjoyed parenting or cooking,
or the other work of hand or brain, glimpsed that self-
fulfilment. But in the twenty-first century work may be
slightly easier to see as a call and a blessing. The technology
developed in the twentieth century has made the abolition
of drudgery in factory or office astonishingly possible in
the industrial or post-industrial nations. The more labour-
intensive technology which is still appropriate in poorer
countries, because it provides jobs and incomes, is more
dignified than the use of human beings as muscle-power.
And the green revolution which is transforming agriculture
can give the farmer a new sense of dignity. Education has
become a necessity in the countryside. The challenge to
the farmer's intelligence is how to produce more without
damaging the soil or the animals, and the rewards held out
to the farmer's ambition are beginning to be substantial. It
is a verdict on the success of the new agriculture that
between 1970 and 1990 a billion extra mouths were fed, and
life expectancy in the "developing countries" taken as a
whole increased between 1950 and 1990 from forty to sixty
years. Those are some of the statistics of the modern dawn
of the kingdom of God.

Science leaves it an open question, whether *homo sapiens*
can learn well and quickly enough to survive. There are
warnings in the record. The dinosaurs were lords of Earth
for about 150 million years – and became extinct. Neanderthal man ruled Europe for about fifty thousand years – and
died out. Probably the changes in the climate caused these
disappearances from history, but now human survival is
threatened not so much by the environment itself as by
emotions preventing behaviour suitable to the environment.
After a long history as a hunter, *homo sapiens* has a fierce
loyalty to a fairly small group defending a territory and a

taste for the violence of the hunt; and after being given evolutionary advantages by breeding vigorously and staying together as man and woman to rear the young, *homo sapiens* remains the sexiest of animals. Today, these territorial and sexual imperatives have no biological value unless they are disciplined in order that a sustainable population may face the tasks of survival in peace. But it is obvious that *homo sapiens* is not finding the required mental and spiritual evolution easy. That is why so many who are not attached to any religious organization feel, perhaps vaguely, that the help of religion is needed if in the next millennium there is to be anything at all like a banquet in the promised land.

GOVERNMENT AND SEXUALITY

Such is a possible modern interpretation of the Bible's use of the image of the banquet to suggest the physical basis of life under the government of God. But what can be said about the life itself? I offer some brief suggestions which I believe reflect a widespread agreement between Christians, although the well-known controversies point to the need to recognize Christian diversity. I concentrate on the role of government and the nature of sexuality. These are subjects whose importance in human welfare or misery during the twentieth century needs no comment: when utterances by religious leaders get reported in the modern media, it is usually because they have touched on politics or sex. People's reactions may be exasperated. Sometimes it is said that religion ought to have nothing to do with politics. Sometimes it is said that the clergy ought to stop being negative about sexuality. But a government by God which did not deal with both these realities would be a farce. To discuss them is not an anticlimax for a theology which has concentrated mainly on Jesus and his Father, the Creator of all that exists.

The twentieth century's political tragedies, although obvious enough, still deserve to be listed and pondered. The pompous European empires, full of Christian symbols but not so full of Christian lives, armed themselves against each other in a way which led to 1914. Communism offered an illusory Paradise when those empires had been bankrupted and discredited, and Fascism appealed as an alternative to inflation, unemployment and humiliation. Europeans often vainly resisted the independence of their colonies; and their ex-colonies, perpetuating the frontiers drawn on the colonial maps and forced to remain economically dependent under neocolonialism, vainly hoped for unity and prosperity after freedom. In their disillusionment these new nations usually accepted regimes which relied on the army, the police, a single party and corruption rather than on ability in economics. The gap between the rich and the poor nations steadily widened. The rich nations developed much new technology but could not provide enough jobs for their citizens. They created unprecedented wealth but in the opinion of many could not create either justice or happiness. The one realistic hope of the poor nations was that the rich might buy more and more of their primary products, selling in exchange machines, manufactures, technical information, loans and (here comes another tragedy) arms. But the rapidly growing populations of the poor nations needed more food than could be grown and more medicine than could be afforded; and rich and poor countries were united by the problem that Earth's resources were being exhausted or polluted. It is a story which contradicts optimism and confirms the Bible's gloomier verdicts on the character and prospects of humanity. It also supports the Bible's insistence that if God is to govern humanity, it must be because that is his will, not because that is the result of accelerating human success.

However, the legacy of the twentieth century will not be completely poisonous. There have been developments in it which may be interpreted as signs of the dawning kingdom of God amid the storm clouds. Popular participation in government has grown despite many reversals, and has been helped by popular knowledge of the misdeeds of the powerful as reported by the media. All adults (excluding criminals, peers of the realm and lunatics) have been allowed to vote, even if the elections have been rigged and the electorates drugged by lying propaganda. Even regimes which have been monstrously cruel to their own peoples have thought it best to call themselves "democracies". This spread of democracy has in the end been welcomed by all the responsible spokesmen of the Christian Churches, despite a long history of preference for more authoritarian regimes. Although many passages in the Bible glorify kings and urge obedience, twentieth-century Christians have paid more attention to passages which teach that the only ruler fit to be entrusted with absolute power is God, since God "is love". The vision has grown that in the government of God there is no room for human dictators, not even for dictatorship exercised in the name of the people or the proletariat.

New forms of human government have emerged which have been somewhat more successful than earlier forms in exercising power in the genuine interests of the governed. Small nations and semi-independent regions within nations have been valued as supports for a much-prized diversity of cultures. Large communities of nations have been accepted as guaranteeing peace and as providing more adequate markets for mass-produced goods and more adequate resources for finance and development. Out of these economic communities unions have begun to grow, with their new forms of organization supplementing or challenging the old authority of the nation-state. Bloodsoaked Western Europe has become the scene of such a growth, while the collapse of the Soviet Union and its empire have been warnings against the imposition of uniformity. The Middle East, where the hope of the kingdom of God was first preached, is only one of the regions where an economic union in the twenty-first century seems the alternative to something very much worse. And the work of the United Nations, despite many manifest weaknesses and failures, has begun to persuade the nations to give priority to the economic tasks of peace which confront humanity as such. Despite many refusals either to understand or to agree, the rich and the poor nations have maintained a dialogue, usually under UN auspices, because they know that they need each other as they begin to see the difficulties of the economic tasks. Despite much acquiescence in the diversion of scarce resources to military and prestige expenditure, both the rich and the poor nations have begun to see that the economic tasks have the inescapable priority; that the war which really matters is against poverty. Despite the dangers of nuclear proliferation, the superpowers' arms race is over. None of these fragile developments is any substitute for the vision of God's reign "on Earth as in heaven". But each is a fraction of that perfect government.

It is widely and sadly agreed that national governments have persistently done either too little or too much in their control over their economies. If they have allowed market forces to operate without restraint (*laissez faire*) they have abdicated from their responsibility to secure survival at an acceptable standard of living for all their citizens – the responsibility which is repeatedly proclaimed in the Hebrew and Christian Bibles as justice for the poor. If they have gathered so much power into their own bureaucratic hands that enterprise and hard work by producers have not been stimulated, their peoples have suffered as much as under governments which have failed to govern. But this century also leaves behind a growing agreement that this choice between disasters, and the sterile debate about the choice, can be avoided. The agreement is not what the New Left proposed when disillusionment with old-style Socialism became general, for the New Left's dislike of all institutions was utopian. Nor is the agreement what the New Right advocated, for the New Right's dislike of government (except when the government was enforcing New Right policies) was also utopian. A third way between Left and Right is open if a government seeks justice first, and knows that justice involving massive public expenditure must be made possible by the profits which can be gained by all as competition in a free market stimulates the production of the goods which consumers want. That is a way which most Christians who could choose have chosen. It is a way which the twenty-first century could take. But no agreement about the details of economic policy has been reached by Christians. Nor is any such agreement either necessary or desirable. When an individual politician or political party appeals for support as being "Christian" there are dangers of hypocrisy, and if the appeal helps to secure political success there are dangers of corruption. A diversity of Christian approaches to day-to-day political and economic problems seems safer. It should not be attacked as "unbiblical", because no detailed political or economic programme is included in the New Testament, as we have seen; there is not the detail that may be found in the Quran and in Muslim legislation inspired by that holy book. A vision of the kingdom of God based on the teaching of Jesus must always be different from any political or economic creed. It is a vision of a glory which shines on Earth from eternity and which endures in eternity when politics and economics are over.

It is a tragic fact that as the twenty-first century draws near no plan has been worked out which will lead to a sustainable prosperity for the rich and to a sustainable life for the poor, without a morally intolerable gap between the two categories of human beings. The causes of this failure are obvious. The rich are seldom sufficiently prepared for any sacrifices. The poor are seldom willing to learn enough from the methods by which the rich have prospered. Each group trusts, without adequate evidence, that Earth's resources will enable present habits to be prolonged. But inexorably such stupidities are checked by the knowledge that the richer and the poorer must survive together or not at all. The richer need the poorer as suppliers of raw materials and markets; the poorer need the richer as purchasers of goods and suppliers of capital and know-how. Both groups will benefit if in the future that often rare commodity, commonsense, can be in better supply, seeing which of Earth's resources can be used safely so as to provide which food products and which manufactured goods; seeing where these products can be produced at the lowest cost to the consumer when the costs and limits of energy-resources have been reckoned realistically; and seeing where free trade is to the advantage of all, and where it has to be limited in order to protect the livelihood of the vulnerable. Already in this mostly stupid century such rethinking has begun and the need for it has been acknowledged in theory almost everywhere. Christian contributions to the intellectual and practical tasks which constitute the next century's agenda can be inspired by the hope of God's kingdom without any pretence that the tasks are not new. Once again the political relevance of the biblical vision becomes clear. It feeds faith and supplies energy. It does not claim that human progress will be automatic. It does not offer a panacea to solve all problems or legislate to cover all details: it allows and encourages a diversity of efforts to interpret and serve the vision. It does say that in the end God's will shall be done and that human co-operation counts. That is the vision which haunts all failures and all successes.

It is no accident that some of the banquets which are presented in the gospels as images of the kingdom are wedding feasts. Sexuality and its fruit, children, are often celebrated in the Scriptures as the best of the Creator's gifts through nature. The letter to the Ephesians compares marriage with Christ's love for the Church (5:25–33). From the time when Adam and Eve were ashamed to be naked, sexuality is also treated in the Bible as a cause of misery – which is no less realistic. In the land which is promised to those who are willing to enter the kingdom, the driving power of sexuality, reproducing life for the last 900 million years, has to be governed by God. And it is not unreasonable that church leaders should be scrutinized as they propound sexual morality. If they are felt to be mistaken in this field, they lose credibility when they also offer opinions on political and economic problems which they are not expected to understand in detail.

The twentieth century is bequeathing many disasters in this area, culminating in AIDS, which in the next century seems bound to devastate many millions of lives, mostly in the Third World. But this century also leaves behind a new vision of what sexuality may become – a more glorious, because more humane, vision than any seen in earlier history. The growing equality between women and men means that modern or post-modern marriage must be essentially friendship based on the mutual enjoyment of sex (meaning the ecstasies of intercourse but also very much more), in contrast with the understanding customary in most old societies that the function of the woman was to serve her husband's physical and economic needs and to bear and rear his children. "Women", said the letter to the Ephesians (5:24), "must be subject to their husbands in everything".

The new understanding of marriage must greatly increase human happiness, but it has produced yet another example of Christian diversity. Many Christians continue to believe that the marriage vows are indissoluble, and this belief has rescued many marriages from dissolution, often (although not always) with happy results. But many other Christians now think that it has become necessary to recognize that some married friendships either die or never begin except in the legal formalities and the physical intercourse.

As we have seen, it was a part of the revolutionary attitude of Jesus towards women that he condemned the Jewish law allowing husbands to divorce their wives (it might be for a trivial cause) as contrary to the Creator's purpose for the sexes. But already in New Testament times this teaching by "the Lord" was not being taken as a completely binding law. Some Christians continue to hold that the only legitimate reason for ending a legal marriage arises when it was not a true marriage: it was never consummated or there was a very serious defect in the intention of one or both of the partners. That is a position to be respected, because it is inspired by loyalty to the teaching of Jesus. But during the twentieth century (as is shown by many studies of public opinion) most Christians have become convinced that it is contrary to the compassionate spirit of Jesus that people who have taken advantage of the laws of their countries to remarry after a divorce, having repented of any contribution they made to the breakdown of the first marriage, should be denied the Church's prayers for the new union and excluded from Holy Communion as a means of receiving God's gracious help. Specially in societies where at least a third of all first marriages are dissolved legally and usually without social disapproval, such treatment of a second marriage, which may suggest that it is an unforgivable sin, seems to most Christians to be no part of essential Christianity.

According to surveys this is the attitude of most Roman Catholics in many countries. The strongly conservative Eastern Orthodox Churches have for long taught that a first marriage may die and a second marriage may be recognized.

Similarly, it seems that most Christians do not now agree that the use of artificial contraceptives is always wrong. The attempts of some church leaders (including successive Popes) to prohibit contraceptives may have been somewhat more justifiable in days when contraceptive devices were primitive and the chief (or only) purpose of sexual intercourse was regarded (at least by theologians) as being the conception of the children who were needed by society in large numbers because of infant mortality and short life expectancy. The justification was, however, always questionable because church leaders had to base their arguments not on the Bible (where the subject is not mentioned) but on a belief that a "natural law" prohibits interference with the natural results of the intercourse (although no such law prohibits interference with many other natural processes). When sexual intercourse is valued chiefly as a means of deepening married love, it seems unloving and destructive to restrict it to periods when fertilization is less likely to occur. In a world where the population is expected to increase from four to six billions in the quarter-century 1974–99, it seems crazy to regard the production of large families as a religious duty. Particularly is this the case in Africa and West Asia, where religion is still very influential and where the growth of the population is running at over three per cent per annum and resulting in a dehumanizing poverty. And as the pollution and exhaustion of Earth's natural resources are increasingly recognized, it becomes increasingly clear that human overpopulation is anti-creation.

The prohibition of artificial contraceptives on religious

grounds seems to most Christians specially wrong in countries where women can quite easily obtain an abortion as the alternative. These countries include European lands famous for their Roman Catholic history, including Poland. Most Christians in the twentieth century agree that as a last resort an abortion, like a war, may be the lesser of two evils. Therefore it seems legitimate for the laws of a country to permit it, for parents to choose it and for medical staff to agree to carry it out, under some tragic circumstances. But the use of abortion as contraception is abhorrent to the Christian conscience because it holds a human, or potentially human, life so very cheap.

When marriage is regarded primarily as a solemnly committed friendship which in intention is lifelong, and when contraceptives are available to the unmarried, it is inevitable that many people should enjoy sexual intercourse without the commitment of marriage but usually with the thought that it will help them to prepare for marriage with this or another partner. Many Christians reject that possibility as the "fornication" condemned in the Bible, and they deserve sincere respect, particularly when self-control is difficult for them personally. But many studies of public opinion have shown that most Christians have either accepted this customary practice of modern societies or do not regard it as a major moral issue. Most would regard the practice as better than the custom of paying prostitutes forced into that "game" by poverty – and better than the custom of buying girls as brides who were allowed no previous sexual experience and no choice about marriage. One tragic consequence is, however, the growth in the numbers of babies born outside wedlock. Another result is much heartbreak. It would therefore seem to most Christians wrong for the Churches to change their traditional teaching that sex outside the commitment and stability of marriage is at best the second best.

It is relevant to this modern discussion that the normal age for women being betrothed or marrying was much lower in many traditional societies, including Jewish society in the first century AD; girls were usually pledged by their families in marriage when scarcely past puberty. Modern society asks young people to contain their sexual drives in the years when these are at their peak, although a modern advance has been the recognition that masturbation is usually harmless in spite of centuries of guilt-producing denunciation by churchmen. Most Christians now agree that masturbation is usually a normal and sensible way for the young to explore their own God-given sexuality and for the unmarried to relieve their sexual tensions.

It is also inevitable that when the scientific understanding of the condition of homosexuality in men or women has increased (although it is far from complete), the Christian attitude has often changed. Increasing numbers of Christians have become convinced that homosexuals are not excluded from the kingdom of God, not even if they express their loving commitment to a partner physically, since homosexuality is caused by a person's inheritance of genes, perhaps influenced by the behaviour of parents. It is no one's fault.

A modern reader of a passage such as Romans 1:26–32 is likely to conclude that Paul's profound understanding of human nature did not include a modern knowledge of the physical and emotional basis of human sexuality. Homosexuals, we now know, are not "perverts". It would not be "natural" for them to love a person of the other sex sexually. The term "homosexual" ought not to include the bisexual feelings which seem normal in the awakening sexuality of adolescence. So at this point Paul's teaching belonged to his culture rather than to the everlasting Gospel. Its indignation is understandable (in the Greco-Roman world many boys

were "loved" by men), but it was like the teaching that
women ought to cover their heads while worshipping "out
of regard for the angels" (1 Corinthians 11:10), which seems
to be a reference to the ancient story that the "sons of the
gods" had intercourse when they "saw how beautiful these
daughters were" (Genesis 6:1–4). The remark ascribed to
Jesus in Matthew 19:12 that "some are incapable of marriage because they were born so" (a remark made in a
society where almost everyone was married) may be closer
to a modern understanding of the homosexual minority. But
in our time most Christians would add two further points.
It is not necessary to fly against the evidence by pretending
that homosexuality is equivalent to marriage as a recipe for
happiness. Nor is it necessary for homosexuals to "have
sex". The factual observation in Matthew's gospel that some
Christians "have renounced marriage for the sake of the
kingdom of Heaven" applies equally to homosexuals. Often
at great cost to themselves, some who have that nature have
renounced all sexual contacts, demonstrating that under the
government of God human beings need not behave like other
animals. Knowing how much unhappiness and damage can
result from homosexual liaisons (partly because the heterosexual majority is prejudiced), they can refrain from physical
sexual activity in order to contribute by other means to the
creation of a humanity fit for eternity. Many teachers and
clergy have been and are in this category, using the rare
spiritual gifts which have won fame for the artistic achievements of other homosexuals.

THE PEOPLE OF GOD

Inevitably it disappoints many people to be told that Christians do not all agree on the questions of politics, economics
and sexual morality which are the questions of the day. It

disappoints people who want a religion which will save them the trouble of thinking for themselves. It also disappoints people who like to think that any religion must be wedded to a political, economic or ethical system which is obviously out of date. But the claim that Christianity offers a simple, authoritative answer to these vexed modern questions cannot be sustained either by an appeal to "what has been believed everywhere, always and by all" or by invoking the teaching of Jesus, a challenging vision which was never meant to be legislation. In different societies Christians have accepted or supported a considerable variety of arrangements in these matters, and have drawn from the Bible various texts which appear to support their views. Their Lord is reported to have refused to give simple answers, saying instead: "Pay Caesar what belongs to Caesar, and God what belongs to God", which "left them completely taken aback" (Mark 12:17); "Who set me over you to judge or arbitrate?", which left two brothers still in dispute over the division of the family property (Luke 12:14); "If a man looks at a woman with a lustful eye, he has already committed adultery with her in his heart" (Matthew 5:28), which left no one entitled to throw the first stone at the flagrantly guilty woman (John 8:7).

In what is permanently relevant in the message of Jesus, the idea of the kingdom of God gives us not detailed instructions but a convincing vision of a people and a God. It is better than any number of regulations with a use-by date on them which religious leaders tend to conceal.

When the supreme purpose of the Creator is fulfilled, there is to be a people. That means more than can be imagined inside the prison of modern individualism. There is a vision of persons-in-community – of persons who become personal not in isolation but by growth in relationships with other people, in the "fellowship of the Holy Spirit". To be happy, we always have responsibilities to other people as parts of love on many levels, as well as rights to fulfil ourselves. Therefore Christian prayer for the coming of this kingdom which is a community is always prayer made by a community – by "us". It does not follow that the institutional Church is the kingdom of God, or is the only place where the kingdom can be prayed and worked for. But the Church is on the right lines when it functions as a community.

And there is to be a government making these persons one people. That means more than the endorsement of any of the modern versions of the defence of a strong political or military or religious regime. In this vision, what draws this people together and guides them is a power which transcends the governments of the world, both because it is truly divine and because it is truly loving, so that all the propaganda of the rulers who are "given the title Benefactor" (Luke 22:25) is discredited. The divine power is motivated by love for all humanity, not for a limited group in competition with other groups. In the tradition about Jesus, as we saw, warnings that few may persevere on the road that leads to eternal life are accompanied by the proclamation of a love for many and for all. In Luke's version of a passage in Q, when Jesus is asked "Sir, are only a few to be saved?" he does not answer directly but says: "Make every effort . . ." (13:23,24). Paul and John, the two Christians of the first century who possessed spiritual genius, saw that the will of God is for the salvation of all, putting in their own language the message of Jesus that the kingdom of God is a banquet to which the world is invited. And because this invitation will not be accepted by all in the world as it is, Christian prayer for the coming of this kingdom on Earth has to wrestle with that tragedy and with its many disastrous consequences, in the passionate hope that in the end the

longing of God that all may accept his love will prove stronger than the human rejection. Probably most Christians now
see that hope as involving a growth and a decision after
death. Even amid the tragedy, the Christian believes that
the all-embracing will of God is already obeyed "in heaven"
– that is, by all who live eternally. Many mortals will always
say that such faith is a sentimental illusion, but it is made
possible by the revelation of God's love in Christ, communicated by the power of the Holy Spirit – an experience which
overwhelms the habits of evil and the hesitations of scepticism. From the personal experience of being governed by
God arises the great hope for all.

I owe more than I can say to the churches which have
accepted and sustained me since I was baptized in a little
white church in Cairo. But modern reflection has shown
that it is ridiculous for the Christian Church to call itself
exclusively "the people of God". The claim is no more
realistic than a similarly exclusive claim made on behalf of
the Jewish or Muslim people. As they have met other
religions on more or less equal terms for the first time in
history, Christians have realized that they have much to
learn from both Jews and Muslims about God and about
community life. They also have much to learn from Indian
and African intuitions about God, from the Buddhist tran-
quillity in meditation, and from the sense of "primitive"
peoples such as the American Indians or the Australian
Aborigines that the land is sacred. And they have much to
learn from secular humanists about being human. Indeed,
they have much to learn from Christian non-churchgoers
about being Christian.

Most Christians do not nowadays approach the adherents
of other faiths assuming that the others will "go to hell" or
"perish" unless they cease to be "heathen" before they die,
for a revolution has taken place in attitudes to "mission" or

"evangelism" during the twentieth century. It is in sharp
contrast with the attitudes taken by most Christians in most
previous periods, but it is a recovery of the attitude of Jesus
of Nazareth to his fellow Jews. There is the warning that it
is possible to reject the message of Jesus in such a way that
a person rejects God and God's offer of abundant and eternal
life. That is the solemnity of the proclamation of the message. But the message itself is good news, the best news
possible, the news for all of God's love in Christ, of his
power in the Spirit, of his will to take action to establish a
kingdom of justice, health, love, joy and peace – and the
motive of evangelism is to share that good news with all. It
is a sufficient motive, although not enough Christians have
yet acknowledged this.

If the Church is "the People of God", it can only be in
the sense in which the Hebrew prophets clung to the belief
that their own sinful people had been chosen by God for
certain purposes. They believed in that choice even while
they denounced the sins of their people and prophesied
disasters resulting from those sins. It is not difficult to think
of disasters which could follow, and already do follow, the
current practices of the Christian Church. Many parts of
the Church have been dangerously slow to adjust their doctrines to the growing revelation of truth, and to adjust their
structures of power to an age which is less and less dominated by white men. The healthy diversity of Christians has
tragically led to a lack of communion between them, so that
the Church is in practice an unattractive and ineffective
model to a humanity which painfully seeks a greater unity.
The Church seems to the outsider to be imprisoned in controversies mostly inherited from the past and mostly irrelevant to the urgent problems and tasks of our time – and
the honest insider will often be close to despair because these
accusations have truth in them. Yet the Christian Church's

astonishing ability to be reformed and renewed is another fact of history.

It is not difficult to imagine a Church which could escape from its tragedies during the twenty-first century. Here are some of my own dreams, although I do not claim that they must be shared by every Christian. The universal Church's President would be the Pope of Rome; no other candidate for that essential post can be imagined. But the bureaucracy of the Vatican would abandon the claim to have jurisdiction over the world's Christians. Encouraged by its President, the Church would be in intelligent dialogue with the Bible and would submit to the Bible's central message. It would be a communion held together by bonds of affection as commanded in the Bible. It would be the Catholic (meaning universal) gathering of the baptized for the Eucharist, and their scattering for service to God's other children. It would identify itself with the poor and would demand justice in society. It would encourage all its members to do all they could to heal the sick. It would exercise pastoral care, calling for this purpose many more priests and other pastors (who need not be either paid or unmarried or male). It would evangelize confidently because it would love to offer the best, but it would no longer claim infallibility either for its own leaders or for its Scriptures. It would admit to past errors, including sad failures to come to terms with science, with freedom and with sexuality. It would admire, welcome and defend all the goodness, natural or human, in the world around it. It would be protestant because it would protest against all that was unworthy in its own life or in the life of the world, but it would not be tied to any nation as a state church, nor to any theological document from the sixteenth (or any other) century. It would be orthodox because it would live and worship in the great tradition inherited from the saints and martyrs of the past, but not because its energy would depend on fossil fuel. It would be enthusiastic without insisting on any one form of enthusiasm. It would treat women in the spirit of Jesus and, being essentially inter-racial, would be colourblind . . .

But greater than any such hopes are the timeless commands, to love God and the neighbour.

The writers of the New Testament begin the unending process of relating those apparently simple rules to different and changing situations. In Mark's gospel (12:28–34) and Matthew's (21:34–40) Jesus answers the scribe's question "Which is the first of all the commandments?" by quoting the Hebrew Scriptures (Deuteronomy 6:4–5 and Leviticus 19:18) – and "after that nobody dared put any more questions to him" because to devout Jews the answer was so obviously right. References in the letters both of James (2:8) and of Paul (Galatians 5:14; Romans 3:9) also show that this was standard Jewish teaching. However, in Luke's gospel (10:25–29) it is the scribe, not Jesus, who gives this teaching – and he follows his Scriptural quotations with the question: "But who is my neighbour?" The parable of the Good Samaritan is now told.

It broadens the idea of neighbourliness from the solidarity of Jew with Jew to the practical response to human need simply because it is human. This parable is provocatively anti-racist instead of being a merely anticlerical story about the layman helping when the priest and Levite did not; and it makes the trained expert in the Jewish religious law think with a startled surprise that the day may come when he needs the despised Samaritan as a neighbour. In Matthew's gospel (5:43–48) Christians suffering from orthodox Jewish hostility are told to forget about the Jewish solidarity which includes "hate your enemy": they are to imitate God's own universal love, so that they must "love your enemies and pray for your persecutors". And the Christian meaning of the ancient command and desire to love God is indicated when a rich young man tells Jesus that he still feels that he lacks something although he has kept the familiar commandments. In his reply Jesus indicates what loving God may involve: "If you wish to be perfect, go, sell your possessions, and . . . come and follow me" (19:16–22). Moreover, in all these Christian gospels there is a warning that the duty to love God must involve mental exertions: "with all your mind" is added to the commandment given in Deuteronomy. And so we are obliged to think out what these familiar commandments mean, as knives which will be surgery for us.

In our time Christians can agree with non-Christians that love for the neighbour is unlikely unless there is first love for the self, in the sense of a relaxed self-esteem which is not bitterly on the defensive or agressively anxious to find in others the faults which one condemns in oneself. And Christians can agree with non-Christians that a full human life needs a vision and a task where the ideal is loved "with all your heart, and with all your soul, and with all your mind", so that the devotion of a lover to the beloved opens the gates of Paradise. But the message of Jesus does not merely reinforce non-Christian wisdom. It brings to our notice the human being whose physical or spiritual needs we usually find it more convenient to ignore. It challenges us to forgive and to love to an extent that makes sense only if we believe in a Father who forgives and loves all. And it warns us that this belief may be very demanding and costly indeed, with a price which is worth paying because if we pay it our own deepest need will be met. If I do not love myself – it may be, because I was not loved as a child without inhibitions or qualifications, or because I have not been loved fully and faithfully as a spouse – the faith that I have been loved and accepted by God is what I need. If I am imprisoned in a narrow loyalty to my own group, or if I am poisoned by hatred of other groups or other individuals, the faith in God the Father of all is what I need. If I condemn myself not because I have an unhealthy "guilt-complex" but because I have behaved wrongly and done appalling damage, what I need to hear is that my Father is running towards me in welcome. But to gain access to this wealth, a price has to be paid. The Father offers the wealth freely, but it costs us our pride to receive the gift we need – for we have to receive it alongside others who, like us, hold out empty hands.

In this light, it is dishonest to dream of the perfect Church without wanting for myself and for all Christians a much closer approach to the moral and spiritual standards of the kingdom of God as expounded so uncomfortably in, for example, the Sermon on the Mount. On that at least all Christians should agree. If the concentration of the Church could be on that quest, everything else would fall into its proper place, in accordance with the principle: "set your mind on God's kingdom and his justice, and all the rest will come to you as well" (Matthew 6:33). This is because Christians can believe with good reason that in the end, when all physically based life has died and the matter-energy from which it has evolved is itself exhausted, spirits can endure, based on the life of God. And Christians can know that the appropriate preparation for that destiny is set out in the Sermon on the Mount. There the Christians' Teacher and Saviour calls for an end to anger, lust, superficiality, bitterness, hatred, hypocrisy, materialism, anxiety, pride and fear. These are the impediments both to the survival of *homo sapiens* on Earth and to the life which is eternity.

The reason why Christian belief in the possibility of eternal life for all the people of God remains reasonable is this: Christians can begin to know how alive is the God revealed by Jesus Christ. It is not necessary to be a Christian in order to think it reasonable to believe that the mental and spiritual activities of *homo sapiens* are on a level of reality different from the physical, although before death they depend on the two fistfuls of pink-grey matter called the brain. About 70,000 years ago Neanderthal man buried his dead in a way that suggested some belief in life after death. Nor is it necessary to be a Christian in order to think it reasonable to believe that the personality as it has developed on this mental and spiritual level can survive the death of the brain. Constant curiosity about the possibility has been rewarded – or so it is widely thought – by some experiences of the dead being alive. What is Christian is the experience of knowing Jesus Christ as alive, confirming his own teaching that God loves so much that he holds the dead in his own life, where they are based on that love for ever. He does not throw them away like cigarette ends. "He is not God of the dead but of the living" – although to be "like the angels in heaven" is to enter a life barely glimpsed and little understood before death (Mark 12:25–27).

I have suggested that in modern or post-modern times the coming of the kingdom of God to the whole people of God can be understood as a process which proceeds through the creation of the universe and the evolution of life, and through the strengthening of emotions appropriate to the survival of *homo sapiens*, to a moral and spiritual preparation for eternity. It would surely be strange to say that such an interpretation is less true or less powerful than the use of pictures which belong to a pre-scientific age. It would also be strange to say that a picture of God painted before the light of science must be superior to one which has been made possible by the gift of the Creator's revelation of his methods through science in addition to the Father's revelation of his love through Christ.

The God who can be believed in after Christ and after

science is the "Source, Guide and Goal of all that exists" (Romans 11:36 in NEB) but we have no evidence that all events happen exactly according to a good purpose. We see much that seems to us chance, waste or evil, and unless we think that God is not as carefully loving as we are (or try to be sometimes) we have to think that for reasons we cannot fully understand he permits these events as part of the freedom which he has given to his creation. There must be some truth in the idea (the central idea of a modern movement of science-influenced Christian thought, "process theology") that God "lures" events as he "lures" people. That is not an understanding which makes him a ruler with absolute power over his subjects. It is, however, an idea not completely unlike the ideal of a truly modern government, which is to serve and persuade a free people in its own interests. The twenty-first century will inherit the idea that the leader of a truly modern people is a servant, even if he or she is an elected President or Prime Minister or a constitutional monarch. And it is likely that this form of politics will increasingly help the Christian understanding of God's own style of government. In John's gospel the crucifixion of Jesus is the greatest sign of the embodiment of the glory of God, but it is not interpreted by retelling the story of the last supper when the bread was broken and the wine poured out. Instead, there is another story (13:1–17). "Jesus, well aware that the Father had entrusted everything to him, and that he had come from God and was going back to God, rose from the supper table, took off his outer garment and, taking a towel, tied it round him. Then he poured water into a basin, and began to wash his disciples' feet and to wipe them with the towel."

To think of God as servant is certainly unusual – as it is unusual to think of God's patient creativity as motherlike, or to think of God's self-sacrifice and suffering as like a martyr's. But it is a Christian insight, based on the strange life, strange death and strange victory of Jesus of Nazareth. In this vision, God rules in a way that always surprises us – the way to persuasion through the power of love, to achievement through the creation of the other's freedom, to a new level of life through the surrender of death. It is the way of the cross. And it is the Christian experience that the strength which God gives to meet each day's troubles is adequate, more adequate than we naturally expected. Christians also learn that the revelation of God's love at the heart of the mystery of life, given in the imperfect Bible and in the difficult dialogue of prayer, is enough for what concerns us: living. The supply lasts through severe tragedies or the lesser disillusionments. After the questions and pains of the twentieth century, that assertion is unlikely to convince anyone who has fully lived in that century – except when it is said by someone who has felt the questions as disturbances in the depths, and who has by great sorrow shared in at least some of our time's agonies. But I can offer my witness with a complete conviction towards the end of the century and, it may be, of my life.

Having compared God's way of governing the world with a servant's washing of feet, one is likely to be asked nowadays whether what one is trying to say is that God is weak. If so, is that really a reflection of the weakness of one's own religious faith? My answer is that a faith which has been formed by God's revelation through science as well as through the Bible, and which has been tested against some of the harshness of twentieth-century experience, is strong enough for the purposes of life and death. A person who has such a faith can lay every need before God like a trustful child, without being so childish as to rely on a convenient miracle coming. According to Mark (14:36) it was with the childlike call to God as "*Abba*, Father" that an agonized

Jesus accepted his tortured death. In such a spirit, a person who trusts in God's way of governing the world can sometimes glimpse the coming triumph in the public history of humanity as well as in the secret story of the individual. Progress is made, although with many reversals. Justice is established, although with many temporary victories for brute force or low cunning. Resurrections come, however mysteriously. That has "happened" even amid the disasters of the twentieth century, and it could "happen" on a much bigger scale if the next century listens to some of the lessons learned so painfully. The believer will interpret these moments of progress as signs of the dawning of the kingdom of which Jesus spoke. When patience is needed as Jesus warned, it will be remembered that according to science humanity has at least two billion years ahead of it on Earth. And when what is good is shattered in the conflicts, the believer will trust that the eternal God who was, and is, dynamic in Jesus and the Holy Spirit will pick up the pieces.

Index